Schoolwork

Schoolwork

APPROACHES TO THE LABOUR
PROCESS OF TEACHING

EDITED BY
Jenny Ozga
at the Open University

OPEN UNIVERSITY PRESS
MILTON KEYNES · PHILADELPHIA

Open University Press
Open University Educational Enterprises Limited
12 Cofferidge Close
Stony Stratford
Milton Keynes MK11 1BY, England

and
242 Cherry Street
Philadelphia, PA 19106, USA

First Published 1988

British Library Cataloguing in Publication Data

The Educational worker: a reader on teacher's
  work. – (E814; v.1).
  Vol. 1
  1. Teaching – Social aspects
  2. Educational sociology
  I. Ozga, Jennifer
  371.1   LB1025.2

  ISBN 0-335-15554-5
  ISBN 0-335-15544-8 Pbk

Library of Congress Cataloguing in Publication Data

The Educational worker.
  Includes index.
  1. Teaching.   2. Teachers – Great Britain – Job
stress.   3. Teachers – Great Britain – Social conditions.
I. Ozga, Jennifer.
LB1775.E33   1987   371.1'02   87-22115
  ISBN 0-335-15554-5 (v. 1)
  ISBN 0-335-15544-8 (pbk.: v. 1)

Typeset by Rowland Phototypesetting Limited
Bury St Edmunds, Suffolk
Printed in Great Britain
by Biddles Ltd, Guildford and King's Lynn

Contents

Acknowledgements

All possible care has been taken to trace ownership of the material included in this volume, and Open University Press would like to make grateful acknowledgement for permission to reproduce it here.

1. Reprinted from Tipton, B. F., 'Educational Organizations as Workplaces', *British Journal of the Sociology of Education* vol. 6 No 1. © BJSE 1985, by permission of the British Journal of the Sociology of Education.
2. Reprinted from Dreeben, R., 'The School as a Workplace', in *The Second Handbook of Research on Teaching*, Chicago University Press/AERA, 1973, by permission of American Educational Research Association.
3. Reprinted from Bergen, B., 'Only a Schoolmaster: Gender, Class and the effort to professionalize elementary teaching in England, 1870–1910', in *History of Education Quarterly* Spring 1982, © Barry Bergen, by permission of the History of Education Quarterly.
4. Reprinted from Apple, M., 'Work, Class and Teaching', in Walker, S. and Barton, L. (Eds), *Gender, Class and Education*, Lewes, Falmer Press, 1983, © Walker and Barton, by permission of Lewes, Falmer Press.
5. Reprinted from Lawn, M. and Ozga J., 'The Educational Worker', in Barton, L. and Walker, S. (Eds) *Schools, Teachers and Teaching*, Lewes, Falmer Press, 1981, © Barton and Walker, by permission of Lewes, Falmer Press.
6. Reprinted from *Labour/Le Travail* with permission of the editor. © Committee on Canadian Labour History.
7. Reprinted from Buswell, C., 'Pedagogic change and social change', in *BJSE* vol. 1 No. 3, 1980, © BJSE by permission of the British Journal of the Sociology of Education.
8. Reprinted from Freedman, S., 'Teacher burnout and institutional

stress', in Lawn, M. (Ed.) *The politics of Teacher Unionism: International Perspectives*, London, Croom Helm, 1985, © Lawn by permission of Croom Helm and M. Lawn.

9. Reprinted from Redican, B., 'Subject Teachers under stress', in Walford, G. (Ed.), *Schooling in Turmoil*, London, Croom Helm, 1985, © Walford, by permission of Croom Helm and G. Walford.

10. Reprinted from Nias, J., 'What it means to "feel like a teacher": the subjective reality of primary teaching', BERA Conference Paper, Bristol, 1986, © Jennifer Nias, by permission of the author. This paper is incorporated into *Teachers and their work* (provisional title) by J. Nias and to be published by Methuen.

Introduction: teaching, professionalism and work

Jenny Ozga

This Reader is part of a taught Masters Module: E814, Educational Organizations and Professionals. There is a companion Reader: *Culture and Power in Educational Organizations*, edited by Adam Westoby, and a number of set books: Ball's *The Micro-Politics of the School*, Ball and Goodsons' *Teachers' Lives and Careers*, Lawn and Grace's *Teachers: The Culture and Politics of Work* and Morgan's *Images of Organization*, as well as the course text and audio-cassette materials. This Reader is designed primarily as part of that package; however, it also represents an attempt to understand changes in the control and structure of teaching work using the organizing principle of teaching as *work* and teaching as a labour process.

There are a number of factors which make such an approach to teachers' work particularly apposite. Teaching is going through a period of crisis, from which it is likely to emerge as different in significant ways from teaching as it was characterized in the 1960s, the 'zenith' of teachers' professional autonomy. The nature of teaching is being fundamentally altered by a number of different policy initiatives, the cumulative effect of which is to greatly increase central government control over the teaching force. These policy initiatives include alterations to the pattern of initial teacher training and retraining, changes in the content of training which are intended to promote technical competence and shift the emphasis away from general intellectual development; changes in the contractual relationship between teachers and employers; in teachers' negotiating rights (their abolition); in their control over the content of curriculum and examinations; changes in the structure of pay and promotion in teaching; and the establishment of a clear demarcation between staff and line members of the teaching force.

Furthermore, less direct policy initiatives – not promoted through specific policies other than the overarching need of the state to respond to economic crisis, which has resulted in reduced public spending on public services – have produced redeployment, redundancy and a loss of morale among teachers which has probably not been paralleled since the days of the Revised Code of the 1860s and the Geddes Axe of the 1920s. Indeed, loss of morale may currently be even more widespread, given the wedge that has been driven between parents and teachers by the rhetoric of accountability.

The historical references point to the fact that the crisis in teaching is not new but forms an episode in a relationship between teachers and the state which is characterized by different degrees of tension, depending on the extent of the need to exert control over the teaching force. In times of economic crisis, foreign competition and political dissensus, the central state tends towards strong, directive management which imposes controls on teacher recruitment, training, salaries and status, and curriculum and examination content. In relatively relaxed periods, when resources available for education are sufficient to permit a broad interpretation of priorities, and there is at least the appearance of consensus, management is less crisis-led, appears more relaxed, is more strategic in nature and consequently relies heavily on the promotion of teacher professionalism as a form of control.

Of course, management systems are rarely perfectly planned and executed, nor without internal contradictions, nor imposed, without contestation or modification, on the workforce, as Edwards (1979) and Burawoy (1979) remind us. Still less is the central state to be conceived of as a monolith, imposing an unquestioned interpretation of professionalism on all levels of the education system. It is legitimate to identify the central problem of teacher–state relations as one of management and control of the tension inevitably generated by employee–employer antagonism. But it is also necessary to trace variations in the management strategies adopted, to relate these to particular historical junctures and to avoid the suggestion that an all-powerful central state consistently directs all of its efforts in its relations with teachers towards management and control. There are divisions within the state – among and between officials and politicians, for example, which do have policy consequences and which need to be taken into account (Ranson 1985). Furthermore, discussion of the state is complicated in relation to teachers by the position of the LEAs as employers, where again there are divisions, both within local authorities and between them and the centre.

Finally, the potential of teachers – sometimes in alliance with LEAs – to exploit periods of less rigid, more indirect control so as to push the ethic of 'legitimated professionalism' (Dale 1981) to its limits, gaining control over curriculum content, classroom work and a voice in policy-making locally and nationally (as happened in the post-war period), should not be forgotten.

Nevertheless, these factors develop the thesis in complex directions but do not undermine it. Teachers are bound to the state in the relation of employee to employer, and the tension engendered by this relation demands strategies of control and management, changes in which may be identified through historical and contemporary analysis.

At the heart of the question of strategies of control is a division between the use of the ideology of professionalism, which fosters worker compliance and co-option but carries attendant risks (already indicated) and more direct, prescriptive strategies, which produce risks of a very different nature, that is hostility, subversion and organized resistance. Both control strategies ultimately produce dilemmas or contradictions for the state.

Professionalism as an ideology which promoted control of the teaching force developed in reaction from the coercive model in operation at the turn of the century, in response to Fisher's concern about the working-class composition and alliances of the teaching force. Fisher promoted responsible, professional behaviour as an antidote to unionism, through such tactics as the (temporary) creation of a teachers' register, plans for a Teaching Council, the creation of Burnham, control of the more extreme reactionary local employers, and the co-option of suitably professional teachers into the policy process. The feminization of teaching, aided by the 1914–18 war, is a significant, if imperfectly understood, factor here (see Bergen, Ch. 3 in this volume).

Eustace Percy, President of the Board of Education from 1925 to 1928, continued and developed Fisher's approach, promoting responsible professional autonomy within limits. His strategy owed a great deal to Lugard's colonial policy of 'Indirect Rule', which co-opted potential opponents of British imperialism into a semi-autonomous local structure (Lawn 1987). The strategy of Indirect Rule had its inherent dangers as a form of management, as the colonial parallel shows. Both LEAs and teachers were able to exploit the scope it gave them at national and local policy-making levels, and to use the double-edged weapon of professionalism to subvert and reduce central control, to the point, perhaps, when a reaction aimed at re-establishing control was inevitable.

Discussion of teacher professionalism which focuses on its ideological component, drawing on the work of Larson (1979) and Johnson (1972), which attempts to disentangle what professionalism meant at different historical periods (Grace 1986) and which dissects the notion of professional autonomy; exploring the limits of licensed autonomy (Dale, 1981) or distinguishing between workplace, occupational and structural autonomy (Grace 1985), is far removed from the functionalist approaches to professionalism which dominated the study of teaching in the 1950s and 1960s and still exert an influence out of all proportion to their intellectual substance. This uncritical view of professionalism, which measured teachers against 'established' professional workers and found them wanting because of insufficiently esoteric knowledge, lack of sufficiently high status or salaries, and preponderance of female membership, has acted to depress the level of debate around teacher professionalism and deny the legitimacy of examining teaching as work.

Critical analyses of professionalism, on the other hand, direct attention to the problem of control, and lead to the examination of different historical phases of control. Furthermore, this approach raises questions about the nature of teachers' work which open it up to comparisons and connections with varied and stimulating fields of enquiry, which draw on many disciplines and research traditions. These include sociology of organizations, industrial sociology, organization theory and labour process theory. The latter category is currently undergoing a revival thanks to Braverman's *Labour and Monopoly Capital* (1974) and reactions to it, while the rapidly developing area of feminist-inspired enquiry into women's work has both general and specific applicability to teaching.

Among the lines of enquiry which are suggested by looking at teaching as work, and critically considering the meaning of professionalism in teachers' work, are those which direct attention to the organization of teachers' work and the workplace context, to teachers' formal and informal groupings and networks, to the division of labour both by function and by gender in teaching, to the role of management and supervision, to performance appraisal and efficiency, to strategies of compliance and resistance, and to job design and quality control in education work.

Furthermore, the analysis of teaching as work which draws on the labour process tradition brings forward to centre-stage the concept of class, the importance of which is denied by functionalist professionalism. Gender, too – hitherto observed, if at all, as the manifestation of a problem preventing professionalization – takes on major significance in the analysis of teachers' work and the control of teachers' work. It is significant, surely, that feminization of the teaching force has taken place during periods of crisis management (see Danylewycz and Prentice, Ch. 4 in this volume).

In different but related ways the recognition of class and gender as central concepts in the study of teachers' work lends support to the putting of professionalism even further into the background and the adoption of proletarianization as a thesis that, at least, merits investigation. Proletarianization, according to Braverman, follows from the imperative towards accumulation characteristic of capitalism and results in the erosion of workers' control over the labour process, the fragmentation of work and the separation of conception from execution. Braverman concentrated on technical deskilling; critics of his work have developed less deterministic approaches which include the discussion of legitimacy and consent (Wood 1982) and broaden the enquiry from the technical process of production to include job design, the formal structure of management control and the place of the work in question on the labour market.

An approach to proletarianization developed from such concerns, may be extremely productive if applied to teachers' work. If we remember the policy context which was briefly sketched in above, it may be all too easy to conclude that teachers are in the process of proletarianization. But a more cautious and less one-dimensional view should be taken, as proletarianization is not a limited technical process but involves alterations in worker consciousness, and, as we have said, it is by no means clear that proletarianization is as widespread or as inevitable as Braverman suggests. The process is not straightforward: the more complex processes discussed in Wood's (1982) collection and Salaman's (1986) attack on labour process theory raise questions such as the following, all of which would repay investigation. Is conception and execution becoming separated in teaching work? Is the concept of skill applicable to teaching? What does it consist of and how is it developed? How is teachers' work controlled and evaluated? Do teachers have workplace autonomy? Is it task-related; does it apply to some functions more than others and to some teachers more than others? In what ways is teacher compliance achieved: through management, by incentives or by manufacturing 'consent'?

This collection is a first attempt to ask some of these questions and to examine some of the issues raised by the critical analysis of the concepts of professionalism and proletarianization, by bringing together some of the material specifically related to teachers which deals with such questions, either directly or indirectly. Not all the authors would agree with the interpretation of material being presented in this introduction, however; reading of the contributions will confirm that, while there is a shared interest in teachers' work, there is no one 'line' on professionalism or proletarianization.

The first section develops the idea of 'teaching as work' through Frances Tipton's analysis of the causes and consequences of the lack of studies of the school as a workplace and teachers as workers (Ch. 1). Her analysis is rather different from that offered here, as it concentrates on the divisions between the disciplines involved in the study of teaching, and she provides a valuable guide to directions for future research. Robert Dreeben, in an article first published in 1973, looks at the school as a workplace from the starting point of comparisons with other organizations, and, using the methods of analysis then current in organization theory, analyses the 'technology' of teaching work (Ch. 2). Although the article was written some time ago, it remains a near-unique example of an analysis of teaching as work.

The second section, 'Professionalism and Proletarianization: The Significance of Class and Gender', looks at discussions of professionalism and proletarianization first in a historical context and then in the light of contemporary trends in teaching. Barry Bergen's article suggests that the working-class origin and/or female gender of the majority of teachers in his period of study effectively debarred them from achieving professional status (Ch. 3). Marta Danylewycz and Alison Prentice take a less unproblematic view of the control of teachers' work in Canada in the same period, where they find that proletarianization was linked to the feminization of the teaching force (Ch. 4).

In the contemporary analyses in this section, Martin Lawn and I argue the case for taking the proletarianization thesis seriously, and using it as a basis for re-examining teacher unionism and teachers' class position (Ch. 5). Michael Apple uncovers the relations between class and gender in teacher proletarianization, and provides examples of the separation of conception and execution of teaching work in the United States (Ch. 6). This leads to the next section, 'Deskilling at Work', which includes a case study by Carol Buswell concerning the effects of the introduction of curriculum packages and teachers' strategies of compliance with and resistance to them (Ch. 7); Sara Freedman's material collected from Boston teachers on the erosion of their skills, increased supervision and consequent stress (Ch. 8); and Bede Redican's investigation of the transformation of pastoral posts into super-visory positions which challenge subject teachers' authority and autonomy (Ch. 9).

In the final section, 'The Social Construction of Teachers' Work', the emphasis is less on the 'technical' aspects of work and the control of work, and more on the social construction of work: Martin Lawn examines social relations in primary schools and their function in modifying management demands and protecting areas of 'skill' (Ch. 10), Mark Loveys discusses the skills required in adapting to the demands of supply teaching (Ch. 11), and Jennifer Nias, through interview data, presents images of teaching work, its rewards and its penalties (Ch. 12).

In their different ways, the readings in this book illustrate the value of looking at teaching as work. A major gain is the displacement of professional-ism as *the* organizing and explanatory concept in the analysis of teaching. Displacement or reassessment of professionalism allows other important concepts – particularly class and gender – their rightful place.

In addition, the study of teaching as work concentrates attention on what teachers actually do, and on how what they do is organized and managed. This, in turn, reveals how little we know about teachers in comparison with other workers. This collection is an attempt to bring together a coherent selection of material which relates to teachers' work; much more detailed empirical study remains to be done.

References

Braverman, H. (1974) *Labor and Monopoly Capital*, New York, Monthly Review Press.
Burawoy, M. (1979) *Manufacturing Consent: Changes in the Labour Process under Monopoly Capitalism*, Chicago and London, University of Chicago Press.
Dale, R. (1981) 'Control, accountability and William Tyndale', in R. Dale, G. Esland, R. Fergusson and M. Macdonald (eds), *Education and the State, Vol. 2: Politics, Patriarchy and Practice*, Milton Keynes, Open University Press.
Edwards, R. (1979) *Contested Terrain: The Transformation of the Workplace in the Twentieth Century*, New York, Basic Books.
Grace, G. (1985) 'Judging teachers: the social and political contexts of teacher evaluation', *British Journal of the Sociology of Education* 6(1).
Johnson, T. (1972) *Professions and Power*, London, Macmillan.

Larson, M. S. (1979) *The Rise of the Professionals: A Sociological Analysis*, Berkeley, University of California Press.

Lawn, M. (1987) 'The spur and the bridle: changing the mode of curriculum control', *Journal of Curriculum Studies* 19(3).

Ranson, S. (1985) 'Contradictions in the Government of Educational Change', *Political Studies*, 33(1).

Salaman, G. (1986) *Working*, Chichester, Ellis Horwood.

Wood, S. (1982) (ed.) *The Degradation of Work? Skill, Deskilling and the Labour Process*, London, Hutchinson.

Section I

The work context of teaching

1
Educational organizations as workplaces

Frances Tipton

As organizations go, schools and colleges may not have been as much neglected by exercises in general social analysis as others. [. . .] But looking at them as places of work is another matter. It will be argued here that the study of educational organizations as workplaces has been bedevilled by the tyranny of taxonomies in organizational analysis, the intellectual isolation of the study of organizations and the management orientation of educational administration as a field.

The tyranny of taxonomies

Organizations are classified in everyday life – as firms, churches, schools and prisons, for example. They are also regularly classified by academics, as standard texts such as those by Silverman and by Eldridge and Crombie indicate.[1] The results produced by academics are not always so different from everyday usage. The influential typology based upon functions used by Katz and Kahn is a case in point.[2] Here firms, economic organizations, have their being because they produce to meet needs: schools, maintenance organizations, have theirs to perpetuate the society that has such needs: both thereby ensure the existence of the society. Time and again such formulations are criticized, as the references quoted illustrate, yet the labels and assumptions stay put. Thus it is neither new to say that the view that schools are schools and firms are firms may be handy in that it highlights the differences between them but also dangerous because it diverts us from their similarities, nor too late.
[. . .]
    The analysis of educational institutions as workplaces requires two

things: firstly, the staff to be shifted into a central focus and, secondly, use to be made of general social science material on employment. Certainly, a shift of focus to teachers has taken place in the subsequent wave of interactionist analysis.[3] A similar movement is illustrated in the contributions to projects with more mixed perspectives.[4] The question remains of whether such change has been simultaneously accompanied by the placement of teachers within a labour market framework or acknowledgement of teaching as employment.

[. . .]

On the rare occasion when a labour market theme does occur, as for example in Ginsburg, Meyenn and Miller's report on teachers, professionalism and trade unionism, the context of the school is lost.[5] This paper is based upon their examination of the views of a small number of teacher union activists drawn from different schools with respect to the topic of professionalism and trade unionism. Thus, as in previous times, the teacher is 'removed' from the workplace for analysis – although the concept used in the process is now ideology rather than role. The organizational analyst, however, would be interested in knowing how these activists handled their views and dilemmas in their relations with colleagues and headteachers within their own workplaces.[6] The unique contribution to the subject of teachers and work is that made by Lawn and Ozga in the last of the three collections of papers mentioned.[7] This also, and understandably, is disconnected from the field of the sociology of educational organizations: yet it is probably the best example available of the form of analysis the latter must embrace for reinterpretation of such organizations as workplaces to progress.

The new sociology of education did not arise without criticism, and not just from systems theorists. Marxists, such as Joan Simon, were instantly on the attack because of its potential for neglecting the structural context of education.[8] And by the mid and late 1970s the increased attention being paid to the idea of political economy in general and Marxism in particular in sociology in Britain and America was being reflected in the study of education.

Such a change of direction looks to be a promising one for the purpose of bringing educational organizations as workplaces into sharper focus. However, little radical thought over the years has been directed at detailed analysis of the design of work in specific work situations even in the traditional industrial setting.[9] Indeed, it was for this reason that Braverman's account of capitalism and work design, to be returned to later, was at first regarded as a break-through and only subsequently taken to task (albeit with due respect).[10] For what he did, by virtue of his publication, was to inspire others to address the finer points of work organization in different capitalist societies.[11] In the light of this, it is perhaps not surprising to find that the initial impact on the sociology of education of Marxist and political economy approaches has been to reopen questions about macro-level relationships – this time concerning knowledge and social reproduction and the role of the state. Once again the teacher has remained in the background: an agent of economically significant cultural messages.[12] When teachers have been the direct focus it has usually been with regard to the determination of their social class position. But great difficulty is regularly experienced in satisfactorily extracting them from the slot of being, thereby, simply state functionaries. The end result from the present viewpoint, is the endorsement, by default if nothing more, of the kind of categorization of organizations already encountered. In other words, schools have become cast as repositories of 'unproductive' or 'mental' labour and thereby passed over as workplaces proper. However, if the analysis is commenced from another direction, that is to say from the assumption that teachers have to earn their living, not only can we study the quality of working life in educational institutions and other employment issues, but a more complicated answer to the question of the class position of teachers may prove necessary. Lawn and Ozga reach similar conclusions through a parallel route.[13]

Turning to the specific field of the study of schools as organizations, it is discernible that the same process of classification has been adopted. L. A. Bell in a recent article in the *British Journal of Sociology of Education* made an appeal for a 'reappraisal' of the study of schools as organizations.[14] An indication of the balance of the article is that of his thirty references, only four are drawn from outside the field of education. His themes, the question of goals, stability of organizational membership and type of technology are by no means inimical to an organization as workplaces perspective. Far from it. The point is that they are stopped short. The problem about schools is that they have unclear goals and unclear technology, says Bell. Thus:

> The external demands which are made on schools . . . often conflict with each other. . . . This, taken with the different views about the nature and content of education which already exists within the teaching profession, has led in many schools to a situation in which it is not very clear what the goals of the schools are.[15]

In addition, there is much uncertainty about the process of teaching and learning. (Incidentally, the state of uncertainty about how to deal with inputs into the production process was the essence of Charles Perrow's concept of technology and theory about the determination of organizational structure.[16]) Together, says Bell, this spells trouble for teachers: they know neither what they should do nor how to do it. So far as it goes this may be true. But unless we know how much importance they attach to work in the first place we cannot tell to what extent teachers are affected by or care about unclear educational goals and teaching technology. As it stands, teachers emerge from this study rather like robots: beings programmed to think only of their work organization's ends and means. Such an approach would be plausible for a society in which teachers were religious functionaries or the effectiveness of teacher education for ideologically 'programming' teachers was potentially 100 per cent and in fact exploited.

The point of this discussion is not actually to win over the opposition to the idea of looking at schools as workplaces. Constructing taxonomies of organizations inevitably forces through either/or decisions. A particular body has to be either an economic or an educational organization. Thus Salaman accepts the fact that organizations have more than one face; he says, for example, that, 'to see, say, economic organisations simply in terms of their production of various goods and materials is to ignore their political importance'.[17] For all that it can be seen that they remain *economic* organizations; in other words, he retains the idea of a core identity. And this seems to have coloured his notion of what is and what is not a work organization. The process of classifying should aid not hinder analysis. Thus a current purpose for looking at organizations should, as it were, interact with existing modes of classification. In this way, the initial classification may be altered as the outcome of the current research and in the context of that issue. It will not, of course, necessarily be changed for all time: the original classification may remain a perfectly satisfactory idea for other purposes.

Thus, to want to examine schools as workplaces does not preclude them from being examined in terms of other criteria posited as the core of a concept of education. But what would be argued is that the most penetrating analyses of schools and colleges as organizations will not be achieved by assuming they are special. Neither will such analyses be achieved by applying alternative perspectives in isolation from one another. It is interesting to look at schools as workplaces as much *because* education is not industrial production as for any other reason; that difference is built into the research design. By the same token no realistic picture of schooling can be created unless account is taken of the idea that teaching and educational administration may also be regarded as work by those who did it. It may be that in the final analysis working in educational organizations turns out to be so fundamentally unlike working in other kinds of organizations that it makes sense to separate them in certain systems of classification.

The isolation of organizational analysis

Paradoxically, organizational analysis has not until quite recently been a good tool for understanding organizations. It has been a subject strangely lacking in realism. One major reason for this has been its isolation from an obvious source of material, that generated by a field itself divided into the overlapping and ideologically warring subjects of industrial relations, industrial sociology and the sociology of work or occupations. This can be illustrated with the aid of two books that attempt to bring the two enterprises, organizational analysis and, what for present purpose will be called industrial sociology, together, but starting from different points. Salaman's *Work Organisations* is one of them. Here Salaman argues quite specifically for an integration of the fields of organization theory, industrial sociology and the sociology of work.[18] The text and/or references set out to fulfil this obligation by covering, in addition to a wide range of British and, as is more usual, American organizational analysis, such subjects as trade unions, the design of work and the labour market. In *Competition and Control at Work* Stephen Hill presents 'the new industrial sociology'.[19] He includes organization theory, albeit on a modest scale, in this enterprise. It comes as some surprise to see the subject referred to as a 'specialised area of industrial sociology' rather than as an autonomous area of study, one predominantly made up of contributions from psychology, economics, politics, sociology and what is known as management theory.[20] However, this does not alter the main point, which is Hill's interest in making more use of organization theory in industrial sociology.

For British users of organizational analysis there is another factor that has contributed to its unrealistic quality. The subject has been dominated by American texts. The following authors, some then living some dead, all widely read in the 1950s and 1960s, are all Americans: Taylor, Barnard, Mayo, Parsons, Etzioni, Blau, Scott, Perrow, Selznick, Cyert and March, Hage, Goulder. The very enthusiasm for the British case studies produced by Woodward and by Burns and Stalker seems to bear this out.[21] The main journal in the field, the *Administrative Science Quarterly*, remains an outlet almost exclusively for American writers. This American influence begins to weaken as far as new contributors to the field of organizational analysis itself in Britain are concerned but remains strong on those outside the field drawing upon it – such as writers on educational institutions. It is no doubt this American domination of the subject that has been responsible for the lack of consideration given to the labour market, especially to trade unionism. Trade unionism, because of its historical connection with socialism, is less accepted in American life and thought than in European. The influence of Macarthy-ism has cast a long shadow even over American academics.[22] A subject that is as linked with management as organizational analysis must be among the last to shake it off.

In addition, organizational analysis has been disconnected from, or highly selective in its use of, general social science theory and ideas. Organizations in mainstream organizational analysis may have had *members*, but these members have rarely been identified in terms of their social class, age, gender or ethnic group. In short, they exist in a socio-cultural limbo. And the organizations as a whole often exist as if in an economic and political limbo: only in rare cases have governmental, legal, macro-economic (as opposed to immediate market) or international factors been taken into account. Mouzelis was a lone voice in the 1960s asking for the subject to turn away from con-sideration of trivial issues, largely pursued by writers in the management tradi-tion, and back to the fundamental ones, particularly of power and democracy, that concerned the classic writers.[23] Some ten years later a response came in the shape of texts such as those by Abrahamsson, Burrell and Morgan and Salaman. For with *Work Organisations*, Salaman says, additionally, that he is returning 'to the preoccupation of Marx and Weber' and trying above all to 're-establish the political nature of organisational structure'.[24]

It is therefore not surprising that when writers on schools have turned to organizational analysis for ideas the results have disappointed as accounts of schools as places of employment. And it is worth noting that three out of Bell's four references to the organizational analysis literature were American sources.[25] The fact that organizational analysis has frequently been bypassed by writers on schools and colleges has indeed been an advantage when it has led instead to a greater use of general social theory. But opportunities have been lost. Thus social class, age and gender have been used as factors in the analysis of schools and colleges to a greater extent than in that of business firms, but in relation to pupil and student rather than staff interaction. Durkheim's ideas on education and the moral order have influenced research on the goals of educational organizations, yet his notion of the occupational community has not been used in the analysis of teachers in the way it has, for example, of architects and railwaymen.[26] Marxist thought has inspired writing on education and the reproduction of the dominant ideology but not on, as has been said, the division of labour and the design of work in schools and colleges.

Educational administration as industrial relations?

The field of educational administration could in many ways be regarded as the industrial relations branch of the study of education. It is based, if precariously, upon a foundation of the social sciences and it aims to provide a service to practitioners through its teaching and research. Organizational analysis has been a strong component of the field of study since its inception. One of the first texts to be produced by the first organized body of university teachers of educational administration, the American NCPEA, contained a commissioned article from Talcott Parsons on organizational analysis.[27] Recent writing indicates that this early emphasis has not waned amongst American academics and that it has travelled unimpeded across the Atlantic.

The British *Educational Administration Bulletin* heralds both points by virtue of the attention it gave to a paper given in an international conference held in London in 1974. The paper, by a Canadian, T. Barr Greenfield, condemned the domination of systems theory in the version of organizational analysis popular in education administration.[28] It was, by the same token, a criticism of the hold of the American academic establishment in the field. This material, or adaptations of it, was used on more than one occasion again.[29]

At the level of theory, British educational administration has been overpowered by the earlier start to the subject in America. Thus systems theory has held sway in American writing, and American writing has held sway in British writing. It is both interesting and sad that the attempt by

Baron and Taylor to develop a British social science foundation to the subject came to nothing.[30] The field of education administration has grown in the sense that more people now study and write under that rubric but no progress has been made in the development of the social science foundation to the subject. Thus the publicity given to the system theory versus phenomenology debate initiated by Barr Greenfield was of great benefit. An alternative paradigm to systems theory became at last available to British students of educational administration. But it is indicative of the state of disassociation between British educational administration and British social science that the earlier and very heated debates in this country on the identical theme of positivism and phenomenology in first sociology and then sociology of education appeared to go unnoticed.[31]

If the main theoretical debate in recent years in educational administration has been the phenomenological attack on systems theory, it follows that what remains largely unnoticed is the renewed interest in the social sciences in political economy and radical thought. Perusal of the index of *Approaches to School Management* will reveal one mention of Marx and this turns out to be a note arising from a passing comment in one article.[32] And neither capitalist and socialist philosophies nor party politics, the labour market context of teaching, nor unions are dealt with in regard to their impact on school management in a serious way in the text. This point is underlined in a recent selection of literature for 'the teaching of education management' provided by a management teachers' group in the British Educational Management and Administration Society.[33] British educational administration, therefore, has been unable to break the American mould. This has consisted of a reliance upon psychology and social psychology and an ignorance or fear of European sociology and political science, party politics and the labour movement. The first manifests itself in a preponderance of writing on leadership characteristics and effectiveness (perhaps through 'participation') and small–group behaviour in organizations. The second is a preference for the politically uncomplicating framework of systems theory.[34] It is unfortunate that the phenomenological critique opened up by Barr Greenfield is not a sufficiently powerful tool in itself to counterbalance these tendencies.

Since the publication of *Educational Administration and the Social Sciences*, the ethos of the field has changed.[35] Greater effort has been put into giving it a management identity. One indication of this is the decision to add the term 'management' to the title of the British Educational Administration Society. Thus the intellectual future for the subject is uncertain. At one time it would have been expected that social science thinking would automatically, if slowly, percolate through to it: radical thought, however, fits uneasily into a management perspective, and thus the response to the Barr Greenfield kind of debate that has taken place in sociology and the sociology of education, and which for organizational analysis is very ably charted by Burrell and Morgan, may bypass the field altogether.[36] Certainly, Burrell and Morgan's publication does not appear among the recommendations of texts in the *Education*

Management Teachers' Newsletter.[37] Nor, in fact, does any British text with a definite sociological orientation. Indeed, of the non-education references, only one British writer, a former professor of management at the London Business School, is included. Thus British and British-based sociological writers on organizations, who as a group have made considerable contributions to the subject and now include such names as Albrow, Mouzelis, Silverman, Salaman, Burrell and Morgan, Eldridge and Crombie, are excluded only to be replaced by, for example, a publication which, on the compiler's own admission, is 'dull' and 'one of a large number of basic block-busters for American students of management'.[38]

The field of industrial relations proper and industrial sociology has always contained a tension between the goals of providing a management service and critical analysis. Indeed, a literature exists on the issue.[39] However, management bias is not an acute problem. There has been a long and rich tradition of research into labour history in Britain, and interest in the analysis of modern trade unionism continues unabated. Thus the subject is copiously recorded and widely taught in colleges and universities.[40] The same cannot be said about unionism in education. Despite the fact that one teacher union alone, the NUT, has consistently remained amongst the top dozen largest unions in the country in the last twenty-five years (in 1960, out of 651 unions in the UK it was eighth in terms of membership size[41]), and another, the ATTI, joined the TUC long before white-collar unions in other sectors, the subject is hardly studied. To the extent that it has been opened up at all it is with respect to the impact of unionism as a pressure group *vis-à-vis* government education and salary policy; published studies of teacher union membership and grass-roots activity remain few. The material consulted by Undy *et al.* when writing about the NUT in 1981 remained (except for additions from recent copies of the *The Teacher* and *Rank and File*) that used also by this writer in the early 1970s, and its sparsity had been noted then.[42] So despite such comment and a subsequent recommendation by George Baron that the industrial relations dimension should be taken more into account in education,[43] a recent and rare look on the subject begins, 'This book is an attempt to generate discussion and research on organised teacher activity, an area of study within education which remains relatively neglected, particularly in terms of reputable studies of union activity on a day-to-day local basis.'[44] If the subject is not dismissed, it is treated unsympathetically. The most recent production on educational administration, *Approaches to Post-School Management*, has gone just a little further in the direction of an industrial relations approach than previous texts.[45] Even so, there is instruction in contrasting it with what will undoubtedly be a widely used reader on industrial relations published the same year, G. S. Bain's *Industrial Relations to Britain*.[46] Parts I and II of the latter deal with, respectively, trade unions and management. These topics are each given a fifth of the text to themselves. Of *Approaches to Post-School Management*, 43 per cent is devoted to two sections on, first, leadership and then management. Only one five-page article in these almost 200 pages is about trade unions. And it is entitled 'Relations *with* Trade Unions' (emphasis added).[47] In other words, it is not about the contribution of trade unionism *per se* to staff security and satisfaction or educational decision-making; rather, the impression given is that the article is there to instruct managements on how to *deal* with unions.

Given that educational administration sets out to be in part a practitioner-oriented subject, but given also its 'management' stance and lack of equivalent interest in unionism, a problem arises of how changes of practice that benefit staff rather than heads, or at the expense of heads, can be pursued. Many of the conclusions that are, to be drawn from discussions about the quality of working life involve basic restructuring of workplaces so as to redistribute tasks and decision-making powers. Positions of headship, and so on, are thereby immediately the centre of concern. So far we have discovered only a head who raises the issue of the abolition of headship in the current literature in the field.[48]

Educational institutions as workplaces: starting points

The temptation is to attempt to begin the study of educational institutions as workplaces from the establishment of a concept of work organization suitably elastic to include them. This is to be resisted on the grounds that such an exercise involves coping with exactly the complications that beset attempts to deal with teachers in theorizing about social class. Instead, it is recommended that the departure point be the simple enough assumption that teachers do work and schools and colleges are workplaces: comparisons with other employment situations will allow more exact meanings to be subsequently established. This demands drawing upon ideas and material used elsewhere in the analysis of work. It also requires ideas about starting points. Two seemingly useful ones would be orientations to employment and the design of work, for between them they tackle gaps in our information about educational institutions, fan out conveniently into a number of issues, and have the advantage of being relatively well-developed themes in the sociology of work.

Where educational institutions are concerned, it is true they have been considered as 'open systems', that is to say in relation to an 'environment'. But the environment will consist either of pupils (the home and neighbourhood) or decision-makers (educational pressure groups, parents and governments). Rarely does it constitute the labour market of the member of staff. Even stepping aside from institutional studies the position is not greatly improved. Thus, though Bradley and Silverleaf give themselves the promising remit of looking at careers in further education, they skate around the core issues of whether their sample of teachers have realistic chances of alternative employment, what exactly the pay-off for them is as between intrinsic job satisfaction and financial reward and, beyond asking whether they will apply for promotion, what kind of action they would be prepared to take in support of their careers.[49] The subject of trade unionism, for example, is simply not raised. The nearest matters come to it is in the form of the question, 'Are you a member of a professional association or body?' Indeed, one is left curious as to what the purpose of such a question could be. Teaching and educational administration, therefore, still awaits its version of an *Affluent Worker* study.

The *Industrial Attitudes and Behaviour* volume of this project by John Goldthorpe and his colleagues remains twenty years after its inception an excellent guide as to how to approach the study of people at work.[50] The point they make about the range of their research *vis-à-vis* previous industrial projects still stands in relation to education ones:

> in subsequent chapters we deal with data relating to the worker and his job, the worker and his work group, the worker and his firm, the worker and his union, and the worker and his economic future. The same range has not always been covered in other studies of industrial employees. Secondly, and more importantly, we also have a considerable amount of material at our disposal concerning our respondents' 'out-plant' lives. Because the perspectives of our research were much broader than those of most specifically 'industrial' studies, we know something about the men in our sample not only as industrial employees but also as husbands and fathers, as neighbours and so on. We have, therefore, the opportunity of seeing their attitudes and behaviour as workers not in the context of the industrial enterprise alone but, rather, in the much wider context provided by family, community and class.[51]

And the questions with which they armed themselves remained difficult to better for industrial or non-industrial settings alike:

> In what degree and in what ways are industrial attitudes and behaviour *patterned* – so that the nature of the worker's relationship, with say, his employing organisation is associated with the nature of his relationships with his workmates, his supervisor, or his union? To the extent that such patterning is in evidence, in what terms is this to be explained and understood? Is it to be seen, for example, as being determined primarily by features of the work situation itself – as being, say, the result of workers' experience of, and reaction to, the work-tasks and roles which they are required to perform? Or is it rather the case that any such pattern may equally, or perhaps more basically, derive from a particular orientation which workers have taken towards employment – from the wants and expectations they have of it, and thus from the way in which they define their work situation rather than simply respond to it? If this latter alternative applies, what are the major determinants, external to the work situation, of the meaning which men give to their work and of the place and function they accord to work within their lives as a whole.[52]

The original importance of the study lay in the decision illustrated here to look at the employee's immediate work task and its organisational setting in relation to his social context in order to interpret his attitude to work. Hence the collection of material on the 'out-plant' lives of respondents. The Goldthorpe and Lockwood thesis about the process by which attitudes to work are formed is both well known and respected, and yet how little material is collected on the social circumstances and out-of-work activities of teachers when constructing school and college case studies. Moreover, these employees will more often than not be women. Given the known importance for many women of outside work identities – those of housewife, mother, or daughter of aging parents and in-laws – an unexplored dimension of schools and colleges as organisations becomes apparent.

Goldthorpe *et al.* concentrated upon manual workers. More recently, Prandy, Stewart and Blackburn have looked at the experience of work of white-collar employees.[53] Their research does not provide us with the same sense of the organizational situation as did the *Affluent Worker* study, but the idea of work orientations is evolved in a direction which carries particular weight for middle-class employment. They dwell on the importance of the development of expectations and on the idea of promotion. Views of promotion are seen as having a significant impact on attitudes to other rewards, that is to say income, status, security, intrinsic job satisfaction and social relationships. Thus 'those with more favourable perceptions of their chances of advancement tend to have lower expectations with respect to the other rewards attaching to their present position', they argue.[54] Promotion, then, is in effect the social bromide: it is one of the factors that helps to reproduce the existing system. If the expectation of promotion declines, much else follows: 'our findings show that a perceived lack of promotion opportunities is the major factor in the development of a critical attitude towards top management'.[55] They also link such responses with the development of 'collective responses', although, it might be added in passing, this is not regarded as synonymous with 'proletarianization'.[56]

It has been said of teaching that little career advancement is possible because the occupational structure of the school is that of a 'flat pyramid'.[57] If this is so, then perhaps teachers do not develop promotion expectations to the same degree as other white-collar workers. On the other hand, perhaps as the outcome of a middle-class socialization, they are every bit as pronounced, thereby giving rise to an occupational group forever operating with a high level of career frustrations. The interview schedule and checklist provided by Prandy *et al.* would enable such points to be explored on a comparative basis.

Certainly, once an analysis of the educational institution is pursued, taking into account the work orientations of staff, different approaches to basic themes in organizational analysis suggest themselves. In fact, this writer has already come to different conclusions about the significance of obscure official goals in education to those implied by Bell, considered earlier, for example.[58] Rather than constituting a source of anxiety, it was this lack of clarity that provided many staff in technical colleges in the 1960s with the opportunity to act entrepreneurially and gain promotion.

Prior to the early 1970s in Britain the subject of the design of jobs was of interest predominantly to a fairly tight-knit group of management consult-ants and psychologists and a few students of labour history and theory. The single most important reason for the rise in interest in the subject more generally amongst sociologists has been the publication of Braverman's thesis on work design and the labour market.[59] The debate surrounding this publication is significant for organizational analysis. Earlier others, such as John Child, had rejected a straightforward technological determinist approach to understanding organizational structure;[60] this debate, however, has provoked interest in the *detail* of job content and the decision-making surrounding it and an awareness of the need for historical research that did not exist to nearly the same degree previously.[61] And Craig Littler sees Braverman's contribution as the opening up of an opportunity for a 'new, *integrated* approach to the study and history of work'.[62]

In one sense, the design of work has had an important place in studies of schools and colleges; there has been a steady output of accounts of the differences between modes of teaching – comparisons of streaming and forms of mixed ability teaching, traditional versus individualized learning, subject based versus team teaching – together with the task of coping in general with recalcitrant clients. This constitutes the stuff of the idea of work design. But these are in the main studies of the effectiveness of pupil learning, the social structures of pupil cultures or of the characteristics of teaching *per se*. They are rarely systematically undertaken as studies of work, work satisfaction, the social relations of staff at work or staff and management control. It is almost as if in the field of education the subject of work design pre-dates the rise of scientific management. Frederick Taylor's view of human motivation may not be morally acceptable in liberal and radical circles, but he did at least make an intellectual contribution by simply positing a link between work design and the goal of efficiency. In education the link between work design, seen from the viewpoint of staff rather than pupils, and the goal of pupil learning is tenuously made, if at all. It is almost as if there is an assumption that anything that is good for the client must be good for staff. Certainly, the proposition that work should be enjoyable for teachers and administrators as a right is as little put either inside or outside social science circles as is the comparable proposition for other workers by boards of private sector companies. When the proposals of 'change agents' for schools are resisted, openly or subtly, by staff the latter's actions are not unusually interpreted unfavourably by different commentators – as moral backsliding or incompetency – rather than as logical actions, from the teachers' view-point, to protect job interests. Even the teachers themselves in the Countes-thorpe experiment were apologetic about reverting to traditional teaching methods because of the strain of using an 'individualized' learning technique.[63]

Braverman's approach to the subject of the design of work differed from the existing literature, much of which had been written by those who could be regarded as members of a 'quality of working life' circle, by being explicitly Marxist in inspiration.[64] His thesis, now well known, is that the capitalist imperative has been responsible for the continual reformulation of jobs, whether blue or white collar, so as to separate the principle of conception from that of execution. The system strives to reduce workers' jobs to pure execution, the essence of the labour process, over which management has complete control. This has become known as deskilling (although it is difficult to find the phrase in Braverman's book). Such a stark analysis has predictably produced reactions: contributors to *The Degradation of Work?* and Craig Littler, for example, have all questioned whether the matter is as simple as Braverman suggests.[65] Unfortunately for those studying education, Braverman's only reference to 'governmental, educational, and health establishments' is as places which reproduce the work processes to be found in enterprises producing directly for the market and containing the 'middle layers' of employment. These are 'a range of intermediate categories, sharing the characteristics of worker on the one side and manager on the other in varying degrees'.[66] In consequence, the main debate over Braverman's thesis is almost exclusively confined to work design and organizational control in the business sector.

In the debate two elements dominate: the question of what *is* happening to skills, to job content, and that of its determination, or management methods. Lawn and Ozga have made a start in the education field with regard to the first.[67] What comes through here and elsewhere is the immense problem of classifying and measuring changes in job content, whether in terms of subjective meanings or objective characteristics. Braverman alone fails to provide sufficient tools for the task. In part this is the outcome of his decision to use only the objective elements of Marx's theory of social class and to leave aside the matter of worker consciousness. It is interesting that in seeking to make good this gap, another American writer who made only partial use of a Marxist framework comes to mind, Blauner. To an extent, Blauner took almost the opposite course to Braverman when he decided to analyse work satisfaction through the concept of alienation but in isolation from the 'objective' element of the ownership of the means of production.[68] There is little doubt that this does grave damage to the final meaning of his research; at the same time, his method of operationalizing the idea of work satisfaction (or alienation in his terms), namely into the four components of control over the task, its meaning and the degree of social isolation and the scope for intrinsic satisfaction associated with it, remains useful for examining shifts in work content. This is equally true of the checklists for measuring attitudes to work developed for the *Affluent Worker* project which followed close on the heels of *Alienation and Freedom* and reflects the same ideas. More recently the Department of Employment's Work Research Unit has produced guidelines for work improvement which contain not dissimilar themes. Modest experiments by the writer in using these with teachers and educational administrators for the self-analysis of jobs indicated that they touch on relevant issues. In turn, the Manpower Services Commission has made prodigious efforts to codify the objective characteristics of jobs.[69] This project has been carried out for the purpose of linking job requirements with youth training. But the process of analysing jobs entered by young people cannot be in principle different from that used for the analysis of jobs in general. As it stands, it provides one illustration of the procedures and degree of detail that would be required as the start of a full attempt at charting movements in the jobs of teachers and educational administrators.

Braverman rests his case about the determination of the design of work on Taylorism: Taylorism, he argues, both represents the capitalist ethic and has been the dominant influence on practice. The implications of his argument for organizational analysis is potentially large for in effect he is replacing the concept of bureaucracy by that of Taylorism as the prime point of departure for the examination of organizational structures. This is an advantage for understanding the design of jobs. The concept of bureaucracy has had a stultifying effect on research in this direction. The division of labour tends to be passed over as simply a manifestation of the distribution of power: how it comes about that tasks are what they are or divided in the way they are so as to realize a system of power distribution is rarely tackled in the degree of detail to which Taylorism automatically lends itself.

However, whether the acceptance and practice of Taylorism has been as widespread, either in Britain or elsewhere, even in industry, as Braverman believes has been disputed. A management method of this kind, it is said, would be unable to deal with a sophisticated workforce and well-organized labour movement. And Craig Littler has added that 'Within capitalism there is a perpetual tension between treating workers as a commodity to be hired and fired and harnessing their ingenuity and cooperativeness'.[70] He returns, therefore, to the question of the role of legitimacy in work relations. But whilst believing in the necessity for the inclusion of a dimension of this kind, he finds the Weberian formulation of legitimacy wanting on the grounds of it being too strong a concept to be able to deal with a lower order of 'day-to-day compliance'.[71] For this he suggests the use of the idea of 'consent'. Work relations may be governed by consent with or without an overarching framework of legitimacy. He continues, here and subsequently in collaboration with Graeme Salaman, by developing a three-part typology for encompassing the ground within which managerial strategies for control at the workplace are formulated.[72] This consists of job design, the formal structure of control and employment relations generally (that is to say, the organization's situation *vis-à-vis* the wider labour market). The dynamic for the managerial search for control strategies is held to be the 'possibility of worker resistance'.[73] This analytical model is put forward as capable of dealing with 'all forms of work organisation'.[74]

Littler plays down the importance of Taylorism and reintroduces the concept of bureaucracy, but at least he keeps the subject of job design in focus. It is unlikely, however, that he had the educational context in mind when recommending the approach for general use (in this he is either less explicit or less ambitious than Braverman). Certainly, the task of analysing job design in the field of education is even more demanding than it is for industrial and commercial settings. One problem is obviously that of the equivalence for the direct role of the profit motive in the determination of job design in workplaces producing goods or services for the market. Another is the phenomenon of professional ideology. This overlays the more generally based sources of legitimacy, or perhaps 'consent', that already start to complicate the understanding of any work situation. Yet the 'Appointments' pages of the national educational press act as a constant reminder that jobs in education have identifiable shapes. So far the explanation for these is confined either to extrapolation from other jobs or to vague suggestions about the role of university subjects as mediated by examining bodies and criss-crossed by professional ideology, or parcelled up in the concept of bureaucratization or the role of the state. All of these points hold water to varying degrees, but a precise account requires the application of a coherent set of ideas to the past as well as the contemporary situation. Braverman and Littler provide between them two examples of potential starting points for such an exercise.

It is not intended that this article should be read as a panegyric for the study of educational institutions through organizational analysis. It could be that it would be better if the subject was permitted a quiet death and the field left to the sociology of work. But if it is to remain in being, then it needs the injection of realism that what could be called the new organizational analysis might be able to bring to it. The alternative to either the death or rejuvenation of the subject is for the style of studying schools and colleges to become so removed from that current in studying other workplaces that it becomes impossible to establish the similarities and differences between the former and the latter.

Notes and references

1. Silverman, D. (1970) *The Theory of Organisations* (London, Heinemann); Eldridge, J. E. T. and Crombie, A. D. (1974) *A Sociology of Organisations* (London, Allen & Unwin).
2. Katz, D. and Kahn, R. L. (1966) *The Social Psychology of Organisations* (New York, Wiley).
3. See, for example, Woods, P. (ed.) (1980) *Teacher Strategies* (London, Croom Helm); Woods, P. (1983) *Sociology and the School: an interactionist viewpoint* (London, Routledge & Kegan Paul).
4. See Eggleston, J. (ed.) (1979) *Teacher Decision-Making in the Classroom* (London, Routledge & Kegan Paul); Barton, L. and Walker, S. (eds) (1981) *Schools, Teachers and Teaching* (Lewes, Falmer Press).

5. Ginsburg, M. B., Meyenn, R. J. and Miller, H. D. R. (1980) Teachers' Conceptions of Professionalism and Trades Unionism: an ideological analysis, in Woods, op. cit., pp. 213–36.
6. Perhaps such a dimension will appear in subsequent reports of the project as a whole, as apparently it does include participant observation in schools.
7. Lawn, M. and Ozga, J. 'The Educational Worker? A re-assessment of teachers' in Barton and Walker, op. cit., pp. 45–64.
8. Simon, J. (1974) 'New direction' sociology and comprehensive schooling, *Forum* 17(1), Autumn, pp. 8–14.
9. This point is developed further in Tipton, B. F. A. (1982) The quality of training and the design of work, *Industrial Relations Journal* 13(1), pp. 35–37.
10. Braverman, H. (1974) *Labor and Monopoly Capitalism* (New York, Monthly Review Press).
11. See, for example, Littler, C. (1982) *The Development of the Labour Process in Capitalist Societies* (London, Heinemann).
12. See, for example, the pioneering Open University projects, Dale, R., Esland, G. and Macdonald, M. (eds) (1976) *Schooling and Capitalism* (London, Routledge & Kegan Paul); Dale, R., Esland, G., Fergusson, R. and Macdonald, M., (eds) (1981) *Education and the State*, Vol. 1, *Schooling and the National Interest*; Vol. 2, *Politics, Patriarchy and Practice* (Lewes, Falmer Press).
13. Lawn and Ozga, op. cit.
14. Bell, I. A. (1980) The school as an organisation: a re-appraisal, *British Journal of Sociology of Education* 1, pp. 193–2.
15. Ibid., pp. 187–8.
16. Perrow, C. (1971) *Organisational Analysis* (London, Tavistock Press).
17. Salaman, G. (1979) *Work Organizations* (London, Longman).
18. Ibid., p. 216.
19. Hill, S. (1981) *Competition and Control at Work: the new industrial sociology* (London, Heinemann).
20. Ibid., p. 77.
21. Woodward, J. (1965) *Industrial Organization: theory and practice* (London, Oxford University Press); Burns, T. and Stalker, G. M. (1961) *The Management of Innovation* (London, Tavistock Press).
22. A brief reference to this is made by Gouldner in Gouldner, A. (1971) *The Coming Crisis of Western Sociology*, London, Heinemann, p. 449.
23. Mouzelis, N. P. (1967) *Organisations and Bureaucracy: an analysis of modern theories* (London, Routledge & Kegan Paul).
24. Salaman, op. cit., p. 216.
25. Bell, op. cit.
26. See, Salaman, G. (1974) *Community and Occupation: an exploration of work/leisure relationships* (Cambridge, Cambridge University Press).
27. Parsons, op. cit.
28. Greenfield, T. B. (1974) Theory about organisations: a new perspective and its implications for schools, paper to the 1974 International Inter-Visitation Programme, London. A symposium on the paper appeared in *Educational Administration* 5(1), Autumn 1976. This was followed by Greenfield, T. B. 'Where does self belong in the study of organisations?' Reply to a symposium, *Educational Administration* 6(1), Winter 1977/8.
29. See Hughes, M. (ed.) (1975) *Administering Education: international challenge*

(London, Athlone Press); Houghton, V. *et al.* (eds) (1975) *Management in Education Reader* (London, Ward Lock); Bush, T. *et al.* (eds) (1980) *Approaches to School Management* (London, Harper & Row).

30. See Baron, G. & Taylor, W. (eds) (1969) *Educational Administration and the Social Sciences* (London, Athlone Press).

31. For the first major examples of published material, see Young, M. F. D. (ed.) (1971) *Knowledge and Control: new directions for the sociology of education* (London, Collier-Macmillan); Filmer, P., Phillipson, M., Silverman, D. and Walsh, D. (1972) *New Directions in Sociological Theory* (London, Collier-Macmillan).

32. Bush *et al.*, op. cit. p. 69.

33. *Education Management Teachers' Newsletter*, BEMAS, No. 3, May, 1983, pp. 4–5.

34. See, for example, the two Open University readers, Houghton, V. *et al.* (eds) (1975) *Management in Education*, Reader 1; Dobson, L. *et al.* (eds) *Management in Education*, Reader 2 (London, Ward Lock Educational).

35. Baron and Taylor, op. cit.

36. Burrell, G. and Morgan, G. (1979) *Sociological Paradigms & Organizational Analysis* (London, Heinemann).

37. Op. cit.

38. The book in question is Hicks, H. and Gullett, C. R. (1976) *The Management of Organisations* (Maidenhead, McGraw-Hill).

39. See, for example, Deem, R. The teaching of industrial sociology in higher education – living with capitalism, or learning to be an organisation person?; Wood, S. Industrial sociology in practice, papers to the 1980 British Sociology Association Conference.

40. For just two recent sources and guides to the literature see Coates, K. and Topham, T. (1980) *Trade Unions in Britain* (Nottingham, Spokesman); Bain, G. S. (ed.) (1983) *Industrial Relations in Britain* (Oxford, Blackwell).

41. Bain, G. S. and Price, R. Union growth: dimensions, determinants and destiny in Bain, op. cit.

42. Undy, R., Ellis, V., McCarthy, W. E. J. and Hulmos, R. M. (1981) *Change in Trade Unions* (London, Hutchinson); Tipton, B. F. A. (1974) The hidden side of teaching: the teachers' unions, *London Educational Review* 3(2), Summer, pp. 20–30.

43. Baron, G. (1975) Some aspects of the 'headmaster Tradition', in Houghton *et al.*, op. cit., pp. 3–4.

44. Ozga, J. T. and Lawn, M. A. (1981) *Teachers, Professionalism and Class* (London, Falmer Press).

45. Boyd-Barrett, O. *et al.*, (eds) (1983) *Approaches to Post-School Management* (London, Harper & Row).

46. Op. cit.

47. Baillie, J. C. N. Relations with trade unions, in Boyd-Barrett, O. *et al.*, op. cit.

48. Watts, J. 'Sharing it out: the role of the head in participatory government', in Bush *et al.*, op. cit., pp. 293–303.

49. Silverleaf, J. and Bradley, J. (1979) *Making the Grade: careers in FE teaching* (Windsor, NFER).

50. Goldthorpe, J. H. *et al.* (1968) *The Affluent Worker: industrial attitudes and behaviour* (London, Cambridge University Press).

51. Ibid., p. 8.

52. Ibid., pp. 8–9.

53. Prandy, K., Steward, A., and Blackburn, R. M. (1982) *White-Collar Work* (London, Macmillan).
54. Ibid., p. 177.
55. Ibid., p. 178.
56. Ibid., p. 178.
57. Purvis, J. (1973) Schoolteaching as a professional career, *BJS* 24(1): 43–57.
58. Tipton, B. F. A. (1973) *Conflict and Change in a Technical College* (London, Hutchinson).
59. Braverman, op. cit.
60. Child, J. (1972) Organizational structure, environment and performance: the role of strategic choice, *Sociology* 6(1), January, pp. 1–22.
61. See, for example, Littler, op. cit.; Salaman, G. (1982) Managing the frontier of control, in Giddens, A. and Mackenzie, G. (eds) *Social Class and the Division of Labour* (Cambridge, Cambridge University Press), pp. 46–62; Wood, S. (ed.) (1983) *The Degradation of Work?* (London, Hutchinson).
62. Littler, op. cit., p. 26.
63. Bernbaum, G. (1972) Countesthorpe College, in *Case Studies of Educational Administration: II at the regional level* (Paris, OECD).
64. See, for example, Davis, L. E. and Taylor, J. C. (eds) (1972) *Design of Jobs* (Harmondsworth, Penguin).
65. Wood, op. cit.; Littler, op. cit.
66. Braverman, op. cit., pp. 405–6.
67. Lawn and Ozga, The Educational Worker? op. cit.
68. See Blauner, R. (1964) *Alienation and Freedom: the factory worker and his industry* (Chicago, University of Chicago Press).
69. See, for example, Manpower Services Commission (1983), *Job Components Inventory: shortened version*.
70. Littler, op. cit., p. 34.
71. Ibid., p. 40.
72. Littler, R. C. and Salaman, G. (1984) *Class at Work* (London, Batsford).
73. Ibid., p. 60.
74. Littler, op. cit., p. 43.

2

The school as a workplace

Robert Dreeben

The word 'workplace' usually conjures up images of factories and crafts-men's shops, places where men mix with tools and things, manufacture products, and perspire. Schools are something else; even though children make noise, dirt and trouble, they are bound up with teachers in activities that are largely mental, bookish and abstract. The point is not to argue that schools are factories and shops after all, but rather that the analysis of social patterns advances more productively when ostensibly different phenomena are shown to be comprehensible in terms of a small set of theoretical propositions. To succeed in such abstract theorizing, of course, is any scientist's dream, and one seldom realized in the social sciences. Usually, however, we settle for less and find pleasure in showing that diverse patterns can at least be arrayed along a few dimensions. That is one reason to consider schools as workplaces: to show that there are concepts and perspectives derived from other areas of the world of work that, when applied to the schools, make them more understandable.

Schools are organizations (as are other kinds of workplaces), which means that they are settings where a variety of occupations are brought together to create some product or provide some service. Organizations also contain work sites, places where particular activities, comprising some process of production, are carried out. Examples of sites are familiar: assembly lines in factories, wards and operating rooms in hospitals, classrooms in schools. In short, by considering certain structural properties of schools and classrooms, it becomes possible to understand the nature of educational work.

But why should one become preoccupied with theoretical notions about social patterns in the first place, and particularly with those pertaining to educational workplaces? The answer is straightforward: it is probably not possible to discover how teaching activities and the classroom experiences of children contribute to what pupils learn in schools (and in other settings) unless we can identify how different teaching activities in different settings create opportunities for and constraints upon learning. In plainer language, the study of workplaces can contribute to our knowledge about what is possible and how things work in schools.

[. . .]

For reasons not altogether clear, the history of education has consisted of a succession of programmatic efforts whose viability has usually been defended through appeals to plausibility, kindness, common sense, the eradication of existing evil, and one or another ideological principle; in short, everything but reasonably firm evidence that if teachers and parents do such-and-such, and if children are engaged in certain activities in certain kinds of settings, then certain known results are likely to ensue. Educational thinking, unfortunately, does not seem to proceed along these lines; but during times when public questioning of the efficacy of the schools has become widespread, it seems not unreasonable to find out, not just assert, what teachers should do and how schools should be built if they are to become more effective or, if not more effective, if children are to become happier learning at prevailing rates and under existing conditions. It is towards this end that the consideration of schools as workplaces gains some justification.

This paper treats the school as a workplace from two perspectives: from the point of view of authority relationships in schools and school systems, and from the point of view of the spatial arrangement of classrooms (work sites). The central theme is that relationships of authority and arrangements of space shape the character of teachers' work activities. There is no attempt here to argue that these are the sole influences on work activities, only that they are central and crucial. The occupational characteristics of teachers (Dreeben, 1970a), for example, undoubtedly influence the nature of teachers' work as does the nature of curriculum materials (Bruner, 1966) and the aggregate social characteristics of pupils. But these topics are beyond the scope of the present effort.

[. . .]

That school systems are bureaucratically organized in many respects (Weber, 1947, pp. 329–33) is unmistakable; but it would be a gross distortion to regard school systems (and particularly schools) as bureaucratic in the same way, for example, that certain government agencies, certain parts of the military, and certain commercial and industrial organizations in which workers are ranked hierarchically to facilitate the 'rational' accomplishment of routine and repetitive tasks for the production of tangible, measurable goods and services are considered bureaucratic.

Certainly, schools and school systems are bureaucratically organized in many important respects: they are hierarchical and governed by rules; workers are appointed to 'offices' (or positions) according to criteria of merit;

and the sequence of positions that workers occupy can constitute a career (actually several different careers). But the work of teachers can be properly understood only if the non-bureaucratic elements of schools are also identified. Among the most important of these non-bureaucratic elements is the teacher's immediate work site – the classroom, a setting subject to administrative direction (at least within the school hierarchy and under the authority of the principal) and yet significantly independent of such direction (Bidwell, 1965, pp. 1014–16).

The term 'non-bureaucratic' is residual and therefore cannot as such denote specific aspects of the external environment having consequences for the work of teachers. Accordingly, it is important to identify some of those aspects. First, the school system hierarchy does not serve as a direct transmission line for the communication of policy decisions designed to influence teachers' classroom activities or for the close supervision of those activities to gauge the accomplishment of school system goals, even though a school system can be viewed as an arrangement of hierarchical positions. This is not to deny that some policy decisions pass down the line, nor to deny that supervision occurs. Rather, the statement indicates that the central *classroom* activities of teachers – instruction and classroom management – are not *primarily* determined by high-level policy decisions; they cannot be viewed as 'following orders', and the reasons are not hard to find. The educational goals of school systems tend to be vaguely defined and refer to present and future outcomes that defy easy measurement and specification into readily identifiable goal-directed activities. Much of the teacher's work, in short, derives its character from the exigencies of classroom, school and community events (Jackson 1968), not from administrative directives.

Second, teaching activities tend not to be defined in terms of conformity to system-wide rules (though clearly certain types of teacher conduct have their origins in rules, e.g. taking attendance, monitoring students in public gatherings and the like). The reasons for the relative absence of rule domination are similar to those described above: activities difficult to codify in terms of sequences of means and ends are also difficult to subsume under general rules. That is, where work situations contain many unknowns and unpredictable exigencies, and where work entails significant loyalties to the needs of clients, work activities will be governed to a substantial degree according to the judgement of workers under the constraints of immediate situational demands (Gouldner, 1954, pp. 105–80; Perrow, 1970, pp. 75–89; Stinchcombe 1959).

Third, the 'quality control' function, to use a term with industrial overtones, tends to be highly attenuated in school systems. If, in fact, it is difficult to define educational goals and to design a 'technology' to effect them, then the meaning of the supervisory rating of workers becomes difficult to interpret and not terribly instructive as far as the overall management of a school system is concerned. Thus, although the rhetoric of supervision has great currency in the vocabulary of school administrators, the practice of supervision and the definition of what it entails continue to be ill defined (Dreeben, 1970a, pp. 42–50). In sum, the fact that the administrative hierarchy does not serve primarily as a 'line' for transmitting and effecting policy decisions, the relative unimportance of administrative rules for the classroom activities of teachers, and the attenuated nature of supervision constitute the more important non-bureaucratic elements that affect teaching.

One should not conclude from these assertions that teachers are essentially autonomous workers whose dealings with administrators are minimal and whose work is largely free of the conflicts usually engendered by hierarchical arrangements. Conflicts between teachers and administrators are legion and arise over such issues as the participation of teachers in the governance of schools and school systems, academic freedom, disciplinary policies, teacher ratings, closeness of supervision, red tape, the assignment of pupils and many more (Corwin, 1970, pp. 105–71). While the fact remains that the character of teachers' work in the classroom is not mainly determined through a bureaucratic apparatus, conflicts with the administration develop to a large extent from the ambiguous position of teaching as an occupation – it is not an autonomous profession nor is it a bureaucratized occupation; the prevailing conflicts frequently develop between the vaguely defined jurisdictional lines separating teachers and administrators.

[. . .]

At least two assumptions about schools and schooling, however, justify asking questions about organizational structure. First, it is possible that schools resemble other organizations like mental hospitals, psychiatric social work agencies and churches (whose efficacy also remains in doubt), all of which are dedicated to changing or influencing complex and variegated patterns of human conduct. This assumption leads to considering the characteristics of 'clients' and of the problems they present, and of the occupational resources – the technology – that workers bring to their jobs. It may be that none of these 'people-changing' organizations has a viable technology for accomplishing its goals, or that any available technology, even if it is otherwise viable, cannot succeed in a large organizational setting.

Second, one can view schools in terms of structural 'responses' to the problem of managing the lives of large numbers of children gathered in confined spaces for long-term instruction. This assumption leads to a consideration of ecological and architectural arrangements.

In any event, and whatever the assumptions, it is necessary to consider the nature of authority relationships in schools because they are hierarchical organizations and because managerial decisions at the minimum put constraints on teachers' work even if those decisions do not define its character. (Questions of architecture and ecology will be discussed later.)

Relationships of authority

The affiliation of teachers and pupils

The manner in which workers are *attached* to an organization and the way others *with whom they have contact* are attached have important consequences for the conduct of workers. The reasons are clear: affiliation determines the nature and level of a worker's placement in the hierarchy and influences the availability of incentives and the nature of contacts between persons in different locations (Barnard, 1938, pp. 139–60). Teachers are affiliated with schools by hiring; hardly an earthshaking revelation, but nevertheless a problematic one. Not all workers associated with organizations are hired – doctors have hospital privileges and lawyers form partnerships, as do architects. Pupils, moreover, are affiliated to schools by conscription (Dreeben, 1970a, pp. 54–7). The variety of affiliative modes suggests that organization members face different constraints and opportunities in their working situations.

Being hired as a salaried employee means that one consents by contract to perform certain agreed upon activities, to accept subordination to hierarchical superiors in exchange for remuneration, and to follow the rules. It means that within agreed upon limits one is subject to the direction of others in the conduct of one's work according to rules binding on oneself and on one's superordinates. (Under arrangements like privilege and partnership, the element of subordination to hierarchical superiors is markedly less, hence the difference in opportunities and constraints.) Among the obligations that teachers assume on being hired is the instruction and control of groups of conscripts – pupils – whose membership is involuntary though not necessarily undesired. This means that teachers must be ready to confront the problems of establishing and maintaining the voluntary participation of pupils in school activities. The situation of the teacher is also affected by the fact that a school district is a catchment area whose social composition (and hence the school's composition) cannot readily be determined or changed by the school. Teachers, then, unlike free professionals, cannot select their clientele and cannot teach only those whom they like or only those who are interested in or responsive to school activities.

Schools, like universities and both mental and general hospitals, all of which include their clients as members of the organization for extended periods of time, depend on the voluntary compliance of their clients with the rules of the organization and on their voluntary participation in activities designed for their welfare (Lefton, 1970, pp. 17–36; Parsons, 1964, pp. 257–91). This means, given the description (above) of how teachers and pupils are affiliated with schools, that in exercising authority teachers must deal with problems of pupils' motivation, not simply in terms of complying with specific teacher requests, assignments and orders, but in terms of gaining pupils' commitment to the enterprise of schooling itself

(Bidwell, 1970, pp. 37–69; Dreeben 1968: p. 37), which entails the expression of goodwill and the establishment of trust. One must naturally distinguish between the voluntariness of membership and the voluntariness of compliance; involuntary members (pupils) may or may not comply voluntarily to the expectations of teachers. But the conscriptive affiliative arrangement creates the problem for teachers of trying to establish and maintain the voluntary participation of some and often many pupils.

The authority problems of school principals *vis-à-vis* their subordinates (teachers) differ substantially from the problems of teachers *vis-à-vis* pupils in part because teachers are affiliated to schools differently from pupils. The compliance of teachers is not really problematic if the terms of employment have really been settled in the labour contract. Violations of the contract (by either side), *de facto* changes in the contract not agreed to by one party or the other, or changes in external circumstances whose effect changes the meaning of the contract (e.g. assigning a teacher to a class with large numbers of children who are very difficult to manage) create problems of authority between employers (principals) and employees (teachers). (Principals, of course, are really managers, not legal employers; but by virtue of the provisions in the labor contract, they are agents of the employer.)

Whether principals can give orders in the bureaucratic sense (Weber, 1947, pp. 324–9) to teachers is debatable. Surely there are certain rules of school operation that they must enforce, rules pertaining more to the internal management of the enterprise than to classroom instruction (e.g. attendance, working hours, free time during the day), and clearly their position affords them both the right and obligation to supervise and judge the work of teachers (Lortie, 1969, p. 11). In these respects, principals occupy a position of bureaucratic superordination relative to teachers.

Teaching, however, is not routine and standardized work, and, moreover, it takes place simultaneously in many classroom locations scattered throughout a school building. The ecological characteristics of schools (a theme to be discussed later) do not resemble those of many factories, government bureaus and business firms whose workers are engaged in repetitive activities readily visible to their supervisors or where the product of their activities can be judged quantitatively and qualitatively. Principals, moreover, have many other responsibilities in addition to the supervision of teachers; and even though they attribute great importance to teacher supervision, they do not spend much time doing it (NEA, 1964, pp. 34, 36, 38). In effect, the situation makes it exceedingly difficult for principals to exercise their supervisory and judgmental functions even if one accepts the highly debatable assumption that there are valid criteria for judging the quality of teaching.

Thus, even though schools have many of the defining characteristics of bureaucracies, a consideration of the modes of affiliation of both pupils and teachers indicates that they do not operate like bureaucracies in some very critical respects. Hiring is an affiliative device that ordinarily makes the bureaucratic direction of work possible; but not in the case of teaching. In fact, the pressures and uncertainties entailed in the running of classrooms often make teachers want more administrative direction than they get (Dreeben, 1970a, pp. 66–75), though the evidence on this point is not completely consistent (NEA, 1964, pp. 41–3); and these same pressures and uncertainties make their work, by its nature, very difficult to direct administratively because principals cannot become well informed about the unique sequence of events in each classroom, nor are they competent to direct the work of teachers in all areas of the curriculum (Lortie, 1969, p. 12). Teaching, then, by virtue of the nature of the school hierarchy and of the characteristics of classroom activities, tends to be self-directed and isolated.

Summary

In the realm of authority relationships, the school as a workplace and the classroom as a work site pose problems for the conduct of teachers. These settings pose *tasks* for teachers, problematic situations for which they must devise strategies, more or less effective, for meeting organizational demands (from the administration), carrying out an instructional program, and coping with the regularities and irregularities of classroom events (Levinson and Gallagher, 1964, p. 38). In a number of crucial respects, schools differ from other organizations staffed by skilled white-collar and/or professional workers, such as hospitals, law firms, universities, social work agencies, insurance companies and the like. They are not bureaucratic in the sense that central work activities are directed by rules or divided into routine, repetitive subactivities. Neither are they professional or craft organizations in which work activities are shaped by esoteric work traditions based on more or less sophisticated technologies in which workers' expert judgments are the primary criteria for making decisions (Etzioni, 1961, pp. 40–54; Stinchcombe 1959).

As a general rule workers (like teachers) engaged in a somewhat unpredictable environment and obliged to provide services for and heed the welfare of clients are not usually governed by bureaucratic rules. The vicissitudes of the classroom cannot be readily subsumed under general formulas prescribing conduct. At the same time and for the same reasons, supervisory direction and review, consistent with affiliation by hiring, do not typically obtain among teachers. Teachers, moreover, lack both a strong craft tradition and a highly developed technology (Dreeben, 1970a, Ch. 4), unlike skilled craftsmen and free professionals, and accordingly have no coherent set of *occupational* (as distinct from organizational) guidelines, based on collectively codified work experiences developed over time or based on research, to cope with the situational demands of their work and to judge the appropriateness of their conduct.

Classrooms, where conscripted children are gathered in confined spaces over long spans of time, engender problems of compliance and order for teachers. From the teacher's perspective the central issue is engaging pupils in the instructional proceedings – keeping them interested, at work and actively involved. The means for doing so, however, are not well understood so that one often finds teachers attempting to keep up with and control the rapid flow of events – in part the director of these events, in part their prisoner, but in any case deeply engrossed in them. Not surprisingly, under the circumstances, the teacher's exercise of authority resembles not that of the director who gives orders, the foreman who supervises or the professional who attempts to apply his expertise to a problem; rather, it is an attempt to instruct (usually by talking, as will be discussed later), to identify and stop violations of rules of conduct, and to play fair – all under pressure. With the endemic uncertainty and unpredictability of classroom events, the teacher, in attempting to instruct and maintain order, becomes more the reactor to than the designer of classroom activities (Jackson 1966).

Spatial arrangements in classrooms

The association between work and authority has deep roots in the history of sociological thinking. Traditional grounds alone would have been sufficient to justify discussing how relationships of authority in schools shape the work of teachers, and of how the nature of their work shapes relationships of authority. But it is easy to forget, given the sociologist's traditional concerns, that not all conduct occurring in hierarchical work settings is best understood in terms of hierarchy, authority and power.

Educators, by contrast, are more likely to think of teachers' work as matters of instruction and curriculum, both topics extending beyond the scope of this paper. But perhaps because classrooms have been constructed according to such a familiar design and because that design has remained so stable (though not without some modifications in a relatively small number of schools), patterns of spatial arrangements in classrooms have largely gone unnoticed for a long time; they have not been considered problematic in terms of shaping the nature of teachers' work. In recent years questions about school architecture and the design of space have risen to educational consciousness – questions, for reasons not entirely clear, that have been heavily weighted ideologically. Proponents of open classrooms (Silberman, 1970) recommend the free use of space within classrooms and the extension of classroom space into corridors; the effect is supposed to be liberating and humanizing for teachers and pupils. Maybe it is; but it is also possible that teachers will encounter unfamiliar difficulties in managing large numbers of pupils in relatively unconfined spaces so that in fact they will have to devote even greater energies to keeping order, gaining attention, and keeping pupils actively engaged in classroom activities (Sommer, 1969, p. 105) than to encouraging pupils to follow their own interests, to inquire freely and to work at their own tempos.

Some architectural critics of current building design see present arrangements as 'mirroring' what they contend to be the authoritarian quality of classroom life (DeCarlo, 1969, pp. 20–1). One looks in vain, however, through this sometimes hortatory, sometimes polemical, literature either for propositions that link the design of space to the conduct of people or for cogent reasons *why* some particular prescribed change in spatial design will produce the changes in conduct its proponents claim for it.

If one has no ideological axe to grind, it seems reasonable to ask how people in a work setting are arranged spatially, how the boundaries of spaces are placed, where physical objects are located, what kind of objects they are, and whether patterns of people's conduct vary (and in what ways) with the arrangement of space (Hall, 1966; Walder and Guest, 1952; Woodward, 1965). [. . .]

Some parameters of classroom life

The evidence to provide a detailed mapping of classroom arrangements and activities, identifying the dominant patterns and variations, does not yet exist. Yet the scattered descriptions that are available seem to indicate some modal consistencies that may in fact have important implications for the nature of teachers' work. One begins, of course, with the familiar observation that most classrooms consist of four walls with rows of desks and chairs for pupils and a single desk for one teacher up front. They contain on the average about thirty pupils (plus or minus fifteen at the extremes) and are crowded.

Classrooms are characterized by high rates of interaction and frequent changes in activities. In one study of thirty-two lessons in sixteen classrooms (grades 1, 6 and 11), some change in 'activity' (not defined) was found to occur once every five seconds in an active classroom, every eighteen seconds in a less active one; 371 'activity episodes' (not defined) occurred during the average lesson; and a change in who talked and who listened occurred 174 times each lesson (Adams and Biddle, 1970, pp. 29–30). Another investigator estimates about 650 individual interchanges (not defined) between an elementary-school teacher and her pupils in the course of a full day of teaching; about 1,000 interchanges when the number of times a teacher talks to the class as a whole (rather than just to separate individuals) is considered (Jackson, 1966, p. 14).
[. . .]

Although no quantitative evidence is presented here on rates of interaction at other work sites, commonplace experience indicates that talk does not fly as fast and as constantly in business offices, law firms, doctors' offices, assembly lines, garages, farms and so on. There is undoubtedly substantial variation among classrooms in rates of interaction, but the fragmentary evidence now available suggests that classrooms are crowded places with lots of talk. But what of the patterns of talk?
[. . .]

Highly suggestive but by no means definitive evidence that runs back to the end of the nineteenth century indicates that teachers run classrooms; they do most of the talking and initiate most of the action. In the relatively short spans of time left to them, pupils mostly reply to questions and less frequently ask them. Evidence on the spatial distribution of talk locates most of it towards the front and center of classrooms (in both secondary schools and college classes). When the teacher talks, the chances are substantial that a large number of pupils will be addressed (not a small group), that the pupil who talks next will be sitting near the front or along a center strip, and that the teacher will be the following speaker (Adams and Biddle, 1970, pp. 63–8; Sommer, 1969, p. 118). Classrooms, in short, are run on the principle of the recitation (Hoetker and Ahlbrand, 1969, p. 146).

If systematic evidence about the past and about current practice, taking full account both of modal patterns and of variations, supports this generalization, we will have discovered a most remarkable phenomenon: the predominance of the recitation. Presumably there are many ways to teach a classroom full of children or to teach them in settings different in structure from classrooms, but for reasons as yet unknown, these alternatives have not gained currency. Of course, one cannot dismiss out of hand the contention that the constraints of classrooms are of such a nature and of such intensity that only one teaching strategy is feasible given those constraints and that alternatives can emerge only against tremendous odds. But that is purely speculation. With proper caveats, however, one can hazard some speculations about the prevalence of the recitation. Why should teachers have discovered this mode of instruction and classroom management? To what set of problematic conditions can the recitation be considered an adaptive response?

The physical design of classrooms, containing one badly outnumbered teacher crowded with some thirty children into a confined space, seems highly conducive to sporadic if not frequent disruption, particularly in the lower grades. The potentiality for disruption may arise from the pupils: because some are restless, immature, uninterested, unmotivated and the like; it may also be provoked by some teachers who are dull, threatening, ill-prepared, tired or who cannot keep children occupied and interested. The teacher's primary task is to design and engage pupils in learning activities sufficiently engrossing that pupils find those activities substantially more attractive than proscribed alternatives (which often have attractions of their own). Under these circumstances, maintaining 'the student's absorption in the task at hand' and getting his attention are tasks of great immediacy and importance both for instructional and managerial reasons (Jackson, 1968, pp. 85, 90).

Teachers' options for gaining attention and engagement are fairly circumscribed. They can command the front of the classroom and attempt to control the proceedings (both for instructional and management purposes) by doing most of the talking (lecturing, questioning and demonstrating) and by controlling pupil participation (presumably reducing its unpredictability) through rapid-fire questioning, which limits pupils' engagement largely to occasions created by the teacher. As Kounin observed, teachers can maintain attention if they ask questions in a way that leaves pupils guessing about who will have to recite – identifying the pupil after the question has been asked, not before (Kounin, 1970, pp. 109–11). Moreover, to the extent that teachers wish to avoid empty time and maintain continuous classroom activity, they will attempt to manage the flow of events from the front of the class by asking questions and directing activities.

[. . .]

Given the spatial constraints of self-contained classrooms and the need for teachers to gain and keep the attention of their pupils (both for adminis-trative and instructional reasons), it is not surprising that the recitation has emerged as an adaptive solution because it can serve both as a means of disseminating knowledge and as a means of control at the same time in a setting whose major parameters are (1) spatial containment and crowding, (2) the inclusion of variously motivated children of different abilities and interests, and (3) the occupational and administrative injunction on teachers to teach – direct an instructional program. Though, as noted earlier, there is no adequate evidence on the frequency of prevailing alternatives to the recitation, one would expect them to take the form of teachers attempting to deal more with individual pupils and small groups, and using a variety of instructional techniques designed to cope with classroom variation (the first alternative to the recitation, mentioned above), not (or not yet) the forms of multiple teacher and open classrooms.

Although this discussion has proceeded mainly along ecological lines, it would be erroneous to advocate an architectural or spatial determinism. In fact, classrooms, at least from a sociological perspective, should be viewed in terms of both technological and ecological attributes. The recitational method is a technology – a way of marshalling means and resources to accomplish some end (whether or not the end is actually achieved, the efficacy of the technology is a distinct question). It is a technology that resides comfortably in a social setting having the organizational properties of classrooms – and comfort has no bearing on whether children learn anything or whether teachers are happy in their work. In recent educational history there have been no innovations in teaching technology of sufficient magni-tude to render the self-contained classroom structurally obsolete; either the technology has changed to fit the constraints of the classroom, or the change proved compatible with existing classroom structure (Stinchcombe, 1965, pp. 153–60).

Classrooms and occupational life

Just as the characteristics of teachers' work are related to the internal spatial arrangements of classrooms, so certain aspects of their occupational life, particularly those pertaining to career development and the diffusion of technology, are related to the spatial placement of classrooms within schools. Perhaps the most important single property of classrooms, viewed from a school-wide perspective, is their spatial scattering and isolation throughout school buildings; and because teachers work in different places at the same time, they do not observe each other working. Even team-teaching arrangements, designed to expand the collaborative efforts of teachers, have not succeeded in making teachers' work activities in the classroom visible to each other, even though team teaching does encourage collaborative planning. The implications of this spatial isolation are far-reaching.

If teachers do not observe each other directly, who does observe them? Pupils, certainly, and with great frequency. Administrators (principals, department heads) also observe them, but rather seldom. If patterns of visibility are construed in terms of who is available to help teachers and to judge their performance, then their isolation appears more than spatial. Pupils, by virtue of their subordinate position and their inexperience, cannot be of much direct help about how to teach and manage a classroom; certainly teachers cannot approach them with questions about what is going right and wrong and expect technically defensible answers. And although pupils can judge the performance of teachers (hold opinions, like and dislike), their judgements cannot be taken as determining criteria for advancement. The inexperience of pupils aside, when workers are hired the job of evaluation is undertaken by hierarchical superiors, not subordinates.

Administrators can legitimately judge and help by virtue of their hierarchical positions and their prior work experience, since they are virtually always former teachers. Their work schedules and job demands are such, however, that they spend very little time visiting classrooms, and when they do, much of what they see is bound to be understood partly out of the context of on-going classroom events that they have not observed.

Because of their work schedules and the spatial dispersion of classrooms, teachers have so few opportunities to see each other at work and accordingly cannot either judge or be helpful *on the basis of direct observation*. This is not to deny that teachers talk shop and talk about each other's problems; they cannot do so, however, on the basis of shared visible and audible experiences. They lack, moreover, written media for communicating about their work because the occupation has no counterpart to a scholarly research tradition (cf. university instructors) in which knowledge is circulated in books and journals, to a collective body of precedent (cf. lawyers) in court reports, to case records (cf. physicians) that document the accumulation of tests and prior medical decisions, and to published designs (cf. architects). And since most educational research is carried out by academics (and without the involvement of teachers) and is published in scholarly or technical journals, teachers tend not to become consumers of it.

The fragmentation of the colleague group, through spatial isolation and the absence of a written tradition of work reports, makes teaching a very solitary and private kind of work. Several observers (Jackson, 1968; Lortie, 1969) have reported that teachers look to the immediate classroom situation both as a source of satisfaction and for signs of their own accomplishment and competence. By implication, this inward-looking perspective on work augurs ill for the cumulative development of a codified body of knowledge about teaching that can be disseminated throughout the occupation. It means that teachers are left very much alone to determine what they are doing right and wrong and to discover what they must do to solve their problems and correct their errors at work. Furthermore, the absence of codified knowledge about teaching puts constraints on schools that train teachers; what precisely shall they train teachers to do, and how shall they design programs to train them, when ideas about the character of the work remain largely in the minds of individual teachers and not part of a publicly shared and reasonably systematic body of knowledge?

Both the spatial distribution of classrooms in schools and their internal arrangements affect the nature of teacher training, particularly practice teaching. Like teachers themselves, apprentices work in isolation from one another, each learning the job most directly from a single 'cooperating teacher'. Although practice teaching is the one phase of the career in which an individual receives frequent and direct supervision from an experienced teacher, the relationship with that teacher tends to be dyadic with the result that the apprentice is exposed mainly to one other person's perspective and mode of doing things. Unlike medical students who undertake much of their training in cohorts and small work groups and who have a great deal of contact with each other and with a variety of instructors (Becker, Geer, Hughes and Strauss, 1961), teacher-trainees lack the kind of support and richness of communication that peers working collectively on the same problems can provide.

Internally, classroom structure limits the extent to which that setting can serve *both* as a work site and as a setting for the training of apprentices. Unlike hospitals and law firms, for example, where new recruits to medicine and law learn their trade as apprentices by performing work tasks of gradually increasing difficulty under close supervision, schools provide a less adequate setting – the classroom – for work and training activities to occur simultaneously. The self-contained, bounded, single-teacher classroom provides the apprentice with two main alternatives: to be observer-listener or teacher. Except for the brief periods of time when trainees are free to deal with individual pupils or small groups of them, the organization of the classroom (to the extent that the recitation model represents the predominant state of things) provides few opportunities to learn the variety of teaching activities that make up the job. The apprentice either does the whole job or watches someone else do it.

One observer has described teaching activities as 'indivisible' (Lortie, 1969, p. 9), meaning that they cannot be readily broken down into component tasks. The recitation is a case in point; it is difficult if not impossible to determine where the instructional component leaves off and the classroom management aspect begins. And if one includes all the attempts to motivate, praise, blame, give instructions, lecture, help, chastize, and the like, it becomes nearly impossible to disentangle the threads. Perhaps teaching is not indivisible but only as yet undivided; occupational activities have not been analysed to identify their components, and *a fortiori*, training experiences like practice teaching cannot be geared to mastering specific skills learned with repeated practice. It may well be, moreover, that the self-contained classroom militates against the identification of the components of teaching activities and accordingly against the development of a division of labor. The reason, of course, is that anyone assuming the position of teacher in such a setting must do the whole job whether or not the parts of the job can be identified.

Summary

It has not been the intent of this chapter to review that enormous, sprawling body of words constituting the literature on the nature and state of the art of teaching. The purpose has been to consider certain *organizational* properties of schools and classrooms that have implications for the character of teachers' work. This accounts for the concern with workplaces and work sites as the central focus, not with the whole range of teaching activities. Certainly, the personal and social characteristics of teachers; the characteristics of pupils, families and neighborhoods; administrative styles; the nature of teacher training; and the opportunities and constraints of the curriculum as well as a host of other considerations affect teachers' work. Important as these considerations are, they were not the subjects of this particular chapter.

The main argument consists of the proposition that certain structural properties of school organization pertaining to relationships of authority and the spatial characteristics of classrooms pose certain problems for teachers, and that the nature of their work can be construed in terms of adaptive responses to those problems.

It would be a gross distortion to conclude from this chapter that teaching is merely teachers talking and keeping order, though much of it has been about those phenomena. It would be correct, however, to conclude that the nature of instructional activities and modes of maintaining order are both central to the enterprise of teaching and strongly affected by those aspects of school and classroom structure discussed here. If teachers saw their pupils one at a time (in tutorial) the way doctors and lawyers see their patients and clients, if pupils were not conscripted, or if teachers had a more viable technology at their disposal, it is reasonably certain that relationships of authority between teachers and pupils would be substantially different than they are. Similarly, if classrooms had different spatial arrangements, if more than one teacher (or other people with classroom responsibilities) were present, or if pupils were freer to use the internal space of learning areas differently, if teachers carried on several distinct instructional programs in a classroom, it is more than likely that alternative modes of teaching (alternate to the recitation) would appear, *if* the component activities of teaching were identified and teachers viewed variations in spatial arrangements as opportunities to combine these components in new ways, and if they wanted to do so.

There is a substantial amount of sociological evidence, based on research in a variety of work situations, that the activities comprising a particular type of work can be performed readily within a certain range of structural settings, but only with great difficulty outside that range (Stinchcombe 1959). This is to say, settings, on the one hand, are constraining; on the other, though they provide opportunities for different kinds of conduct, there is no guarantee that these opportunities will be exploited. The difficulty with the ideologically inspired plans to change the nature of teaching, to make it more effective, more imaginative, more humane, is that they ignore the prevailing structural constraints of schools and classrooms and provide no clear guidelines for using the opportunities. The questions that need to be asked are: given existing structural arrangements in schools and classrooms, what are the alternative forms that teaching activities can take? What are the alternative structural arrangements that can serve educational purposes? And what opportunities and constraints do they create for the character of teachers' work?

References

Barnard, C. I. *The functions of the executive*, Cambridge, Harvard University Press, 1938.
Becker, H. S., Geer, B., Hughes, E. C. and Strauss, A. L. *Boys in white: Student culture in medical school*, Chicago, University of Chicago Press, 1961.
Bidwell, C. E. Students and schools: Some observations on client trust in client-serving organizations, in W. R. Rosengren and M. Lefton (eds), *Organizations and clients*, Columbus, Ohio, Charles E. Merrill, 1970, pp. 37–69.
Bruner, J. S. *Toward a theory of instruction*, Cambridge, Mass., Harvard University Press, 1966.
Corwin, R. G. *Militant professionalism*, New York, Appleton-Century-Crofts, 1970.
DeCarlo, G. Why/how to build school buildings, *Harvard Educational Review*, 1969, 39(4): 12–34.
Dreeben, R. *The nature of teaching*, Glenview, Ill., Scott, Foresman, 1970 (a).
Etzioni, A. *A comparative analysis of complex organizations*, New York, Free Press.
Gouldner, A. W. *Patterns of industrial bureaucracy*, Glencoe, Ill., Free Press.
Hall, E. T. *The hidden dimension*, Garden City, NY, Doubleday, 1966.
Hoetker, J. and Ahlbrand, W. P., Jr. The persistence of the recitation, *American Educational Research Journal*, 1969, 6(2), 145–67.
Jackson, P. W. The way teaching is, in Association for Supervision and Curriculum Development and the Center for the Study of Instruction of the National

Education Association, *The way teaching is*, Washington, DC, NEA, 1966, pp. 7–27.

Kounin, J. *Discipline and group management in classrooms*, New York, Holt, Rinehart & Winston, 1970.

Lefton, M. Client characteristics and structural outcomes. Toward the specification of linkages, in W. R. Rosengren and M. Lefton (eds), *Organizations and clients*, Columbus, Ohio, Charles E. Merrill, 1970, pp. 17–36.

Levinson, D. J. and Gallagher, E. B. *Patienthood in the mental hospital*, Boston, Houghton Mifflin, 1964.

Lortie, D. C. The balance of control and autonomy in elementary school teaching, in A. Etzioni (ed.), *The semi-professions and their organization*, New York, Free Press, 1969, pp. 1–53.

National Education Association, Evaluation of classroom teachers. Research Report 1964–R14, Washington, DC, National Education Association, 1964.

Parsons, T. Definitions of health and illness in the light of American values and social structure, in T. Parsons, *Social structure and personality*, New York, Free Press, 1964, pp. 257–91.

Sommer, R. *Personal space*, Englewood Cliffs, NJ, Prentice-Hall, 1969.

Stinchcombe, A. L. Bureaucratic and craft administration of production: A comparative study, *Administrative Science Quarterly*, 1959, 4(2), 168–87.

Stinchcombe, A. L. Social structure and organizations, in J. G. March (ed.), *Handbook of organizations*, Chicago, Rand McNally, 1965, pp. 142–93.

Walker, C. R. and Guest, R. H. *The man on the assembly line*, Cambridge, Harvard University Press, 1952.

Weber, M. *The theory of social and economic organization*, trans. A. M. Henderson and T. Parsons, Glencoe, Ill., Free Press, 1947.

Woodward, J. *Industrial organization: Theory and practice*, London, Oxford University Press, 1965.

Section II

Professionalism and proletarianization: the significance of class and gender

Historical and Contemporary Analysis

3

Only a schoolmaster: gender, class and the effort to professionalize elementary teaching in England, 1870–1910

Barry H. Bergen

Introduction

'TEACHING is by common consent a profession,' begins a 1917–18 parliamentary report on teachers' salaries. But, the report continues,

> at the same time it suffers from the fact that its membership is not so strictly defined as that of law or medicine. For this as well as other reasons, historical, economic, and social, the English public has not realized its great importance to the national welfare, and have not accorded to its members the position to which their education and the importance of their work entitle them. We may however look forward to a time when admission to the profession will be limited to persons who have reached accepted standards of education and training, a result which will be of great benefit to national education.[1]

Thus did the Parliamentary Committee give voice to the long-standing, persistent complaint of the elementary-school teacher: his social position was not as high as that to which he felt entitled. The terms of this complaint remained essentially the same in 1918 as they had been in 1855: 'What in short the teacher desires is, that his "calling" shall rank as a "profession", that the name of "schoolmaster" shall ring as grandly on the ear as that of "clergy-man" or "solicitor".'[2] The fact that the occupation of elementary school teacher did not ring very grandly on the ears of the English in 1855 should be no surprise. Popular education, elementary education for the masses, was still more idea than reality, dominated by denominational schools as concerned with dispensing doctrine as with teaching the rudiments of the '3

Rs,' and not far removed from the time when teachers were generally acknowledged to be fugitives from failure at other vocations. Government certification of teachers had begun less than ten years before.

By 1918 English education and English elementary school teachers had changed considerably. Major changes following the Education Acts of 1870 and 1902, with many minor adjustments in between, had opened elementary education to a large segment of the population and secondary education to a larger segment than ever before. Certification of teachers, if not universal, was far more widespread than it had been in 1855, and teacher training now included secondary schooling, and perhaps a university degree. A national association had been promoting the position of teachers since 1870.

In spite of the 'common consent' to teaching's place as a profession, teachers perceived their occupation as lacking its rightful position alongside law and medicine. Even an 1899 register of teachers, modelled after that of doctors was abolished in 1908. In spite of some of the trappings of professionalism, teaching was not a profession in the sense of law or medicine. It is my intent in this paper to demonstrate the ways in which class, gender and the relationship of elementary teaching to the state not only led teachers to seek the professionalization of their occupation but ultimately prevented it. The English elementary school teacher was destined to see thwarted his desire that 'he shall feel no more that awful chill and "stony British stare" which follows the explanation that "that interesting young man" is only the "schoolmaster." '[3]

Elementary education in England developed from charitable attempts to educate the poor and the working classes. Thus it bore the stamp of charity from above and of its religious foundations into the twentieth century. As a function of middle-class charity, however, its aims were not always solely charitable. Thus, for example, an 1839 report to Parliament in support of the expansion of elementary education for the working classes cited the utility of education in encouraging 'religious and moral training and habits of order, good breeding, and cleanliness and attention to neatness and dress', and in building 'a link of good feeling and sympathy between the master and his work-people, the want of which is, I am persuaded, the main source of most of the evils that have been sometimes found to arise out of the unions and other combinations of work-people.'[4]

Thus the expansion of elementary education for the working classes would function, in part, as a means of inculcating bourgeois values in the working class and as a means of social control of that class. Bourgeois values and social control are inextricably linked, not only with one another but as well with the idea of an education which would be suited to the worker and his eventual position in society. Thus, P. W. Musgrave writes:

> The middle classes defined the education of the working class as a necessary free service in a minimal form. It is difficult to conjure up the full range of meaning implied by the word 'elementary' when applied

to education during the last part of the nineteenth century. Briefly elementary education was seen as free – hence, tainted by charity it must be cheap – hence, also it must be given in large school classes and consist merely of the three R's. It must have a curriculum sufficient to ensure a meagre literacy and be suited solely to the lower classes – hence, in an elitist age, it must be entirely unconnected with the ruling class.[5]

Popular education, then, was to be both separate and unequal. And it was not free. Elementary education was to be aimed specifically at the lower classes, purportedly to serve their needs but equally clearly to protect middle class interests and class lines:

> We do not profess to give these children an education that will raise them above their station and business in life: that is not our object, but to give them an education that may fit them for that business. We are bound to take a clear and definite view of the position of the class that is to receive instruction: and, having obtained that view, we are bound to make up our minds as to how much instruction that class requires, and is capable of receiving, and we are then bound to have evidence that it has received such instruction.[6]

Thus the prevailing attitudes among the middle class during the period leading up to the greatest expansion of elementary education contained vestiges of condescending charitability mixed with a healthy dose of regard for an educational system functional for middle-class society, i.e. functional for business and industry and protective of class boundaries.[7]

The great explosion of elementary education in England and Wales

Table 1   Percentage of school-age children* attending elementary
               school, England and Wales

Year	%
1871	26
1881	46
1891	57
1901	62
1911	70
1921	68
1931	80

Sources: Average number of students attending elementary schools for 1871, 1881 from *Statistical Abstract for the United Kingdom 1870–1884*, p. 172, for 1891 from *Statistical Abstract for the United Kingdom 1886–1900*, p. 256; for 1901, 1911 from *Statistical Abstract for the United Kingdom 1898–1912*, pp. 412–413; for 1921, 1931 from *Statistical Abstract for the United Kingdom 1913, 1918–1931*, pp. 48–49. Figures for school-age children from B. R. Mitchell, *Abstract of British Historical Statistics*, Cambridge, Cambridge University Press, 1962, p. 12.

*Ages 5–14. Figures for average attendance before 1921 may include students over 14 years old.

Table 2 Teachers in public elementary schools, England and Wales, with sex ratios

	Total number of teachers	Number of female teachers per 100 male teachers
1870	13,729	99
1880	41,426	156
1890	73,533	207
1900	113,986	287
1910	161,804	306
1920	151,879	315
1930	157,061	366

Sources: Figures for 1870, 1880, 1890, from BPP, 1897 XXVI: IXXXiii. Figures for 1900, 1910, from *Statistical Abstract for the United Kingdom 1898–1912*, pp. 412–13. Figures for 1920, 1930, from *Statistical Abstract for the United Kingdom 1913, 1918–31*, pp. 48–9.

followed the Education Act of 1870, which divided the country into school districts and created Local School Boards to administer local 'rates,' or taxes, in the expansion and operation of elementary education. The percentage of school-age children attending elementary schools rose rapidly, from 26 per cent in 1871 to 46 per cent in 1881. It continued to rise steadily, though somewhat less rapidly, to 57 per cent in 1891, reaching 62 per cent at the turn of the century, and 70 per cent in 1911 (Table 1). (These figures are based on average attendance. The number of students registered is much higher.)

There was a corresponding increase in the number of schools: from 9,521 in 1871 to 17,614 in 1881, to 19,508 in 1891 and to 20,100 in 1900.[8] Similarly, expenditure on elementary education increased from £903,978 in 1871, to £2,854,067 in 1881, to £4,392,126 in 1891 and to £10,241,532 in 1900.[9]

The number of teachers in elementary schools rose accordingly (see Table 2). The number of teachers increased by more than threefold between 1870 and 1880, from 13,729 to 41,426. By 1910 it was more than ten times the 1870 figure – 161,804. Of course, the population itself was not static during this time, but if we look at the number of teachers as a proportion of the

Table 3a Number of elementary teachers per 1,000 of the occupied population (census years)

1871	.89
1881	3.39
1891	5.07
1901	7.00
1911	8.82
1921	7.85
1931	7.46

Table 3b   Teachers as a proportion of the occupied population

Year	Number of male elementary teachers per 1,000 occupied Males	Number of female elementary teachers per 1,000 occupied Females
1871	.83	1.88
1881	1.83	6.49
1891	2.39	11.04
1901	2.64	18.59
1911	3.08	22,61
1921	2.76	20.28
1931	2.86	18.24

Sources: Figures for number of teachers for 1871, 1881, 1891, from BPP, 1897, XXVI: lxxxiii. For 1901, 1911, from *Statistical Abstract for the United Kingdom 1898–1912*, pp. 412–13. For 1921, pp. 48–9. Figures for Occupied Population from Mitchell, *British Historical Statistics*, pp. 60–1.

working population, we can get an even better sense of the significance of this growth (Table 3a). Thus for 1871 we find teachers constituting less than one-tenth of 1 per cent of the workforce, 0.89 teachers out of every 1,000 workers. By 1881 there were more than three teachers in every 1,000 occupied people. This figure rose to five per 1,000 in 1891, seven per 1,000 in 1901, and a high of nearly nine per 1,000 in 1911. This represents a tenfold increase in the proportion of teachers in the workforce, spread out evenly from 1871 to 1911.

It is, then, against this background of extraordinary growth that the changing position of teachers must be examined. It remains, however, to determine just what changes in the professional position of teachers we wish to look for. The existing theoretical literature on professionalization is dominated by the functionalist followers of Parsons; who generally construct an 'ideal-type' of a profession, generally modelled after the quintessential profession, medicine. These vary somewhat, but most appear similar to that offered by Bernard Barber:

1. A high degree of generalized and systematic knowledge.
2. Primary orientation to community interest rather than self-interest.
3. A high degree of self-control of behaviour through codes of ethics internalized in the process of work socialization and through voluntary associations organized and operated by the work specialists themselves.
4. A system of rewards (monetary and honorary) that is primarily a set of symbols of work achievement and thus ends in themselves, not the means to some end of individual self-interest.[10]

Occupations, then, are analyzed in terms of this ideal construct to determine their degree of professionalization. A more recent literature has evolved, based on the early work of Carr-Saunders, which treats certain occupations as being of a different nature than the professions, with their own ideal-type, called the 'semi-professions.'[11] These semi-professions – nursing, teaching and social work constituting the most frequently named examples – are generally defined with reference to the ideal-type of the full, or established, professions. That is to say, their ideal-types remain, in reality, a partial fulfilment of the ideal-type based on medicine or law, their position one of an uncompleted journey towards full professionalization.[12] In addition, semi-professions are generally viewed as subject to a much higher level of bureaucratization than the established professions, a process generally seen as antithetical to professionalization. Further, both these processes, professionalization and bureaucratization, are seen as characteristic of 'modern' society.[13]

Two useful critiques of the sociology of professionalization exist: Jean-Michel Chapoulie's 'Sur l'analyse sociologique des groupes professionels,' and Magali S. Larson's *The Rise of Professionalism*.[14] They are to a large degree complementary.

Chapoulie begins with a critique of the Parsonian tradition. Chapoulie finds implicit in Parsons, and explicit in those who follow him, an apologetic interpretation of the role of the professional: the professional is seen as mediating between individual needs and functional necessities. The professional is neutral *vis-à-vis* the different social classes to whom he offers the same services. Thus Parsonian analyses tend to examine the professions by themselves, rather than with regard to their role in the social structure. The ideal-type tends to be constructed by isolating 'important' characteristics of the established professions and, writes Chapoulie, it is easy to show empirically that no occupation approaches this model.[15]

Thus, for Chapoulie, the difficulties found in functionalist analyses proceed from both the method of constructing an ideal-type, and from questions about the nature of social reality raised by the empirical research of interactionists like E. C. Hughes and the Chicago School.[16] These functionalist studies adopt the point of view of the middle class on the division of labor, the importance of institutionalized knowledge, the professional ethic, and occupation as defining social position. This is why, writes Chapoulie, the ideal-type of the professions turns out almost identical to the professional model.[17]

Chapoulie rejects, also, the application of this ideal-type to the semi-professions, as they become no more than 'imperfect realizations' of the ideal-type. In fact, says Chapoulie, they possess extremely diverse objective characteristics, and they share only a middling social status and the fact of not being established.[18]

Chapoulie suggests a reversal of the relational causality between knowledge and professionalization, suggesting the need for a study of the social conditions of the monopolization of knowledge and the consequences for it of the development of a corps of specialists.[19] In place of functionalist theories, which for Chapoulie 'constitute no more than the restatement of the professional model in scientific language' and not a scientific theory, Chapoulie suggests the need to study the daily practice ('la pratique quotidienne') of the professions.[20]

Larson's critique shares certain ideas with Chapoulie's. Ideal-typical constructions, says Larson, tell us not what a profession is but what it pretends to be. The professions' characteristic attributes of special status and prestige would seem to link them to the system of social stratification, but the ordinary emphasis on the 'cognitive and normative dimensions of profession tends to separate these special categories of the social division of labor (i.e., the professions) from the class structure in which they also are inserted.'[21]

Thus, says Larson, both the sociological ideal-type and the professions themselves present the professions as independent from, or at least neutral *vis-à-vis* the class structure.[22] Drawing heavily on Eliot Friedson, Larson stresses the processual nature of professionalization: 'Particular groups of people attempt to negotiate the boundaries of an area in the social division of labor and establish their control over it.'[23] Thus professions are not automatically autonomous, they gain autonomy in a process which is both internal struggle and externally directed persuasion. This internal struggle concerns who shall be included in or excluded from the profession. The persuasion is directed at relevant élites, for, as Friedson noted, 'Professions ultimately depend upon the power of the state, and they originally emerge by the grace of powerful protectors. The privileged position of a profession is thus secured by the political and economic influence of the elite which sponsors it.'[24] Further, for Larson this process of professionalization is undertaken in order to turn special knowledge and skills into social and economic rewards. That is, 'the process by which producers of special services sought to constitute *and control* a market for their expertise.'[25]

Several salient points emerge from these two critiques: first, the need to examine 'daily practice,' the social reality of the professions rather than the professional model perpetuated by them; second, the need to see professionalization as process, the monopolization of knowledge, the constitution and control of the market for that knowledge. I would stress the need to see this as historical process. Third, there is the need to consider aspects of class and power and the role of the state of professionalization.

We can see, then, that a simple measuring of teaching against the functionalist ideal-type would not be particularly useful. We could easily identify the start of certification and the pupil-teacher system in 1846; the foundation of various voluntary associations, and the founding of the first national association in 1870; many examples of the prevalence of the ideal of service among teachers; and finally, the creation of a register of teachers in 1899. Such an enumeration would yield a picture of elementary teaching as a semi-profession, an imperfect realization of the ideal-type. But it would not go far in explaining the inability of the elementary teachers to realize fully the ideal-type in spite of their consistent efforts to do so.

Let us turn, then, to the idea of professionalization as the process of constituting and controlling a market for special services, expertise or knowledge. Two problems appear immediately in considering English elementary teaching. First, to a large extent elementary teaching involved no special knowledge or expertise. Up until 1918, and perhaps even beyond, the training of most elementary teachers was primarily or entirely academic, rather than what we would consider 'professional'.

The first teacher training college was founded by Joseph Lancaster's British and Foreign Society in 1805. The National Society established one in 1812. But the numbers of training colleges grew extremely slowly, and they bore the marks of the system they were designed to serve and of the religiosity of the age. Dr James Kay's (later Sir James Kay-Shuttleworth, who originated the pupil-teacher system) proposed National Training College of 1839 included a regimen of 'heavy outdoor labour, simple diet, incessant vigilance and religious training'.[26] Designed to produce teachers for schools providing a minimum of education, the training colleges, often associated with one or another denomination, strove to impart to their students a level of academic knowledge just slightly above that of the students they would be teaching and a high degree of moral training. Until the 1890s all training colleges were residential. Thus, also, the monitor system which was prevalent up until the late 1840s in the British and Foreign Society schools admittedly sacrificed intellectual attainment for 'sound moral and religious influence'.[27]

Two major changes instituted by the Committee of Council of Education under Kay-Shuttleworth in 1846 did little to promote teacher training beyond the meager academic level it already occupied. From 1846 until 1908 the government paid the salaries of apprentices to the schoolmasters, called pupil-teachers, for a period of five years. At the end of this time the apprentice would compete by examination for entrance and scholarship to the training colleges. As often as not, pupil-teachership represented apprenticeship in the use of the cane rather than in the fine points of pedagogy.[28]

In the same year, 1846, the certification of elementary teachers was begun. The certificate was earned either by examination at the end of the training college program, or by 'external' examination for non-trained teachers. These examinations were primarily academic, and their yearly validation was dependent upon the good graces of the school manager and Her Majesty's Inspectors.[29] The stimulus for certification on the part of the teachers came from the direct supplement to their salary paid to certificated teachers.[30]

In spite of these changes, uncertificated teachers remained a significant proportion of the employed elementary school teachers. Even as late as 1920, public elementary schools employed 36,087 uncertificated teachers and 114,136 certificated teachers.[31] Complaints about the fact that teachers were not being taught how to teach are frequent.[32] Thus the first problem with the constitution and control of a market for a special knowledge is the lack of a significant special knowledge. That knowledge which elementary teachers were imparting to their students was, in a sense, common knowledge. For the middle-class reformers and legislators setting up this system, the knowledge not only of the students but of the teachers as well, was of a low order, far below that of the educated members of their own class, set by them at what they considered the appropriate maximum level. The special knowledge of how to teach was one to which the elementary teachers had no systematic exposure, and, though they may have possessed it to a certain extent, they had no hope of establishing a monopoly of such knowledge.

The second problem for elementary teachers in the constitution and control of a market for a special knowledge was their unclear relation to a particular market. With the establishment of direct supplementary grants to teachers for certification in 1846, teachers began their long tenure of uncertainty somewhere between civil servants and private employees. But the Revised Code of 1861, the odious system of payment by results was instituted. Direct payments to teachers were abolished. Instead, monies were paid to the school managers, a certain amount per child, with deductions for unsatisfactory attendance or performance on yearly exams conducted by Her Majesty's Inspectors.[33] Thus the elementary teacher was employed by the state and the school, and at the mercy of the school manager and Her Majesty's Inspectors. After the Education Act of 1870, the teachers were employed by either school managers or the newly created local school boards, funded by local taxes or 'rates'. Far from having a clearly defined market over which they could assert control, it was not even clear who the teachers' clients were. To whom were they providing their service? Students, school managers, local school boards?

Also at this time the local school boards began to adopt, especially in the larger urban areas, scales of salaries for elementary teachers based on years of satisfactory service. With the Education Act of 1902 and the creation of the Local Education Authorities, which superseded the local school boards, the use of scales of salaries became widespread, and these scales were eventually set by the state. Thus a 1918 Committee on the determination of scales of salaries noted the unique position of elementary teachers: though 'exercising a profession', they were public servants; though members of local public services which formed a single national service, they were not centralized like the civil service; and though controlled primarily by local authorities, the legislature itself was directly concerned with their training, salaries and efficiency.[34]

Clearly, the efforts of elementary teachers to professionalize were undercut before they began by the lack of a special knowledge to be controlled and the lack of a clear market for such knowledge. But though the elementary teachers strove to change these limitations on the professionalization of teaching (a point we will have cause to return to), other factors contributed to ensure that elementary teaching would not become a profession. Two factors in particular contributed to this: first, as we mentioned above, class, power and the role of the state; second, gender.

It would be difficult to overemphasize the degree to which elementary education in England in the nineteenth century constituted an imposition of the middle class on the working class. As R. H. Tawney wrote, 'The elementary schools of 1870 were intended in the main to produce an orderly, civil, obedient population, with sufficient education to understand a command.'[35] The state machinery of education, from the Committee of Council through the Board of Education, was primarily middle class. So also were the important and powerful Her Majesty's Inspectors. In fact, Inspectors were generally appointed directly from Oxford or Cambridge; an elementary teacher could not become an Inspector, and complaints are frequent about the lack of compassion and understanding on the part of Inspectors.[36]

The teachers themselves, however, were all of the working class. Teaching, except at the university level, was not highly regarded by the middle class to begin with, and teaching in the elementary schools was the lowest rung on the teaching ladder.[37] The middle class did not view elementary teaching as a means of upward mobility.

But the elementary teachers seemed to view themselves as having risen above the working class, if not having reached the middle class, and the system of pupil-teachership and training college clearly promoted this view. Thus the early associations of teachers promoted only 'mutual improvement', and 'self-improvement rather than self-advancement', insisting that they were not trade unions.[38] The National Union of Elementary Teachers, founded in 1870, declared itself 'no aggressive association', and, interestingly, dropped 'elementary' from its title in 1889 because it was degrading.[39] One of its stated aims was to 'raise teaching to a profession by means of public register of duly qualified teachers'.[40]

In 1895, the recently renamed National Union of Teachers, at their annual conference, voted two to one against affiliating with the Trades Union Congress, already nearly ten years old. Yet two years later they voted to send £150 to a group of striking quarrymen.[41] This example illustrates nicely the confusion about their class position in the minds of elementary-school teachers. Certainly, the rigorous process of selection for pupil-teachers,[42] the separation from their working-class peers from the age of 13, their position of relative authority, the competitive scholarships for training college places, their certification and the superiority of their education, meager as it was, over that of the rest of the working class led the elementary teachers to consider themselves as 'better'. Clearly, the varied attempts of elementary teachers to professionalize constitute an attempt to raise their class position from an interstitial one between the working class and middle class to the solidly middle-class position[43] of a profession.

Thus we begin to see the roots of the constant complaints that teachers' prestige was not equal to their place in society. The teachers would have felt

Table 4   Indices of teachers' average salaries compared with average wages of selected occupations and with retail prices

			1890 = 100			
Year	Men	Teachers Women	Shipbuilding and engineering	Cotton factory workers	Coal-mining	Retail* prices
1855	75	82	59	n.a.†	126	
1860	78	79	68	n.a.	111	
1865	73	84	71	n.a.	107	
1870	78	84	81	n.a.	113	
1875	91	94	90	n.a.	113	
1880	101	90	87	71	107	
1885	101	92	80	73	96	
1890	100	100	100	100	91	
1895	101	98	101	84	84	
1900	105	108	107	116	89	
1905	108	106	110	94	91‡	

*Retail prices based on 1850 = 100.
†n.a. = figures not available.
‡1905 figure unavailable, 91 is 1902 figure.
  Sources: Figures for teachers' average salaries from A. Tropp, *The School Teachers*, London, Schoolmaster Publications 1957; wages of selected occupations from Mitchell, *British Historical Statistics*, pp. 349–50. Retail price index from Mitchell, ibid., pp. 344–5.

acutely that they were not being adequately rewarded around the turn of the century, when they were in the midst of a period in which their income was increasing more slowly than that of other occupations.

As we can see in Table 4, prices declined overall in the period from 1850 to 1900, from an index of 100 in 1850 to an index of 89 in 1900. At the same time, wages increased. However, in the period from 1880 to 1900, teachers' wages increased more slowly than those of other occupations. Male teachers, for example, increased from an index of 101 in 1880 to 105 in 1900, an increase of 4 points. Cotton factory workers, in the same period, increased from an index of 87 to an index of 107, an increase of 20 points; and coal-miners increased from an index of 71 to 116, an increase of 45 points.

In addition, we can see in Table 5 that, with the exception of a minor fluctuation, teachers' incomes declined as a percentage of the net national per capita income in the period from 1880 to 1920. Thus, although their incomes rose absolutely, all these figures show a worsening economic position for teachers relative to the gains being made in other occupations. And it is, indeed, between 1895 and 1910 that the greatest agitation for professionalization of teaching occurs.[44]

Nevertheless, before we discuss the details of the agitation for professionalization around the turn of the century, we must turn our attention to one of the most important, and perhaps the most striking aspect of elementary teaching in England: gender.

Table 5   Teachers' average income as a percentage of net national per capita
Income

		Net national	
Year	Per capita income (£s)	Male teachers (%)	Female teachers (%)
1855	22.9	393	266
1860	24.1	390	257
1865	27.5	316	244
1870	29.9	312	191
1875	33.9	322	192
1880	31.1	389	235
1885	31.0	390	239
1890	36.9	325	205
1895	36.9	332	217
1900	42.5	295	199
1905	41.3	315	213
1910	44.2	328	226
1915*	45.3	266	188
1920	129.6	209	154
1925	88.2	380	300
1930	86.2	387	295
1935	87.6	356	277

*1915 income estimated.

In 1870, before the growth of elementary education in England, there were a few more male than female elementary teachers: 6,882 men and 6,847 women, which, as we can see in Table 2, is the equivalent of ninety-nine female teachers for every 100 male teachers. This fleeting glimpse of male numerical superiority disappears immediately, never to return. By 1880, there are 156 female teachers for every 100 males. In 1890, this figure had risen to 207, in 1900 it was 287, and in 1910 it was 306. To take a single year as an example, in 1896 there were 94,943 elementary teachers. Of these, 26,547 were men and 68,396 women. Expressed as above, this means there were 258 women teachers for every 100 male teachers in 1896.[45] This phenomenon has been called the 'feminization' of teaching. In forty years women had come to constitute three-quarters of the elementary teachers in England.

Pupil-teaching exhibited the same gender differentiation. For example, in 1870 there were 14,300 pupil-teachers, of whom 6,200 were boys and 8,100 were girls. By 1896, with a total of 35,874 pupil-teachers, there were 7,737 boys and 28,137 girls: 364 girls for every 100 boys.

This feminization of elementary teaching is even more striking when one examines the proportion of the workforce that was teaching. Thus we can see clearly in Table 3b that, although there was a significant increase in the proportion of elementary teachers among the occupied male population, for

Table 6 Average annual salary of certificated teachers

Year	Male (£s)	Female (£s)
1855	90	61
1860	94	62
1865	87	55
1870	93.5	57
1875	109	65
1880	121	73
1885	121	74
1890	120	76
1895	122.5	80
1900	125.5	84.5
1905	130	88
1910	145	100
1915★	150	110
1920	271	200
1925	335	252
1930	334	254
1935	312	244

★1915 incomes are estimates.

Source: Figures for teachers average salaries from Tropp, *The School Teachers*, pp. 273–4. Net national per capita incomes from Mitchell, *British Historical Statistics*, pp. 367–8.

women the increase was substantially larger. Thus between 1871 and 1911 the number of male elementary teachers in every 1,000 occupied males increased from 0.83, or less than one per 1,000, to three per 1,000, just over a threefold increase. Over the same time period, the number of female elementary teachers in every 1,000 occupied females jumped from just under two per 1,000 to over twenty-two per 1,000, better than a tenfold increase in forty years. Clearly, also, elementary teachers constituted a much more significant proportion of the female workforce than of the male workforce.

Although women teachers outnumbered their male colleagues, their salaries remained significantly lower throughout the period under consideration. This differentiation is clearly illustrated in Table 6, where we find women's salaries generally hovering around two-thirds those of male teachers.

This difference between male and female teachers manifested itself in other ways as well. Right from the time of application of pupil-teachership, the girl who intended to become a teacher was treated differently from her male peer:

> Female pupil-teachers, before admission, must produce a certificate from the schoolmistress and managers that they possess reasonable competency as a seamstress; and, at the annual examination, must bring certified specimens of plain needlework to the inspector, together

with a statement from the schoolmistress specifying whether they have been receiving practical instruction in any other kind of domestic industry.[46]

Women in the training colleges, which were overwhelmingly sex-segregated, received a different course of instruction, generally less rigorous than that for the men, substituting subjects like 'sewing and cutting out', and 'domestic economy' for geometry or economy.[47]

Women were only gradually allowed to teach male children at all, and even during the severe shortage of male teachers during the First World War, boys over 12 were placed in larger classes rather than have them taught by women.[48]

The comments of the 1917–18 Committee looking into the establishment of scales of salaries, regarding the difference in pay between men and women elementary teachers are extremely revealing: 'The admitted fact that we have to deal with is that women teachers almost invariably receive lower salaries than those paid to men of similar qualifications and the same standing in the service of the same authority.' This difference was seen to vary from £15 to £60, but 'it is perhaps worth remarking that a relatively small ultimate difference is always associated rather with a low scale for men than with a high scale for women.'[49] Though well aware of the inequity of this difference, the Committee decided that, in the interests of frugal government, they should not challenge this wage difference. After all, reasoned the Committee, if we are able to find women teachers who will work for less, should we not hire them?[50]

The difference between male and female elementary teachers can be seen in their voluntary associations as well. For example, in 1895 83 per cent of all certificated male teachers were National Union of Teachers (NUT) members, but only 35 per cent of the certificated female teachers had joined.[51] This ratio, of course, had profound implications for their role in the organization. In spite of their numerical superiority in the occupation, no woman was president of the NUT until 1911, and equal pay for equal work by women was not added to the aims of the NUT until 1919.[52]

It appears, then, that the low social status of elementary teaching combined with the lack of alternative work opportunities for women produced a female-dominated occupation. This disparagement, in turn, contributed to the continued low status of elementary teaching, a contributing factor in the inability of elementary teaching to achieve the status of 'profession'. It should be remembered, however, that the willingness of the government and schools to hire more women because they worked for less was a significant factor in the feminization of elementary teaching in England.[53]

As we have seen, complaints about the low status of elementary teaching predate the enormous growth of elementary education in the last part of the nineteenth century. So, also, do suggestions for raising the status of elementary teaching. The primary focus of the movement to professionalize teaching centered around the establishment of a register of teachers, administered by teachers, based explicitly on the model of the Medical Act of 1858 and later on the Dental Register of 1878. Such a register was one of the explicit aims of the National Union of Elementary Teachers at its founding in 1870. In 1871 it appointed a Special Committee on the Certification and Registration of Teachers.

A parallel movement, begun in the 1840s, existed among secondary-school teachers, led primarily by the College of Preceptors. They submitted bills in 1879 and 1893, both of which would have excluded elementary teachers: 'The main object of the Bill is the advancement of education by making teaching a closed profession.'[54] In 1899 the creation of a register was ordered, a special committee discussed the problem, and in 1903 a register of teachers was created, with six column headings: alphabetical listing of teachers, column A, column B, address, date of registration qualifications and experience. Column A was to indicate certificated elementary day school teachers, Column B secondary-school teachers.[55] But the NUT and the elementary teachers had not supported this version of the register. Rather than having won the fight for professionalization, they had lost. In order to understand why, it is necessary to examine the struggle to expand secondary education surrounding the Education Act of 1902.

The Bryce Commission of 1894 had been appointed to look into the condition of secondary education. The need for an expansion of secondary education was almost universally acknowledged. At that time secondary education was virtually limited to the middle class, by 1900 in some 100 schools with about 30,000 students.[56] Most of these schools had developed into private élitist institutions from the endowed grammar schools. Thus, outside of the few courses beyond the elementary level offered by the local school boards and the little technical education provided under the Department of Science and Art, working-class access to secondary education was blocked.

With the prospect of an expanded system of secondary education, a struggle ensued over just what form that system would take, which directly concerned both elementary and secondary teachers. The secondary-school teachers, led by the various headmasters' organizations, sought the development of a separate system of secondary education, subsidized by the government, staffed by secondary-school teachers, open to elementary-school students only in cases of exceptional ability.[57] Thus Brian Simon writes:

> To plan secondary education as something quite different from elementary education, different, in particular, from what had been provided in the higher grade or science schools, inevitably meant recourse to the academic tradition perpetuated in the grammar and

public schools. . . . All such schools were envisioned as middle class
schools taking only a small proportion of their pupils from elementary
schools.[58]

The elementary teachers, on the other hand, sought the establishment of a
single system of education, subsidized, free, with easy access from one part of
the system to another. That is, they sought the opening up of secondary
education to those in the elementary system, a *de facto* democratization of
secondary education, with a single teaching profession and advancement
from one part of the system to another, that is the opening up of secondary
teaching to elementary teachers.

Thus we find a correspondence between the professional needs and
class interests of the secondary-school teachers: already somewhat *déclassé*,
a single system of education would end their monopoly on secondary
(and middle-class) education and place them closer to the elementary
teachers on the social scale, perhaps even eliminate the distinctions between them. The hopes of an autonomous profession of secondary-school
teachers would be ended. For the middle class as a whole, the creation
of a unified system of education would constitute the end of a distinct
élite education, the merging of lower-class and middle-class education,
the end of minimal education for the working class. This system would
then open the possibility, in teaching and elsewhere, of working-class
entry into middle-class occupational territory. For the middle class
a 'democratization' of secondary education could only mean an attack on
class boundaries.

The professional interests of elementary teachers demanded a single
system of education. Only with a unified system of education and the
creation of a unified corps of teachers could elementary teachers find social
mobility. Thus their immediate goals coincided with those of the Trades
Union Council and the left in general: the opening up of higher education to
the populace in general, to the working class.[59]

With the lines of class conflict thus clearly drawn, the elementary
teachers and the left faced a difficult situation indeed. The Bryce Commission, all 'public' school and university men, all middle class,[60] reported in
favour of a separate national system of secondary schools, with access only for
children from the elementary schools of exceptional ability. Sir John Gorst, a
Radical-Tory, said:

> While primary instruction should be provided for, and even enforced
> upon all, advanced instruction is for the few. It is in the interest of the
> Commonwealth at large that every boy and girl showing capacities
> above the average should be caught and given the best opportunities for
> developing these capacities. It is not in its interests to scatter broadcast a
> huge system of higher instruction for anyone who chooses to take
> advantage of it, however unfit to receive it.[61]

The Act of 1902 was itself ambiguous on secondary education. It replaced the Local School Boards with Local Education Authorities (LEAs), extended grants from the 'rates' to sectarian elementary schools, and empowered the new LEAs to use the 'rates' to finance education beyond the primary level. It is thus often viewed as the opening step in the democratization of secondary education in England. But, as Brian Simon has forcefully demonstrated, it was the interpretation of the Act by the Board of Education under Robert Morant which set the new system of secondary education on its separate and élitist course.[62]

It is in view of this struggle that the Teachers' Registration and Organization Bill must be examined. It was concurrent with the attempts of the Board to establish separate secondary education that Parliament's 1899 call for a register was acted upon. The 1902 register and creation of the purely administrative Teachers' Registration Council constituted yet another confirmation of separate secondary education, represented by separate column headings for elementary and secondary teachers.

The triumph of separate middle-class secondary education meant the triumph of separate middle-class secondary teachers and the defeat of the elementary teachers' attempts to constitute a single, unified and closed teaching profession. It did not, however, completely satisfy the attempts of secondary teachers to professionalize, in part because the Teachers' Registration Council with the membership of elementary teachers, and with its purely administrative function, bore little resemblance to the Medical Council which secondary teachers held as a model. When the register and Council were abolished in 1906, it was because of administrative problems and disputes over who should be included in Column B.[63]

It seems clear that the efforts of elementary teachers to professionalize were doomed to failure. Without a specialized body of knowledge or a clearly delineated market to be controlled, it seems unlikely that any attempt to make elementary teaching a profession could have succeeded. Increasingly, the 'feminization' of teaching was added weight to the continued low status of elementary teaching. And, probably most important, the working-class backgrounds of elementary teachers and the identification of them with a system of education designed for the working class was an insurmountable barrier to the middle-class status of 'profession'.

Nevertheless, the actions of elementary teachers in the last part of the nineteenth century and the early years of the twentieth – establishment of voluntary associations, attempts to 'close' the profession, attempts to remove uncertificated teachers and to establish a body of work on the 'theory of educational practice' – suggest that elementary teachers had accepted the professional model: the ideological portrayal of the established professions by themselves. Explicit references of Medicine and Dentistry confirm this acquiescence.

The middle-class legislators, councillors and Her Majesty's Inspectors seem never to have discouraged this view; in fact they may have encouraged it to a point. The reasons for this are obvious. Striving to achieve the attributes of the professional model in order to achieve professional status would lead teachers to adopt approaches to work extremely useful to the middle-class administrators of elementary education: a high degree of self-control of behaviour through internalized codes of ethics, a primary orientation towards service to others and the community rather than self, the importance of honorary, non-monetary rewards. Along with these, of course, would come identification with the middle class, middle-class values and thus a tendency away from unionism and other ideas of the left, revolutionary or not.

Thus we see that it greatly served the needs of the middle class to promote the professional model and a striving for professionalization among elementary teachers. We can also see the large degree to which elementary teachers adopted the professional model as their goal. But the support of the ruling élite, a necessary prerequisite to professionalization, went only so far. When it came to the hiring of cheap, uncertificated teachers, the Board would not hesitate. Thus, also, the maintenance of lower pay and lower status for women teachers.

And, finally, when the elementary teachers' push for professionalization came to threaten the strict class lines of the separate systems of education and the security of the middle-class secondary teachers, the élite acted unequivocally. In the end, class lines and class conflict constituted the greatest barrier to the professionalization of teaching as the teachers themselves concieved it. The barrier was insurmountable.

Notes and references

1. *British Parliamentary Papers* (hereafter *BPP*). 1917–18.XI. Report . . . Scales of Salary for Teachers in Elementary Schools.
2. *The School and the Teacher*, October, 1855, quoted in Asher Tropp, *The School Teachers* (London, 1957), p. 26.
3. Ibid.
4. *Effects of the Educational Provisions of the Factories Act*, King Collection, Vol. 227.
5. P. W. Musgrave. *Society and Education in England since 1800* (London, 1968), p. 61.
6. Robert Lowe, during the 1862 debates on the Revised Code following the Newcastle Commission Report of 1861. Cited in Tropp, *School Teachers*, p. 89.
7. One can hardly speak properly of a system of education in England before the Education Act of 1902. Inasmuch as Parliament, by the 1860s, endeavoured to deal with all elementary education at one blow, and for the sake of convenience, I refer loosely here to a system of education meaning only elementary education in general. These clearly drawn class distinctions in education in England persisted in explicit form well into the twentieth century. Indeed, they persist to a certain extent today. This subject is treated masterfully and extensively for our period by

Brian Simon in his classic study *Education and the Labour Movement 1870–1920* (London, 1965). On these aspects of elementary education in particular, see especially pp. 112–64.

8. *Statistical Abstract for the United Kingdom 1870–1884*, p. 172; *1886–1900*, p. 250.
9. Ibid.
10. Bernard Barber, 'Some Problems in the Sociology of the Professions', *Daedalus*, 92/4 (1963): 672. See also, for example, M. L. Cogan, 'Toward a Definition of Profession', *Harvard Educational Review*, 23 (1953): 33–50; A. M. Carr-Saunders and P. A. Wilson, *The Professions* (London, 1933); Howard M. Vollmer and Donald L. Mills (eds), *Professionalization* (Englewood Cliffs, NJ); Richard H. Hall 'Professionalization and Bureaucratization', *American Sociological Review* 33(1968): 92–103: William J. Goode, 'The Theoretical Limits of Professionalization', in Amitai Etzioni (ed.), *The Semi-Professions and Their Organization* (New York, 1963), pp. 266–313. This is, of course, only a partial listing of a vast literature. For a summary of this literature, see also J. A. Jackson (ed.) *Professions and Professionalization* (Cambridge, 1970). I have not distinguished here among those who would separate ideal-types of professions from those of professionalization or professionalism. And, finally, see also Talcott Parsons, *Essays in Sociological Theory* (New York, 1954), esp. 'The Professions and Social Structure', pp. 34–49.
11. See especially Etzioni, *Semi-Professions*.
12. See, for example, Nina Toren, 'Semi-Professionalism and Social Work: A Theoretical Perspective', in Etzioni. *Semi-Professions*, pp. 141–5. Here Toren follows Carr-Saunders in identifying 'new' and 'would-be' professions, as well as established and semi-professions. Her dependence upon the standard ideal-type is explicit.
13. See, for example, Harold L. Wilensky 'The Professionalization of Everyone? *American Journal of Sociology* 70 (Sept. 1964); 137–58; Hall. 'Professionalization and Bureaucratization', *American Journal of Sociology*; Toren, 'Semi-professionalism and Social Work,' *American Journal of Sociology*; Dan C. Lortie, 'The Balance of Control and Autonomy in Elementary School Teaching', in Etzioni, *Semi-Professions*, pp. 1–53; W. Richard Scott, 'Professional Employees in a Bureaucratic Structure: Social Work', in Etzioni, *Semi-Professions*, pp. 82–140; Richard L. Simpson and Ida Harper Simpson 'Women and Bureaucracy in the Semi-Professions', in Etzioni. *Semi-Professions*, pp. 196–265; G. Harries-Jenkins 'Professionals in Organizations', in Jackson, *Professions*, pp. 51–108.
14. Jean-Michel Chapoulie, 'Sur l'analyse sociologique des groupes professionels'. *Revue française de sociologie*, 14 (1973): 86–114: Magali S. Larson, *The Rise of Professionalism*, (Berkeley, 1977). I refer here specifically to Larson's introduction, in which her critique is stated (pp. ix–xviii), but her critique has obviously informed her entire study. Other critiques of the sociology of professionalization do exist, for example, V. Olesen and E. W. Whittaker 'Critical notes on sociological studies of professional socialization', in Jackson, *Professions*, pp. 179–221; and Jackson's own introduction to the same volume, but I have found Larson and Chapoulie most useful.
15. Chapoulie, 'Sur l'analyse sociologique', pp. 92–4.
16. Ibid., p. 95, cf. for example, E. C. Hughes *The Sociological Eye* (Chicago, 1971).
17. Chapoulie, 'Sur l'analyse sociologique', p. 95. It is the professional model, and

the acceptance and internalization of the moral rules of professional conduct which justify the status not only of the established professions in society, but of their study in sociology.

18. Ibid., p. 97.
19. Ibid., p. 96.
20. Chapoulie, 'Sur l'analyse sociologique', pp. 96, 98, ff. This summary constitutes a gross simplication of Chapoulie's suggestions, but I believe I have faithfully rendered his critique of functionalism. He is, indeed, critical of the interactionists. In fact, this critique constitutes most of the rest of the article, but he is far less critical of them than of the functionalists.
21. Larson, *The Rise of Professionalism*, pp. xii–xiii.
22. Ibid., p. xiv.
23. Ibid., p. xii.
24. Ibid. That the cognitive elements of the professions help define them means, for Larson, that a determination of their class position will revolve around a treatment of the role of intellectuals in society. Her discussion of this, however, lies outside the realm of this paper, though it has great bearing on its general theoretical questions. We will see, however, that elementary teachers in England lacked a discrete body of generalized and systematized knowledge, and that their class position is best understood outside Mannheim's category of *freisehwebende intelligenz*, which Larson applies to the professions.
25. Larson, *The Rise of Professionalism*, pp. xvi–xvii (emphasis Larson's).
26. Tropp, *School Teachers*, p. 14.
27. Ibid., pp. 16–17.
28. Simon, *Education and the Labour Movement*, p. 115.
29. See, for example, Tropp, *School Teachers*, pp. 18–19.
30. In 1846, 10–30 for men, 6–20 for women.
31. *Statistical Abstract for the United Kingdom 1913, 1918–31*, pp. 48–9.
32. See for example, BPP, 1887, XXVIII, 738.
33. Tropp, *School Teachers*, pp. 58–98.
34. BPP 1917–18, XI, Report . . . Enquiring into . . . Scales of Salary for Teachers in Elementary Schools, pp. 449–512.
35. R. H. Tawney *Education, the Socialist Policy* cited in Simon, *Education and the Labour Movement*, p. 119, 145, ff.
36. Tropp, *School Teachers*, pp. 30–1, 41. See especially Simon, *Education and the Labour Movement*, pp. 118–19.
37. Tropp, *School Teachers*, pp. 15, 22–3, 34–5, 147–50.
38. Ibid., pp. 44–54.
39. Ibid., pp. 108; 109; n. 6.
40. Ibid., p. 111.
41. Ibid., pp. 147–50; 150, n. 33.
42. Candidates for pupil-teacher needed testimony from the school manager not only on their own character, but on that of their parents. Illegitimate children could not be pupil-teachers. In the case of unsatisfactory parents, the child could become a pupil-teacher if he or she moved, but not to any public house. Every candidate had to satisfy a test of his or her religious knowledge, and girls had to provide examples of their needlework.
43. See Larson, *The Rise of Professionalism*, p. xvi on the middle-class nature of the professions.

44. I am painfully aware of the difficulties involved in assessing the relative economic position of elementary school teachers in England for this period. The significant differences between urban and rural teachers, secular and religious schools, certificated and non-certificated teachers do not appear in these tables. The only such difference which does appear is that between men and women, because it is so well documented. But I do feel that I have shown as, well as possible, the basic relative economic position of elementary-school teachers for the period. My thanks to Steven Ruggles and Roald Euller for assistance with the tables.

45. *BPP*, 1897, XXVI, lxxxiii.

46. *BPP*, 1871, I.V, Minute . . . Establishing a New Code of Regulations, 317.

47. *BPP*, LVI. Syllabus . . . , 231.

48. *BPP*, 1917–18, XI, Report . . . , 6.

49. *BPP*, 1917–18. XI, Report . . . Enquiring into . . . Scales of Salary for Teachers in Elementary Schools, 8–9.

50. Ibid.

51. Tropp, *School Teachers*, p. 157, n. 46.

52. Ibid., p. 157, n. 46; p. 158.

53. For treatments of the feminization of teaching in America, see for example, Sheila M. Rothman, *Woman's Proper Place* (New York, 1978), esp. 'Defining Woman's Work: Typewriters, Salesgirls and Teachers,' pp. 42–62; W. Elliot Brownlee and Mary M. Brownlee, *Women in the American Economy* (New Haven, 1976), esp. 'The Designation of Teaching as "Women's Work,"' pp. 266–70; and Michael B. Katz, *The Irony of Early School Reform*, (Boston, 1968), esp. pp. 56–9, 153–9.

54. *BPP*, 1890–1, XVII. Special Report . . . On the Teachers' Registration and Organization Bill, 224.

55. *BPP*, 1962, I.XXVIII, 6.

56. Simon, *Education and the Labour Movement*, pp. 99–112, on the development of the public schools out of the endowed grammar schools.

57. Tropp, *School Teachers*, pp. 175–7; Simon, *Education and the Labour Movement*, pp. 208–16.

58. Simon, *Education and the Labour Movement*, pp. 242, is actually discussing the implementation of the 1902 Act, rather than the debate leading up to it.

59. Ibid., pp. 224–34. I am, for the purpose of this paper, taking an extremely narrow view of the issues involved in the Education Act of 1902.

60. Tropp, *School Teachers*, p. 179; Simon, *Education and the Labour Movement*, p. 238.

61. Quoted in Simon, *Education and the Labour Movement*, p. 238.

62. Ibid., pp. 208–46, see esp. pp. 238–46.

63. Tropp, *School Teachers*, pp. 195–9; *BPP*, 1902, LXVIII, 791; 1906, XC, 407; 1908, LXXXIII, 799; 1890–91, X, 287; 1890–1, XVII, 199. The abolition of the register in 1906 is really only the beginning of the continuing struggle for registration and the establishment of a Council. The events become inextricably linked with the relations between elementary and secondary teachers, but the failure of the Council and register established in 1912, which lapsed in 1949, owe more, I believe, to the nature of teaching and its position in English society. As I hope this paper shows, the inability of teachers to professionalize is deeply rooted. See also, Tropp, *School Teachers*, pp. 267–9. The changing professional status of

elementary teachers in England after 1908 must be linked to the end of the system of pupil-teachership, and the establishment of bursarship, which did much to place entry into elementary teaching outside the financial abilities of the working class.

4

Teachers' work: changing patterns and perceptions in the emerging school systems of nineteenth- and early twentieth-century central Canada

Marta Danylewycz and Alison Prentice

The contract of Miss Ellen McGuire, dated 1 June 1880, spelt out government teachers' duties as they were understood at that time in the province of Quebec. As mistress of District School No. 3 in the township of Lowe, she agreed to

> exercise an efficient supervision over the pupils attending the school; to teach such subjects as are authorized and to make use only of duly approved school books; to fill up all blank forms which may be sent her by the Department of Public Instruction, the Inspectors or Commissioners; to keep all school registers required; to preserve amongst the archives of the school such copy books and other works of the pupils which she may be ordered to put aside; to keep the school-rooms in good order and not to allow them to be used for any other purpose without permission to that effect; to follow such rules as may be established for discipline and punishment; to preserve carefully the *Journal of Education*; in a word to fulfill all the duties of a good teacher; to hold school every day, except on Sundays, and festivals and on the holidays authorized by the Commissioners or granted by proper authority.[1]

Miss McGuire's contract stated that it was 'in conformity with' the Quebec School Act of 1878 and, like many teacher contracts of the period, was on a printed form provided by the Quebec Department of Public Instruction. Her duties, as spelt out in the printed engagement, were those put forward by the department as the standard for any government school teacher in the province.

In subsequent years, provincial regulations and contract forms included further detail. Indeed, the very next year, the contract of Philomène Lachance of the parish of St Croix, St Flavien, already stipulated that it was the teacher's duty to supervise pupils, whether they were in or out of class, as long as they were 'under her view'. It was further agreed that Mlle Lachance would keep the school register and children's books in a cupboard especially designed for that purpose. The teacher was expressly forbidden to use any of the school-rooms to entertain unauthorized visitors. The contract also sounded a cautionary note regarding the use of corporal punishment, which was to be discouraged. Finally, the teacher was to be properly dressed and to set a good example of 'cleanliness' and 'savoir vivre'.[2]

Teacher contracts such as those of Ellen McGurie and Philomène Lachance outline the major areas of teachers' work in state-supported elementary schools in the latter part of the nineteenth century. They deal with the subjects to be taught, the paperwork and the discipline of both pupils and the teacher herself. They speak, if only briefly, of the teacher's duty to take care of the schoolroom and its property. On the other hand, the contracts say nothing about the responsibility of the school commissioners towards the teacher and the school. Although they failed to mention class size, the state of school buildings, heating and cleaning arrangements, or even the locations of schools, these factors too affected teachers' work. Teacher's contracts, therefore, left much unsaid.

They nevertheless serve as a useful starting point for examining the history of teachers' work in a vital period of transition. The following discussion, which is part of a larger, on-going study of Quebec and Ontario public school teachers, focuses on the crucial years in the nineteenth and early twentieth centuries when state school systems were in the process of being established and teacher workforces were becoming disproportionately female across both provinces. We have probed elsewhere some of the major problems addressed by our explorations in this history, such as teachers' class and ethnic origins, the question of their changing ages, marital and household status, and the overwhelmingly important issue of gender as it affected all of these questions, or was addressed by school reformers and teachers of the time.[3] In this exploratory essay, our focus is on the actual work of teachers in the schoolroom, as this appears to have been understood and as this under-standing changed during the crucial years of school system development in the nineteenth and early twentieth centuries. It is taken as a given that, increasingly, the teachers we are studying were women.

As we analysed the history of teachers in this period, we were struck by two interesting lacunae in most previous historical considerations of the subject. Educational historians have tended on the whole to treat turn-of-the-century school mistresses and masters as incipient professionals or, more disparagingly, as professionals 'manqués', shying away from any concrete consideration of the work that they actually did. The story has often been told as a tragedy: an account of the failure of teaching to become a 'genuine profession'. In one Canadian analysis, this failure was explicitly attributed, at least in part, to the influx of inexperienced and malleable young girls into the occupation and the resulting devaluing of the work of experienced and well-trained males. Equally, labour historians have not seen teachers as part of the changing workforce that needs to be examined in their analyses of the emergence of industrial capitalism. As Graham Lowe has shown to be the case with clerical workers, teachers also have not fitted very well into the classic model of workers perceived to be men doing manual, as opposed to intellectual or managerial, work.[4] Teachers, on the contrary, have been seen and portrayed as 'brainworkers'; and as either actually or ideally the managers, at the very least, of children if not of other adults. In addition, they were very clearly not working *men*, since so many, as time went on, were in fact women. Thus teachers *as workers* have been left out of nineteenth- and early twentieth-century labour history, just as they have been ignored in the history of education. Recently, investigations by Michael Apple on the position of twentieth-century American teachers, and Barry Bergen, Jennifer Ozga, and Martin Lawn on their late nineteenth- and twentieth-century British counterparts, have called into question both the tendency to focus exclusively on teachers' status as either incipient or failed professionals and the tendency to ignore them as workers. By looking carefully at the meaning of changes in teachers' work and working conditions, and by introducing the concept of gender, these studies begin, rather, to develop a convincing argument for the 'proletarianization' of the teacher labour force.[5]

Our task, in the light of these considerations, was to try to come to grips more concretely than has been the case in the past with what teachers did in their daily work and how this work changed during the period of state school system construction in central Canada. As our concern was to try to get a general picture, we have ignored many details and interesting comparative questions, perhaps blurring very real differences between teachers' work in Quebec and Ontario, in Catholic and Protestant, or rural and urban schools. Nor have we focused very sharply on emerging differences between the roles of teaching assistants and principal teachers or even between those of men and women. Our concern, rather, has been to look at what was going on in nearly all nineteenth-century state-supported elementary schools, in both provinces, in all their regional, religious and ethnic variety, to try to find the common denominators that seemed to have been affecting nearly all teachers, whatever their backgrounds or places in schools and school systems. In a reading of the annual reports of the Ontario and Quebec provincial departments of public instruction, the reports of the Montreal Catholic School Commission and the Toronto Public School Board, the *Journal of Education for Upper Canada* and the *Educational Record of the Province of Quebec*, as well as a sampling of the correspondence of the two provincial education departments and other scattered sources, we in fact discovered a number of recurring themes. These included the introduction of new subjects and new teaching methods into nineteenth- and early twentieth-century schoolrooms; the introduction and phenomenal growth of paperwork; and a growing emphasis on discipline and hierarchy, as well as on uniformity of practice and routine. Pupil and teacher health and the question of the physical maintenance of schools and classrooms also emerged as important questions for analysis. Documents of the period make it clear, in other words, that an understanding of teachers' work must include a consideration not only of their tasks but also of the changing conditions under which they performed them. Finally, teachers' work was affected by less tangible factors. Their own perceptions, and the perceptions of their employers, regarding the economic and social position of schoolmistresses and schoolmasters, as well as assumptions about what work was compatible with that position, also played a role. Here great tensions were generated, tensions that explain the contradictory policies pursued by the women teachers' associations which emerged at the turn of the century, as they sought to improve their members' conditions of work and to define the position of women teachers in the labour force.

New subjects, more teaching

Despite the profound differences in the organization and structure of the Ontario and Quebec public school systems, both were settling into an era of consolidation and growth by the 1880s. Having weathered the storms of local opposition to the intervention of central authorities in the establishment of schools, and having asserted their dominance over teacher certification and classroom instruction, provincial educational leaders were now in a position to expand the functions of the institutions they increasingly controlled. The lengthening of the period of formal schooling and the broadening of the public school curriculum were part of that expansion and both developments directly affected the work of teachers. As children remained in school longer, class sizes and schools grew proportionally; and as students had to master a broader range of subjects, the workload of many teachers increased.

The 1871 Ontario School Law, which made schooling compulsory for children between the ages of 7 and 12, also called for the addition of agriculture and drawing to the long established elementary school programme of reading, writing, arithmetic, geography and grammar. The 1880s saw the introduction in Ontario of hygiene, temperance and calisthenics into the curriculum, and the turn of the century brought in manual training and domestic science. The annual reports of the Department of Education recording the number of children learning the new subjects following their introduction attest to the widening of teachers' responsibilities during the last quarter of the nineteenth century. The number of children studying drawing, for example, increased eightfold between 1870 and 1900;

the number taking hygiene increased sixfold; and the number taking drill and calisthenics increased threefold between 1880 and 1900.[6]

Similar developments occurred in Quebec, producing comparable alterations in the work of teachers. Although compulsory education was not legislated until 1940, a rise in school attendance, owing to growing enrollment and the lengthening of the period of formal schooling, was evident by the last quarter of the nineteenth century. Moreover, as was the case in Ontario, so too in Quebec were agriculture, drawing, hygiene, calisthenics and domestic science beginning to be integrated into the public elementary-school curriculum during the closing decades of the nineteenth century.[7]

In both provinces curricular reform created much consternation among teachers. Not having been consulted about or forewarned of changes in elementary-school programmes, they were frequently overwhelmed by the new demands being made of them. 'Can anyone tell us where we are drifting to in this matter of additional textbooks and increasing number of subjects?' asked one Montreal teacher of a teachers' journal. It was this teacher's hope that the editor would throw some light on the 'impossible goal' towards which teachers were 'expected to hasten'.[8] Teachers such as this correspondent were often troubled by their lack of preparation to teach the new subjects. Many responded by simply ignoring the pressure to introduce them, arguing that this was justified as long as the central authorities did not provide proper instruction manuals or opportunities for teacher retraining. Because both provinces were slow in helping teachers out of the conundrum the new subjects created, such resistance endured.[9]

Central authorities, for their part, may have counted on the high turnover rate among teachers to flush out the older and ill-equipped masters and mistresses who would, they must have reasoned, eventually be replaced by normal school graduates trained in the teaching of the new subjects. But normal school training remained the exception rather than the rule in both Ontario and Quebec. The majority of teachers moved into the occupation through other channels, generally by attending model or convent schools and then presenting themselves to local boards of examiners. Moreover, within the teaching corps there were increasing numbers of persisters or career teachers whose training predated curricular reform. If in the early days educational authorities satisfied themselves by assuming that such teachers would train themselves in the new subjects or by reminding the recalcitrant that 'the *clever* teachers' would be able to master them 'without the aid of a manual',[10] by the last decades of the nineteenth century they began to supply some assistance. During the holidays, after school and on weekends, school-mistresses and masters were urged to attend provincially or locally organized classes and institutes, to learn not only the new subjects but the more modern methods of instruction and classroom management popularized by the 'new education' movement of the period. These extracurricular courses, *ad hoc* at first, soon became a regular part of teachers' work.[11]

Paperwork

If new subjects added to the teacher's workload, so did the rapidly growing mounds of paperwork. As early as 1847, the chief superintendent of schools for Upper Canada had foreshadowed this work when he wrote to a local school officer to the effect that what was not put in writing did not, for the purposes of the school system, exist. What was communicated 'verbally', he commented then, could not be considered 'official'. In this brief remark, tossed off so casually to an obscure Upper Canadian educator who must have failed to put some information crucial to his purposes on paper, the chief superintendent enunciated a principle which was to haunt teachers as well as the officers of school systems from then on.[12]

It may have been the local school officers who were legally required to fill out the forms demanded by provincial authorities – and by the 1860s in Ontario, local trustees' reports covered over a hundred different items – but it was usually the teacher who had to supply the basic information. And of the 'blank forms' mentioned in the Quebec teachers' contracts of the early 1880s, the most time-consuming, as well as the most vital, was probably the individual class or school register. In Canada West the daily attendance register seems to have made its appearance as early as the 1840s. In 1850 it took on a crucial role for local schools, and parents and taxpayers, for after that date the Upper Canadian school grant was distributed on the basis of average attendance rates, with the highest grants going to the schools with the best attendance. Woe betide the teacher who did not keep an accurate daily account of pupils' presence or absence in the school, for falsification of the attendance register, according to the chief superintendent's report for 1859, met with 'punishment'. Failure to keep it altogether jeopardized the entire school grant to the section.[13]

By the 1880s in Quebec, it was clear that individual teachers had paperwork that went beyond the compiling of the daily registers. A correspondent to the *Educational Record* explained the methods whereby teachers could compute the averages from their daily records for half-yearly reports.[14] Rural Quebec teachers reported to local commissioners rather than to boards of trustees for individual schools, and an 1883 report from the country of Soulanges is evidence of some of the information that they had to include. This document, dated 19 February 1883, came from the pen of Marie Argonie Viau, *institutrice* of a school in the sixth *arrondissement* of the Municipalité Scolaire de St Joseph. It was two pages in length. One page listed the scholars in the school, along with their ages and the numbers of boys and girls who were studying various subjects or reading particular books. The other page consisted of a letter introducing this material, explaining its deficiencies and requesting that the commissioners supply the teacher with a notebook so that she could comply with the requirement that an on-going record be kept of inspectors' and commissioners' visits to her school.[15]

In the city of Toronto, the annual reports of the Public School Board are evidence of the reporting tasks that could be added to the work of urban teachers as school systems grew larger and more complex. In 1872, in addition to the statistical summaries of their schools' registers that were periodically required, headmasters and mistresses were asked to provide monthly lists of absentees for that month, along with the reasons for their non-attendance. In 1881, it was announced that every teacher had to keep a written record of all homework assigned to pupils. Finally, in 1891, written assessments of individual students' progress were added to the teachers' work. At the end of the school year, every teacher had to produce a 'mind chart' for each pupil, along with his or her recommendations regarding the individual pupils' promotions.[16]

If reporting to their superiors produced one kind of paperwork for teachers, the advent of written tests and examinations produced another. Gone was the era when everything depended on the oral questioning of both pupils and teachers. Examinations for teacher certification, on the one hand, and the correction and assessment of students' workbooks and examinations, on the other, loomed ever larger in the work of schools. Another part of the teacher's work lay in dealing with the anxiety that examinations inevitably produced. On the occasion of the introduction of provincial examinations in Quebec in 1895, a sarcastic letter from '*Amicus*' appeared in the *Educational Record*, revealing the extent to which one correspondent, at least, felt that schoolmistresses and masters in Ontario had already become slaves to the unreasonable central authorities who controlled such exams. *Amicus* produced a list of injunctions which reflected what this author clearly believed were the sins the Ontario examiners had all too often committed. Failing to phrase questions simply or arrange them clearly, or to proofread the printed copies of the examinations, were only a few among many. Moreover, it was really the teachers who were being examined, not their pupils. What provincial examiners wanted, *Amicus* seemed to imply, was confusion and anxiety – in short, more work for the people who were actually on the firing line in the schools, their already overburdened teachers.[17]

The work of supervision – and being supervised

Both *Amicus* and Marie Argonie Viau outlined the difficulties teachers had in complying with the control mechanisms set in place by provincial schoolmen, and their comments reveal how wide the gulf could be between the expectations of central authorities and the realities teachers faced on the local level. If the laws and departmental or local regulations were problematic, even the pressures generated by reformers' supposedly helpful suggestions could have a disquieting effect. A teacher writing to the *Educational Record* in the mid-1880s captured the anxiety of many. The *Record*'s advice was good, the letter implied, but hard to follow in this teacher's country school. The *Record* had suggested a school museum, but that was impossible. The 'scholars would likely kill one another with the mineral specimens'. Even the more standard activities of needlework and scripture reading were counted 'a loss of time' in this teacher's school, where pupils no doubt continued the tradition of attending only when farm or domestic work permitted them to do so: 'You have never taught schools in this country. I feel as I felt one summer when I rode for a month a very vicious horse, coaxing him a little, yet not too much, lest he should think, or rather find out, that I feared him, for then he would be sure to run away with me'.[18]

Individual teachers were caught between the exigencies of local conditions and the demands of their superiors, and both fell heavily on them. In the 1840s it had been possible for an elderly rural teacher from the Upper Canadian District of Gore to lie on a bench and allow the pupils to read out loud to him as they gradually drifted into the school over the course of the morning. But the district superintendent, on observing this approach to school teaching, had been shocked. As he related to the chief superintendent of the province, when all the pupils were assembled he had lectured both teacher and taught on the importance of punctuality; later on he had seen to it that the old man's certificate to teach was not renewed.[19] The situation of the teacher from Gore anticipated that of his successors for, as the nineteenth century wore on, the teacher's role in matters like punctuality was increasingly emphasized. One graphic illustration of how important such issues became was the astonishing drop from 69,456 cases of 'lateness' reported for Toronto board schools in 1874 to only 5,976 cases in 1880. This constituted a great improvement in the eyes of the city's newly appointed school superintendent, James Hughes; how it had been achieved was not explained. Clearly, though, classroom teachers must have been involved in Hughes' campaign to reduce tardiness.[20]

Teachers were also increasingly expected to take responsibility for the behaviour of students outside the classroom. This included pupils 'on their way to and from school' as well as during lunch hours and school breaks. Recognizing the fact that some parents sent children to school when they were sick, the Toronto board required each school to appoint a teacher to stay inside with such pupils during recess. All other teachers, according to a new regulation of 1879, had to be in the schoolyard during that period.[21] The supervision of children outside of the classroom, most educators believed, involved not just one's presence but also setting a good example. Thus an 1885 *Educational Record* article entitled 'Noontime' exhorted teachers to eat 'decorously' and use a napkin when having lunch with their pupils. After a short lunchtime rest, they were also encouraged to organize games for the children to keep them happy and occupied.[22]

As school officials increasingly used teachers to tighten the reins of control over students, they also introduced measures to ensure that the teachers themselves performed their work as specified in the regulations. Through local institutes teachers were instructed in matters as personal as their tone of voice and as trivial as how many times to pull the rope when ringing the school bell, as well as in matters more clearly related to academic instruction.[23] But the more obvious controls were exerted by the visits of school inspectors and, where schools were growing larger, by principals or head teachers. The frequency and character of rural school inspection depended on a variety of factors, ranging from the personality of the inspector to the location of the school. Schools that were hard to reach were sometimes missed altogether when the inspector made his rounds.[24] Conversely, urban teachers were inspected more regularly than rural teachers and were subjected to more systematic and closer controls. In Toronto, for example, Public School Board teachers were visited by an increasing number of 'specialists', who supervised the teaching of subjects like drawing, domestic science and drill. Schoolmistresses and some masters who taught for large urban boards were also visibly compartmentalized in the lower rungs of growing educational bureaucracies which subjected them to several levels of inspection, beginning with the school principal and ending with the district and provincial superintendency.[25]

Working for better health

The superintendency concerned itself not just with teachers, of course. It was also part of the inspector's job to supervise the local school boards themselves, with a view to enforcing the laws requiring decent school accommodation. Ontario authorities, for example, specified in 1871 exactly how much land, floor space and air each school should have, depending on the number of pupils. Requirements governing fences, ventilation and heating, drinking water, school privies and equipment were vaguer, stating only that these items should be 'sufficient' or 'suitable'.[26] But whether they were specific or vague, the regulations were hard to enforce and teachers all too often found their employers delinquent in these matters. As a result, their work frequently had to be performed under the most trying conditions.

In a typical letter, dated 23 March 1883, a local inspector described to his superiors in the Quebec Department of Public Instruction the failure of the commissioners for St Jean de Rouville to provide proper accommodation for their village school. The school, he reported, was exactly as he had found it the year before, despite promises to repair and renovate it. The building was so cold that parts of it were uninhabitable; the rooms were so small that some of the children were literally 'crushed one against the other'. The inspector clearly felt that only provincial pressure could bring about an improvement and he buttressed his case by referring to the feelings of the school's two teachers. These schoolmistresses not only suffered considerable 'malaise' because of the conditions in their school, but, according to the inspector, were reluctant to complain because when their predecessor had done so, he had been reprimanded and forced to retract his complaints by the St Jean de Rouville commissioners.[27]

In Montreal, teachers employed by the Catholic School Commission did not even need to submit a grievance to be reprimanded. City health inspectors might achieve the same result, as in the case of Mlle Thibodeau in 1877. Because they found the conditions in her two-room school 'injurious to the health of the pupils' and reported that finding to her employers, Thibodeau's subsidy from the commission was cut off. This teacher, her employers decided, would be reinstated only after the required renovations were made or after she found a new building to house her 150 pupils.[28]

Thibodeau's predicament was not an isolated one in the history of Quebec schooling. Many Montreal women teachers toiled in poorly ventilated, ill-equipped, insufficiently lit and overcrowded classrooms. When health inspectors presented a damning report, they and not their employers, the commissioners, faced the consequences, because schoolrooms and buildings were their responsibility.[29] Thibodeau was laid off for a month and a half; she needed that much time to find more suitable accommodation for her school. In the meantime, she and others like her suffered the loss of their salaries while moving from one site to another. Thibodeau, like many other teachers, also suffered from poor health, fatigue and physical breakdown as a result of her working conditions, and eventually had to resign.

Clearly, if the health of the students was endangered by the poor condition of many schools, so too was that of their teachers. Léocadie Généreux, a contemporary of Thibodeau and mistress of a neighbouring school, requested a leave of absence in 1879 due 'to the precarious state of her health'. It was granted along with a $50.00 bonus in recognition of fifteen years of service to the school commission.[30] Généreux returned to the classroom one year later, to take up the front line in the battle against smallpox, diphtheria and tuberculosis being waged by school officials and public health reformers. In the wake of scientific findings that many of the contagious diseases could be contained by vaccination and proper diet, late nineteenth- and early twentieth-century teachers increasingly found themselves instructing their pupils in hygiene and correct eating habits, ensuring that they were vaccinated, inspecting them for contagious diseases and sending the ill to the school clinic or home.[31]

The combination of poor working conditions and exposure to a variety of contagious diseases debilitated teachers, forcing many to take periodic leaves of absence. In recognition of this fact, the Toronto Public School Board in the 1870s began to hire 'occasional teachers' to replace those on sick leave.[32] While from the students' and employers' point of view substitute teachers were a solution to the absent teacher problem, they were hardly the answer as far as the ailing schoolmistresses were concerned. Their only recourse at times of sickness was family, kin or charitable institutions. In this regard their situation was no different from that of nineteenth-century labourers, who also relied on these traditional, albeit frequently inadequate, support systems.

At the same time, however, teachers were pressuring provincial governments to make amends to pension funds (established in 1853 in Ontario and in 1856 in Quebec) in view of the ill effects working conditions had on their health. Individual and isolated requests of schoolmistresses like that of Eliza Pelletier from L'Islet, Quebec, for an early retirement with a pension due to her anaemic condition, became by the turn of the century collective demands voiced at meetings of teachers' associations.[33] The associations of Protestant and Catholic teachers of Montreal stood united in the early 1900s in an effort to pressure the provincial government to lower the age of retirement for women teachers from 56 to 50. Reasoning that 'the great majority of women teachers break down before reaching the present retiring age, and are utterly unfit to follow other occupations', they demanded revisions to the pension fund scheme as well as, at least implicitly, a recognition by school officials that the work of women teachers was far more exacting than that of the men.[34]

In the same vein, women teachers began to publicize their concerns about health and working conditions through the medium of the press. Whenever the occasion presented itself, and it did in turn-of-the-century Montreal with the founding of the *Ligue d'enseignement*, they pleaded their case with the public.[35] They also rejoiced when support for their cause or recognition of the difficulties under which they laboured appeared outside their own circles. In 1891 the *Educational Record* reprinted an article from one of the province's newspapers that had taken notice of the teacher's plight and outlined ways in which teachers could prevent fatigue, anaemia or mere discouragement.[36]

School maintenance and housekeeping

If poor working conditions and health care were dominant themes for teachers in the second half of the nineteenth century and carried on unabated into the early twentieth, a related and muted theme was the teacher's continuing role in the physical maintenance of the school. The school had once been located in the teacher's home, a rented house or a room in someone else's house; then, as provincial school systems were put into place, in most locations the school house became public property and, in theory, the responsibility for its maintenance shifted to local boards of trustees or commissioners. But, for the women who taught under the Montreal Catholic School Commission, as we have seen, this theory did not even begin to be put into practice. And for a long time the boundaries of responsibility for the maintenance and upkeep of school property remained blurred in other regions as well. Often school boards insisted that at least the minor work of school maintenance still belonged to teachers.

In Ontario, debate on the subject can be traced back to the 1840s. Queries to the office of the chief superintendent of schools suggest that Upper

Canadian trustee boards and their teachers had already entered into dispute in two areas: who should lay the fires in schools and who should clean the schoolhouses. In 1848, Egerton Ryerson wrote that these were matters of negotiations between teachers and trustees, the law not specifying who was responsible for the work of school maintenance. He suggested that the trustees could give the teacher a higher salary in return for the work, grant a special allowance for the purpose or agree to it being done by the pupils under the teacher's direction.[37] But arguments on the subject continued to reach the chief superintendent's desk, as trustees pressed the housework of the school on reluctant teachers who clearly regarded such tasks as 'extra' work or beneath their dignity. By 1861 the provincial Education Office took a stronger stand on behalf of such teachers. The housekeeping work of the school, Egerton Ryerson now argued, was no longer a matter for negotiation; such work, he implied, did not belong to the men and women whose employment educational reformers were trying so hard to define as 'professional'. Under the heading 'Official Replies of the Chief Superintendent of Schools to Local School Authorities in Upper Canada', the *Journal of Education for Upper Canada* published the following brief statement: '*Teachers are not required to make Fires*. The Teacher is employed to teach the school, but he is not employed to make the fires and clean the school house, much less repair the school house'.[38]

Provincial educational authorities' pronouncements did not necessarily sway local school boards, however, and in an 1863 trustees' minute book for School Section No. 1, North West Oxford, building fires as well as ringing the school bell were explicitly laid out as the teacher's contracted work. In 1865, however, the superintendent from Oxford County reported that the more common solution in the country schools under his jurisdiction was to hire a lad to do the 'extra work' or to press it onto the pupils.[39]

Anna Paulin, who taught in the Quebec parish of Ste Marie de Manoir Rouville in the 1880s, engaged to keep the school clean and the path to the school clear, according to her contract.[40] But in Quebec as well, such work was subject to debate. Under the heading 'Enquiries', the *Educational Record* dealt with the topic in 1885. Was it 'part of the teacher's duty' to light the school fires each morning? The answer was unequivocal: 'Certainly not. The trouble and expense of lighting the fires must be provided for by the school commissioners through the school manager of the district'.[41] In 1889 the *Educational Record* argued that it was the teacher's job, with the help of her pupils, to keep the schoolroom neat and clean, but only provided that a proper caretaker cleaned it thoroughly once a week. The issue was of sufficient importance to merit attention once again in an 1893 editorial on how teachers could improve their position in society. Schoolmistresses and masters were advised to see to it that their contracts were signed and sealed and that no one dictated to them on the subject of where they should board. Last but not least, they were told to arrange 'if possible, with the trustees to make someone look after the cleaning of the schoolroom and making the fires'.[42]

If these issues continued to be problematic for rural teachers as late as the 1890s, in the cities they were less often debated. At least, wherever urban schools were larger than one or two rooms, the need for a separate staff of caretakers was generally recognized. By 1876 the Toronto Public School Board employed nineteen caretakers; fifteen years later their number had almost tripled. City school caretakers in the nineteenth century frequently lived on the school property; indeed, it seems often to have been a family occupation and even a job for women. Wages compared favourably with those of teachers: in 1889 the top annual salary for a male caretaker was $600, for a woman $375. In 1891, nine women were among the board's fifty-three caretakers. Two of these women were succeeded, when they died, by their sons.[43]

If the heavy work of school cleaning and laying fires was a thing of the past for city schoolteachers, this did not mean that their jobs were entirely free of housekeeping tasks. Urban and rural teachers alike were exhorted to keep their schoolrooms tidy and to 'beautify' them.[44] Even the Montreal daily, *Le Canada*, in its support for the 'new education' movement, decried the unattractive appearance of Quebec schools compared to American ones: 'Our [schools] are devoid of decoration, while in the public and catholic schools of our neighbours, professors and students pride themselves on giving their schools as beautiful an appearance as possible'.[45] Schoolroom tidying and decorating, indeed, gradually moved in to replace the more mundane tasks of sweeping and dusting for late nineteenth-century teachers.

Tidying became important for both rural and city teachers because of the growing stock of globes, maps and other material goods that modern schools required. In the city of Toronto as well as in rural and urban Quebec, school documents express concern about this work. As one of them put it, now that the teacher was responsible for school property it was only fair that each school or classroom should contain a cupboard for its safekeeping. In Toronto, the school board recognized in 1873 that teachers occasionally needed extra time for the work of tidying and organizing the schoolroom and its contents. That year, at least, the day before the Christmas holidays was set aside for teachers to put their rooms 'in good order'.[46]

The advent of caretakers also meant another kind of work for urban teachers: the work of negotiating when their interests and those of the caretakers clashed. Such a conflict occurred when the women employed in Toronto schools noticed that the oil used by the caretakers on the floors soiled the hems of their skirts. If it was part of the teacher's work to set a good example by looking clean and presentable – and Ellen McGuire's 1880 Quebec contract was not the only one to state explicitly that this was the case – then a measure initiated to reduce costs or caretakers' labour in maintaining floors had resulted in increased costs and labour for the women who taught in Toronto public schools.[47]

Resistance and perceptions of the woman teacher's ambiguous position

It was this issue, along with those of their wages, that the Women Teachers' Association of Toronto brought to the trustees of the city twenty years after their organization's founding in 1885. Indeed, these were the problems, along with other long-standing concerns about health, working conditions and the reorganization of the pension fund in light of the particular needs and experiences of women teachers, that eventually drove schoolmistresses to band together and establish protective associations. In central Canada, Toronto led the way with Montreal and then, somewhat later, rural teachers in both Ontario and Quebec followed suit. By the turn of the century, urban women teachers were speaking with collective voices, not only echoing the grievances their predecessors had so frequently raised in individual exchanges with their local and provincial superiors but also winning some concessions from their employers. In Toronto, for example, organization helped to bring the women teachers a salary scale based on seniority rather than grade level and the election of a woman to the school board.[48] In Montreal the associations of Catholic and Protestant women teachers succeeded in persuading the provincial government to make the pension plan more favourable to women teachers and to raise the annual pension by 50 per cent. The Catholic association also guaranteed ill or unemployed teachers some assistance during times of need.[49]

When schoolmistresses should be allowed to retire and the presence of women on school boards were hardly the major concerns of those promoting school system development and professionalism among teachers in the nineteenth and early twentieth centuries. The former were of such profound interest to Ontario and Quebec women teachers, on the other hand, that eventually they began to view themselves as a class apart from their male colleagues and state school employers. A sense of separateness, nourished by years of working conditions harsher than those endured by men (who generally could look forward to administrative positions or at least teaching the more advanced grades) and of a shared experience of inequality in salary and opportunity for advancement in the occupation, led many of the career women teachers to express their particular demands and grievances increasingly openly. As part of her contribution to the pension debate, a Quebec schoolmistress, who had 'roamed professionally' from one rural county to another for nearly twenty years, remarked in no uncertain terms that she, as a teacher, did 'more work for [her] country than some of our politicians'. This conviction prompted her to ask why no provision could be made for 'the few women' who made elementary teaching 'their life-work' and to offer the provincial government a list of suggested improvements.

I would suggest that our Government provide a work house for superannuated female teachers, taxing highly-salaried teachers and school inspectors for its support. Another suggestion I beg leave to make is that women be eligible for the office of school inspector. It would be a comfortable berth for some of us that have been too long on starvation salaries.[50]

Such sentiments were behind the founding of separate women teachers' associations in both Ontario and Quebec. The frustrations and aspirations expressed by teachers making suggestions of this kind were also a reflection of the transition teachers' work had undergone in the period since 1840. Prior to the establishment of government school systems as well as during the early years of their creation, schoolmistresses and masters worked within informal, more personal and less hierarchical structures. Centralization and the development of provincial elementary school systems brought about a major change in the form and content of schooling. Athénais Bibaud, the principal of Marchand Academy in Montreal, noted in 1911 that in the past 'the programme of studies was not as heavy', leaving time for frequent breaks and 'cordial chats between teachers and pupils, chats which were very useful because they *shed light on everything*'. But, as she further remarked, as all things go, this type of interaction between student and teacher had come to an end, and not just in her own school. Discipline had become 'more severe', pupils and teachers alike 'worked a bit harder', and younger mistresses were now supervised by the older, more experienced ones. By this time, too, the Montreal Catholic School Commission exercised more control over the academy.[51]

The reorganization of time, work, and discipline in the school did not improve the lot of the teacher. 'One thing that did not keep pace with the changing times', added Bibaud in her reflections, 'were the salaries of teaching assistants'.[52] A similar observation of the disjuncture between the enduring regime of low salaries and the changing mode of schooling led Elizabeth Binmore, a founder of the Montreal Protestant Women Teachers' Association, to speculate on the nature of the woman teacher's work in the public schoolroom and its relationship to her status in society. Did her employment fit with the title 'lady teacher' which was still so much in use? Elizabeth Binmore seemed to think not.[53] Her work was not leisure; therefore it was not appropriate to refer to the schoolmistress by using a term implying that it was. 'Lady teacher' belonged to a genteel past which by the turn of the century was but a dim memory to the vast majority of overworked and underpaid women teachers in Montreal.

While Binmore was able to make such a statement in the mid-1890s, a moment when Montreal teachers' salaries, owing to depressed economic conditions, may have been at a particularly low ebb, she and her colleagues in the three women teachers' associations that late nineteenth-century conditions spawned in Quebec and Ontario nevertheless had great difficulty grasping permanently a vision of themselves as workers. Wayne Urban has argued that in the three American cities he studied, the women teachers who organized were aware of their interests and fought mainly as interest groups rather than as incipient professionals, although their approaches varied according to local conditions.[54] It is very clear that Canadian women teachers, like their American counterparts, also formed their associations with bread and butter issues such as wages, working conditions and pensions chiefly in mind. Yet, unlike the most radical Americans, Canadian teachers were reluctant to ally themselves with working-class organizations or identify with working-class groups that had comparable problems. In Toronto, the Woman Teachers' Association toyed with a labour affiliation in 1905, but backed off.[55]

Perhaps the key word here is 'comparable'. For, with hindsight, we can now see that the position of turn-of-the-century women teachers was similar to that of beleaguered industrial workers but, as the women teachers of the time perceived, it was also different. Women teachers had not necessarily been 'deskilled'; on the contrary, new skills were constantly being demanded of them. Nor were they necessarily subjected to seasonal unemployment and layoffs to the same extent as labourers, especially those who worked in the light manufacturing industries. Moreover, their work was supposedly intellectual and not manual, a division which, at least according to Harry Braverman, was 'the most decisive single step in the division of labour' taken by industrial capitalist societies.[56] Yet as 'brainworkers' they also at times toiled manually, beautifying their schools, keeping the path to the schoolhouse clear in the winter, and inspecting pupils for contagious diseases. They spent hours on the busy work of maintaining school records and looking after the objects that increasingly filled their classrooms. In fact, in their work they straddled both sides of Braverman's great divide and laboured on the margins of both. As far as their working conditions and salaries were concerned, however, they did share the plight of nineteenth-century workers.[57]

It was the uncertainty of their position in the labour force that helps to explain how women teachers could flirt with the mystique of professionalism while at the same time their members referred to themselves as the exploited or as toilers and hirelings. In recalling their double bind one returns, finally, to feminists' recognition of the need for a more nuanced analysis of work and a less dichotomous vision of the social order if we are to understand the work of women.[58] Elizabeth Binmore began to glimpse these truths in the mid-1890s. Teachers, she saw, were not 'ladies'. Nor, however, could they fully see themselves as workers, in spite of the poor wages and difficult working conditions they endured.

Michael Apple has rightly argued that teachers' 'deskilling and reskilling, intensification and loss of control, or the countervailing pressures of professionalization and proletarianization' that have affected the occupation, and continue to affect it to this day, are complex processes. They cannot be explained solely in terms of the sexual division of labour. Nevertheless, as he also contends, that division has been an essential component in these processes.[59] This brief study of central Canadian teachers during the period of state school systems formation confirms Apple's contention. Turn-of-the-century women teachers in Ontario and Quebec were increasingly aware of their special problems and some were already aware of the ambiguity of their position. Many also knew that a major source of their difficulties was the fact that they were women in school systems largely designed for and controlled by men.[60]

Notes and references

1. Engagement of Ellen McGuire, 1 June 1880, Education Records, E 13, Archives Nationales du Québec (hereafter ANQ).
2. Engagement of Philomène Lachance, 11 July 1881, E 13, ANQ.
3. Alison Prentice, 'The Feminization of Teaching in British North America and Canada, 1845–1875', *Social History/Histoire sociale*, 8 (1975), 5–20; Marta Danylewycz, Beth Light, and Alison Prentice, 'The Evolution of the Sexual Division of Labour in Teaching: A Nineteenth Century Ontario and Quebec Case Study', *Social History/Histoire sociale*, 16 (1983), 81–109; Marta Danylewycz and Alison Prentice, 'Teachers, Gender and Bureaucratizing School Systems in Nineteenth Century Monreal and Toronto', *History of Education Quarterly* 24 (1984), 75–100.
4. André Labarrère-Paulé, *Les Instituteurs laiques au Canada français, 1836–1900*, (Québec 1965). J. G. Althouse, *The Ontario Teacher: A Historical Account of Progress, 1800–1910* (1929; Toronto 1967) focuses on the 'rise' of the professional teacher, but avoids discussing the question of gender. Graham S. Lowe, 'Class, Job and Gender in the Canadian Office', *Labour/Le Travail* 10 (1982), 11–37.
5. Michael W. Apple, 'Work, Class and Teaching', in Stephen Walker and Len Barton (eds), *Gender, Class and Education* (New York 1983), 53–67; Jennifer Ozga and Martin Lawn, *Teachers, Professionalism and Class: A Study of Organized Teachers* (London 1981); Barry H. Bergen, 'Only a Schoolmaster: Gender, Class and the Effort to Professionalize Elementary Teaching in England, 1870–1910', *History of Education Quarterly* 22 (1982), 1–21.
6. *Annual Reports of the Chief Superintendent of Schools for Ontario*, 1870–1900.
7. *Ibid.* and *Annual Reports of the Superintendent for the Province of Quebec*, 1870–1900.
8. *Educational Record of the Province of Quebec* 13, 1 (1893), 28.
9. *Educational Record* 9, 12 (1889), 324. Resistance to curricular reform in Quebec can be traced in a variety of sources. For references to complaints coming from rural schools, see the letters in Education Records, E 13, 615–44, 614–50, 615–200, and 615–82, ANQ.
10. A reference to parent resistance to too many new subjects, and the fact that the Toronto Public School Board supported the complaint against their introduction by the provincial government, may be found in the *Annual Reports of the Toronto Public School Board*, 1872 and 1873. Reports for the remainder of the 1870s and 1880s record the work of special subject masters hired to deal with new areas like music, drill, and drawing, including the introduction of after-hours classes to train the teachers. The tone of the special subject masters' reports suggests that many urban teachers were as slow as rural teachers to accept the new subjects.

11. Miss Reid, 'How to keep the Little Ones Employed', *Educational Record* 2, 10 (1882), 413.
12. Egerton Ryerson to C. Gregor, 5 May 1847, Education Records, RG 2, C-1, Letterbook C, 355, Public Archives of Ontario (hereafter PAO). On the role of the Ryerson administration in the increase of paperwork in Ontario Schools, see Alison Prentice, 'The Public Instructor: Egerton Ryerson and the Role of the Public School Administrator', in Neil McDonald and Alf Chaiton (eds), *Egerton Tyerson and His Times* (Toronto 1978), 129–29.
13. *Annual Report of the Chief Superintendent of Schools for Ontario*, 1859, 16–7.
14. *Educational Record* 6, 3 (1886), 81–2.
15. Report of Marie Argonie Viau to the commissioners, 19 February 1883, E 13, ANQ.
16. *Annual Reports of the Toronto Public School Board*, 1872, 12–5; 1881, 16; 1891, 28 ff.
17. *Educational Record* 15, 3 (1895), 91–3.
18. *Ibid.*, 5, 2 (1885), 57.
19. Patrick Thornton to Egerton Ryerson, 22 January 1849, RG 2, C-6-C, PAO.
20. *Annual Report of the Toronto Public School Board*, 1880, 11.
21. *Ibid.*, 1873, 66; 1879, 29.
22. *Educational Record* 5, 1 (1885), 7–8.
23. *Annual Report of the Toronto Public School Board*, 1886, 18–9.
24. J-P. Nantel to Hon. Surintendant de l'Instruction Publique, le 29 March 1884, E 13, 637–50, ANQ.
25. *Annual Report of the Toronto Public School Board*, 1891, 33 ff., describes the addition of an assistant superintendent and four 'supervisory principals' to the Toronto administration.
26. *Annual Report of the Chief Superintendent of Schools for Ontario*, 1870, 59.
27. J. B. Delage to Gédéon Quimet, 23 March 1883, E 13, ANQ.
28. Registre des délibérations du Bureau des Commissaires, Vol. II, 27 April, 4 May, 19 June 1877. Archives de la Commission des Écoles Catholiques de Montréal (ACCM).
29. The Montreal Catholic School Commission was unusual in requiring women teachers to find accommodation for their own schools. The commission did not, until the 1900s, build schools for female teachers and students. A discussion of its policies may be found in Marta Danylewycz, 'Sexes et classes sociales dans l'ensiegnement: le cas de Montréal à la fin du 19e siècle', in N. Fahmy-Eid and Micheline Dumont, *Maîtresses de maison, maîtresses d'école* (Montréal 1983), 93–118.
30. Registre des délibérations. Vol. II, 5 March 1879; Généreux worked for the commission until her death in 1890, ACCM.
31. For a discussion of public health reform and the role of teachers in it see Neil Sutherland, *Children in English-Canadian Society: Framing the Twentieth Century Consensus* (Toronto 1978).
32. Teachers were permitted to take sick leaves of up to one month. For longer absences they had to pay for the substitute teachers out of their own pockets. See *Annual Reports of the Toronto Public School Board*, 1872, 98, and 1874, 85–90.
33. Eliza Pelletier to V. T. Simard, 19 January 1884, E 13, 637–12, ANQ.
34. 'Miss Ferguson's Address to Convention on Pension Act', *Educational Record* 28, 12 (1903), 392.

35. See the following in *La Patrie*, 'Causerie – Une Grande Fondation', 6 December 1902; 'Autour de l'école', 11 October 1902.
36. *Educational Record* 11, 1 (1891), 4–12.
37. Egerton Ryerson to John Monger, 26 December 1848, RG 2, C-1, Letterbook D, 360.
38. Letters of inquiry on the subject include C. W. D. De l'Armitage to Egerton Ryerson, 27 June 1849; Meade N. Wright to Ryerson, 26 June 1859; and Teacher to Ryerson, 1 April 1859, RG 2, C-6-C, PAO. 'Official Replies . . .', *Journal of Education for Upper Canada* 14, 3 (1861), 40.
39. North West Oxford Trustees' Minute Book, School Section No. 1, 15 January 1863, RG 51, 10816, No. 1, PAO, and *Annual Report of the Chief Superintendent of Schools for Ontario*, 1865, Appendix A, 53.
40. Engagement of Anna Poulin, 1 June 1882, E 13, 826–13, ANQ.
41. 'Enquiries', *Educational Record* 5 7/8 (1885), 199.
42. *Educational Record* 13, 10 (1893), 286.
43. *Annual Reports of the Toronto Public School Board*; see especially 1876, Appendix 1, 10, and 1891, 14–5 and 37–9.
44. See *ibid*, 1876, 18; and 'Something for Country Teachers', *Educational Record* 4, 2 (1884), 51–3.
45. 'Les écoles primaires à Montréal et aux États Unis', *Le Canada*, 26 August 1903.
46. *Annual Report of the Toronto Public School Board*, 1873, 87.
47. Wendy Bryans, 'The Women Teachers' Association of Toronto', paper presented to the Canadian Association for American Studies, Ottawa, 1974.
48. *Ibid.*
49. Marie Lavigne and Jennifer Stoddart, 'Women's Work in Montreal at the Beginning of the Century', in Marylee Stephenson (ed.), *Women in Canada* (Toronto 1977), 139. Marise Thivierge, 'La Syndicalisation des institutrices catholiques, 1900–1959', in *Maîtresses de maison*.
50. 'Correspondence', *Educational Record* 11, 9 (1891), 241–2.
51. Athénais Bibaud, 'Nos écoles de Filles', *Revue Canadienne* 2 (1911), 138–9. In 1905 the Marchand Academy had been listed as 'receiving subsidies', but not 'under the control' of the Montreal Catholic School Commission. By 1909, the Catholic School Commission had replaced the former school with a new one built by itself and now directly under its control. Many girls' schools in Montreal underwent a similar transformation at this time.
52. *Ibid.*, 139.
53. Miss E. Binmore, 'The Financial Outlook of the Women Teachers of Montreal', *Educational Record* 13, 3 (1893), 69–74.
54. Wayne Urban, *Why Teachers Organized* (Detroit 1983). The three cities studied were Chicago, New York, and Atlanta.
55. Bryans, 'The Women Teachers' Association of Toronto', 13–4. See also Alison Prentice, 'Themes in the History of the Toronto Women Teachers' Association', in Paula Bourne (ed.), *Women's Paid and Unpaid Work* (Toronto forthcoming). The most radical Americans were the leaders of the women teachers' associations in Chicago.
56. Harry Braverman, *Labor and Monopoly Capital* (New York and London 1974).
57. Michael W. Apple has argued that twentieth-century teachers are 'located simultaneously in two classes', being members both of the petite bourgeoisie and the working class. See his 'Work, Class and Teaching', 53.

58. Joan Kelly, 'The Doubled Vision of Feminist Theory', in Judith L. Newton, Mary Ryan, and Judith Walkowitz (eds), *Sex and Class in Women's History* (London 1983), 259–70.
59. Apple, 'Work, Class and Teaching', 64.
60. Prentice, 'Themes in the History of the Toronto Women Teachers' Association'; Bryans, 'The Women Teachers' Association'; John R. Abbott, '"A Man's Task": Women Teachers and the Turn-of-the-Century Public School Inspectorate in Ontario', paper presented to the Canadian Historical Association annual meeting, Montreal, 1985.

5

The educational worker?
A reassessment of teachers

Martin Lawn and Jenny Ozga

This paper is an attempt to put together various strands of our work on
teachers and our criticisms of existing work. Two principal directions have
informed our work: a re-examination of teacher union history, and a
re-examination of the concepts of professionalism and class as applied to
teachers.
[. . .]

Professionalism

The quest for the signifying characteristics of professionalism is one on which
researchers on teaching seem constantly engaged. Its dominance in the
research on teachers seems at times to lie not just within the contributing
disciplines or ideological viewpoints of the research, but in an overwhelming
'commonsense' view that there is no other conceivable position. Professionalism and teaching seem synonymous. [. . .] For example, Tropp
holds the view that teachers, by their own efforts, within a consistent strategy
followed by most of them for at least a hundred years, and with the eventual
tacit or active support of the state, have become professionals.[1] By professionals he means *de facto* controllers of the education service. There is no
general agreement in most 'professionalism' theory on whether the state
helped to license them as a group acting in its interests or whether teachers
won the grudging support of the state by acting in mildly contrary ways.

Our opposition to or unease about this view of professionalism is
probably generated by a disbelief in the hegemonic nature of the concept – the
idea that a group of people with different locations and contradictions, during
a long period, could hold to a consistent strategy or view of themselves which

is divorced from the conditions in which they worked and the social movements in which they were involved. This is not to deny a value in understanding and applying the term professional to teachers, but to argue the need for an awareness of the complexity of the idea.

Our argument, expressed briefly, would be that the term 'professionalism', in its use by teachers and the central and local state, changes; includes variations of meaning and contains elements remarkably similar to the aims and actions of other (and not only white-collar) workers.

We would suggest that at least one way in which the term was used by the state, from about 1918–20 onwards, was as a means of controlling the radical and extended actions of teachers as to their work conditions.[2] It was also connected to the shift in attitude towards the education service by the state itself in this period (from the Fisher Act to its eventual, partial dismemberment). The role of the elementary teachers was to alter due to this new function, determined by working-class demand, technological change and their own unrest. Questions as to the 'right to strike', 'Labour affiliation' and civil service membership were all raised, but it is the growth of the professional ideology which dominates the actions of central and local government and co-opts elements of the teachers' organizations. There are also other ways in which professional demands may be seen. In our view, they may represent commitment to a craft ethic similar to that of other skilled, craft unions.

[. . .]

Professionalism is a complex concept, involving contradictions and group and historically specific meanings. [. . .] At times, professionalism figures as a means of resistance or a means of control or both. At periods of crisis, even the elements of a rhetoric of control may lose their dominance over some teachers as there appears a recognizable gap between rhetoric and reality – the situation prevailing in the disabled education system today. In periods of relative 'calm', a rhetoric of state professionalism may exercise more 'commonsense' influence over larger sections of teachers.

What we are hinting at is a recognition that the term generates meanings according to the material basis and shared ideological view of different parties. The major contradiction is still between the meanings generated by the employers and employees, but these are not always historically distinct nor are they always possible to separate.

The idea of 'service' appears, in variations, on both sides of the contradiction. Earlier this century the belief of teachers, municipal employees and civil servants in public service responsibility was not at odds with elements of the employers' views. That the rhetoric and the reality of that 'service' became separated is the lesson of the later part of the twentieth century.

[. . .]

Instead of asking 'are teachers really professionals or not?', let us ask 'what has been excluded from our understanding of teachers through the

dominance of *a priori* assumptions about professionalism and its significance?' In asking the latter question, it may then be possible to return to
professionalism and question its nature and its material base.

For us, there are two interesting areas which produce fruitful ideas on
teachers and their work; first, the socialist and neo-Marxist class analyses of
skilled and white-collar workers which have created some insights into the
problems involved in understanding class and teachers, if not the solutions;
second, the growth of new historical research on teachers' own work
experience, allegiances and organizations suggests new complexities in
analysing teachers' work.

Class and Teachers

Underlying most commonsense usage of the term 'professionalism' is an
association between professionalism and the middle class, and, indeed, this is
also the connection made by theorists in this area whether ideologically of the
Left or Right. For example, Asher Tropp saw a gradual move this century
away from the working-class social origins (and some political or educational
sympathy) of teachers, by a process of partially successful professionalization
(increased remuneration, higher qualifications and some policy-making
influence) towards a recognized middle classness. There is a general agreement with Tropp's thesis from the politically opposed perspective adopted
by Finn, Grant and Johnson (1979): 'Professionalism can be understood as a
petit bourgeois strategy for advancing and defending a relatively privileged
position.' (p. 170)[3] Both views, though differently interpreted, are based on a
simplistic view of professionalism and its relation to class. There is no
recognition of the contradictions involved in the term as it is used by different
groups over historical periods nor how it may have positive and negative
aspects, from the point of view of a progressive standpoint.

Recent neo-Marxist or structural Marxist analysis of class position
(threading through Althusser, Poulantzas and Erik Olin Wright,[4] in its
attempt to throw over the lack of 'hard' explanation of social change and the
role of the state that they felt was the major weakness of Marxist scholarship,
have taken positions which seem to us to view class as a static entity. Class
takes on an unacceptable degree of abstraction from concrete work situations, and ignores the dynamic role which people have in society in resisting
and creating alternatives.

In education as a service, teachers are generally viewed as state functionaries with the main responsibility for ideological control and social and
cultural reproduction of capitalism. This view accords with the economic
analysis of Crompton,[5] who sees teachers, amongst others, as paid for out of
surplus value created by industrial workers, and garnered by the state to
reproduce itself. The two general arguments – a group paid for out of surplus
value to act as the state's agent, and for its ideological, cultural and economic

reproduction and domination – set up teachers in ways which make them irretrievably lost to the progressive or labour movement. [. . .]

This proposition is simplistic in essence, if not in its explanation. Teachers may be state functionaries but this is not, nor could it ever be, a comprehensive explanation of their behaviour or analysis of their position.

All education does not serve the purposes of the state all the time. [. . .] The blanket use of the term 'state functionaries' hides too many historical, local and particular possibilities and, importantly, ignores teachers' attempts at working–class alliances on education and their varied interpretation of their role as perceived by the state, and their resistances to it.

The question of payment from surplus value is a difficult area for all Marxists. The invisibility of the product is real enough. Yet (following Hunt),[6] isn't it necessary to recognize the increasing complexity and changing operations of capitalism in its drive to increase the accumulation of capital? [. . .] As capitalism has become increasingly sophisticated so the growth of bureaucratic, service and distribution functions has grown. The production of value now needs a related body of work associated with its *realization*. A greater proportion of capital is devoted to the creation of invisible commodities generating the thesis of the 'collective labourer'. The generation of value is now undertaken outside as well as inside the factory and, since the 1920s, the state has taken a more direct role in this process – for instance, the creation of apprenticed skilled labour is now undertaken in universities, schools and the Manpower Services Commission. Aren't teachers part of this 'collective labourer', producing a labour force, a commodity improved in value?

The recognition that teachers are workers, by nature of their economic position as employees, and yet still acting as agents of the state, introduces us, whatever its other faults, to the notion of contradiction in the teachers' position.[7] But let us take the notion of contradiction further. All workers suffer a contradiction between themselves and their work; this is based, at root, on the fact that they are cheated every day of some of the value of their labour and that, in continuing working, they are reproducing capitalism. There are further contradictions based on gender, race, hierarchical and geographical factors plus their historical memory of their position (within their family, factory or skill). Yet, with all these contradictions, the capitalist or the state cannot simply override and dominate the worker. There has always been conflict and resistance, and economic and ideological initiatives based on them, at different historical periods and, hence, an accumulation of experience paralleling the accumulation of capital. Why then should teachers be different? [. . .]

If class is an important concept in the understanding of teachers, it cannot be reduced to an economic relationship nor to a cultural or ideological function *alone*. The material base is essential for understanding the world, but it is not its only creator. Class is also a relational concept involving several factors (economic, political or social) and a process (not static condition) taking place over historical time.

E. P. Thompson takes a position on class which opposes the structural Marxist position and, we argue, would better serve the exploration of teachers, their class and labour process. In Thompson's words:

> class is not, as some sociologists would have it, a static category – so many people standing in this or that relation to the means of production – which can be measured in positivist or quantitative terms. Class, in the Marxist tradition, is (or ought to be) *a historical category*, describing *people in relationship over time*, and the ways in which they become conscious of their relationships, separate, unite, enter into struggle, form institutions and transmit values in class ways.
>
> Hence class is an 'economic' and it is also a 'cultural' formation: it is impossible to give any theoretical priority to one aspect over the other . . . what changes, as the mode of production and productive relations change, is the *experience* of living men and women. And this experience is sorted out in class ways, in social life and in consciousness, in the assent, the resistance and the choices of men and women.
>
> (Thompson 1979)[8]

To look at teachers in this way we need evidence about their actions, contradictions and labour processes – their consciousness and their condition.

Historical evidence has been limited and mainly confined to incidents related to 'professionalism', though Asher Tropp's book does provide interesting cases which are seen as aberrations by Tropp in the development of teachers as a professional group.

One particular period, from 1916 to 1920, was a watershed in the relation between teachers and the state. During this period the teachers were involved in an extensive series of guerilla strikes and disputes with over half the local education authorities in the country; they were considering the affiliation of the major teachers' union to the Labour Party and were also involved in a series of formal discussions on alliances with other white-collar workers. To these events (footnotes in Tropp's book) may be added the researches of Brian Simon in this period – the swing to Labour was so strong in the country that Special Branch reports on leading radicals amongst the teachers were included in a special Board of Education file 'Drift of Teachers to the Labour Party', which also includes a report on a deputation to Baldwin, the Prime Minister, by prominent Conservatives concerned at the national drift to Labour and pleading for a positive Conservative educational policy.[9]

The significance of a period like this has been lost over the years. The bare bones of the relationship between teachers and the state are revealed in the issues raised in the national press at the time. Should teachers strike? Should they become professionals? Does the state have a new responsibility to workers' education? The degree of the conflict between teachers and their

86   *Martin Lawn and Jenny Ozga*

employers can now, in retrospect, seem both tentative and fundamental. For instance, to many rural teachers their immediate oppressor was the local vicar or parish council and was becoming their county council; yet for urban teachers, questions not just about the local authority but the nature of education under capitalism were being raised. The drift to the Labour Party, and beyond to the Communist Party, was both a recognition of class interests and a recognition that education was a shared interest with the working class. The significance of this tentative, open alliance nationally was not lost, in this period, on Lloyd George, who allegedly pointed out to his Cabinet, when supporting Fisher's new, expensive education Bill, that at the head of each continental revolutionary movement were ex-teachers.

Progressive elements in the state produced a more sophisticated policy with regard to teachers than the previous use of local authority henchmen acting as fairly omnipotent cost-cutters, etc. The proposal to make teachers civil servants with a new 'status' was rejected, as it would have created a direct employment link between teachers and the central state – the Board of Education was unwilling to make that relationship open and said so. The creation of a new 'professionalism', combined with the better financial conditions built into the Burnham Scales, was a policy which, if not the sole prerogative of the central state in the 1920s and 1930s, made it the beneficiary – it encouraged responsibility and autonomy of classroom decision-making in conjunction with a consistent policy of breaking the ideological and strategic alliance between the teachers and the Labour movement – by sacking militants, etc.[10]

The teachers' movement and strength through this period was part of, and cannot be isolated from, the resurgent working-class militancy in the second decade of this century, which was in retreat by the early 1920s. For the purpose of our argument, this was not an isolated, discrete event, but indicative of, and revealing about, the main antagonistic contradiction between the teachers as employees and the central and local state as employers. Their relationship has never been merely reducible to crude physical and economic exploitation. Different contending factions within capitalism can have quite different educational policies – the consecutive post-war governments could move from the Fisher Act to the Geddes 'Axe' on spending. These policies were made strategically and tactically – Fisher's Act was not just far-sighted investment in 'human capital' (his phrase), but was a tactical response to the war, and the enormous working-class demand for education. Teachers have also taken a number of different actions which have been used to construct a theory of consistent professionalism; at times in apparent harmony with central controls, at other times in open conflict. Each helps us to interpret the other.

Proletarianization

Our assumption is, in this tentative thesis, that there is a connection between the increased proletarianization of teachers' work, deskilling and reskilling, and 'class in itself' actions of teachers. These are all part of the same thing – the nature of work, degrees of autonomy over decision-making, political and social actions as individuals or in a group, and resistance to change and promotion of changes. If class is a relational concept, proletarianization of work is an economic and a social process – a process of change and resistance expressed in individual, school-based and national developments. In passing, we have referred to evidence of discontent about the nature of the education service and the working-class/Labour movement alliance; what we will try and offer here is evidence that work processes and the quality of work are subject to similar forces in education as they are elsewhere, particularly in white-collar work. Again, our difficulty lies in the fact that while this subject is developing in many work areas, education is still treated as an area apart, patrolled by professionals. Hence we are forced, at this stage, to make our case by inference, and by extrapolation from the experiences of other workers.

The changing nature of capital has led to a growth of white-collar, service-sector workers. These workers are, we believe, in the process of proletarianization earlier undergone by industrial workers. Proletarianization follows from the removal of skill from work, the exclusion of the worker from the conceptual functions of work. Worker autonomy is eroded, the relationship between employer and employee breaks down, management controls are strengthened and craft skills and the craft ethic decline.

The lack of clear outlines of a production process has allowed sociologists to see only reproductive or hidden functions of the state expressed in education and to continue to treat teachers as separate from other workers and public servants.

Today, most of the working class in Britain is in service industries, which may be treated as theoretically non-productive. Yet one has to recognize that without the specialized, fragmented processes that capitalism has created – such as personnel management, supervisory staff, warehousing staff, financial and administrative offices, distribution and sales – *value* could not be *realized*. In the production and realization of value, many different workers, in many places and often unconnected from each other, act, in total, as 'collective labourers'. Education is one of the more specialized parts of the means of production and the role of the state, since the 1920s, has been to take over some of the functions of private capital and integrate and reorganize them.

Proletarianization is a process which affects all work – directly at the point of production but of necessity, sooner or later, at the points of distribution or realization of value. If education is part of the creation of value, expressed as a trained work force, then this process will be analysed and restructured to increase its efficiency (productivity). This process will be constant; that is, it will always be occurring in some place at any time, but it will also occur in varying degrees as moments of crisis necessitate strategic restructuring. This change will not only be a response to the crisis (production of new grades of trained workforce, etc.), but will take into account the degree of resistance likely to result. [. . .]

It is only relatively recently that the idea of proletarianization has come to be applied to white-collar workers. Crompton, for example, has developed it in relation to insurance workers, where, she argues, proletarianization through the introduction of technology and the rationalization and centralization of control 'substantially transformed' the class situations of insurance employees in the 1960s.[11]

It is this argument that Bowles and Ginitis used in relation to the development of the United States education service.[12] Although their arguments might not be directly used in relation to our own very different educational history, they tried to show, like Raymond Callahan (in *Education and the Cult of Efficiency*)[13] that the education service was influenced by the application of business methods generated in the pursuit of industrial efficiency by Taylor, etc. The development of the scientific management movement, involving task allocation, detailed curriculum control and text selection, they argue, introduced the 'social relations of the production line'. This view of teachers places them, like other workers, firmly against the background of the constant transformation of the production process by capital in its drive to extract and accumulate – the education system is affected in the same way as other areas of work.

The use of a guided, limited 'professionalism' and the creation of a mock partnership with central and local government is the British equivalent of this transformation of the education service. Business efficiency methods have been slow to reconstruct British industry and their use in education, are a recent phenomenon. Instead, as Lord Eustace Percy (President of the Board of Education in the 1920s) made clear in his autobiography,[14] the extremism of some teachers could be controlled by a system of licensed autonomy. He borrowed from British colonial experience notions of 'indirect rule' – the emancipation of parts of local authority and teacher work was not intended to endanger 'real tactical control' of (the) social service[15] but to remove *unnecessary* central powers. The sophistication of Whitehall and the Board of Education in the 1920s has been further explored by John White;[16] to his tentative conclusion that the centralized system was dismantled in anticipation of the first Labour victory at the polls should be added our own suggestion, that it was part of the development of a means of controlling teachers ideologically (with the generation of a limited 'professionalism') and by means of finely tuned tactical control in a system which now needed guiding not directing.

In what senses are teachers proletarianized? How have their conditions of work in teaching altered to illuminate the possibility of proletarianization?

Further to this point, in what ways has the purchase of labour power from teachers been realized by increasing control of organization, by mechanization, and by growth of supervision?

Using the general process, as analysed by Harry Braverman,[17] as our starting point, we suggest that in teaching, as in other kinds of work:

> There is a long term tendency through fragmentation, rationalization and mechanization for workers and their job to become deskilled, both in an absolute sense (they lose craft and traditional abilities) and in a relative one (scientific knowledge progressively accumulates in the production process). . . . Thus the worker, regardless of his or her personal talents, may be more easily and cheaply substituted for in the production process.[18]

We recognize that there are problems in describing teachers as skilled workers, but argue that skill is not only a technical term, denoting control over a complex process and involving an understanding of that process – it is also a social term. Skill is a creation of labour control over the workplace and the job content.[19] Skill implies a relationship to the process of conception *and* execution, the strength – or weakness – of the relationship to these processes is demonstrated by the terms 'skilled', 'semi-skilled' and 'unskilled'. Today, even skilled work, whatever the length of the training period, is confined to execution, and excludes conception. Planning is divorced from execution and, in turn, is now (in the draughtsman's office, in engineering) able to be described as skilled, semi-skilled and so on.

Earlier this century, teachers trained each other, mainly in the workplace (the school) but increasingly in pupil-teacher centres and the new municipal colleges. Generally, experienced teachers, the senior or head teacher, taught the inexperienced the trade. The need for certification, the clear recognition of skill, was recognized by teachers. The role of the state, in its indirect control of local authority colleges (the intake and numbers in teaching) and its influence on the content of the courses was often seen by teachers as the opponent of a teacher–controlled skill. By the 1920s elementary teachers felt that they were in greater control of their workplace and job content, after the serious conflicts of the previous decade and the gradual weakening or dismantling of parts of the education code. Increasingly, it appears as if the definition of skill has been created by the teacher but in response to interventionist financial investments or initiatives taken centrally. Skill is a contested concept. The relative autonomy is a recognition of this contestation and of teacher definition of work/education. Skill has been seen recently in terms of technical attributes, specialized tasks and career structures and scale posts, reflecting the increased intervention by the employer, consistent with the changing nature of the labour process elsewhere. It has been weakened in terms of teacher definition of the conception and execution of work (education).

This weakening has occurred during periods of teacher overproduction and a decline of the ideology of working-class guardianship over the education service (which was how it was increasingly seen by 1920 through the initiative of the Bradford Charter of 1917 and the education alliance with the TUC) and an acceptance of ideas of partnership. It resides in a rhetoric of autonomy. The fight against cheap teaching labour was a fight over the quality of education for the working class – resistance to the dilution of craft skill by the introduction in the First World War, and after, of unskilled, untrained teachers was a conscious act in defence of education and training, defined by the teachers or their allies themselves. Deskilling involved a political response similar to that created in the industrial working class in this period.

Teachers and the labour process

The proletarianization of work involves a number of different aspects. The major aspect is, obviously, the loss of skill or craft or traditional knowledge. This is a continuous process which may have sudden changes and swift movements, depending on technological change and its applications, the nature of the production process and the ideology and history of the workforce. There are also a number of contingent aspects; the loss of autonomy, the increase of supervision, creation of reskilled specializations and increase in stress – all a recognized part of proletarianization. Proletarianization may move through a number of steps in relation to work. First, by treating the worker like a machine: the Taylor movement in production control, systems management, behavioural objectives, etc., all try to reduce the variability and creativity of the individual in relation to the work process, reducing the 'irrationality' of the worker. Second, the worker is tied directly to the machine – as an appendage – where the machine controls the pace and content of the work. Third, if possible, the machine may, if cheaper, be substituted for the worker.

Braverman, writing about white-collar clerical work, describes it in its early days as a craft, with master craftsmen (the bookkeeper or chief clerk) maintaining total control of the record-keeping process and young apprentices or journeymen (clerks, ledger clerks, office boys) learning their trade in the office. As the accounting of value becomes more complex:

> The intimate associations, the atmosphere of mutual obligation, and the degree of loyalty which characterized the small office became transformed. . . . The characteristic feature of this era was the ending of the reign of the bookkeeper and the rise of the office manager as the prime functionary and the representative of management.[20]

Work is now reduced from being an understanding of the whole process and becomes more and more the steady, unvarying, part of the whole. Thought, or conception, is eliminated from the work, though not the worker, and the mind is used as 'the equivalent of the hand of the detail worker in production'.[21]

This description has parallels with the historical development of schools from being small enterprises, not created by but (in practical process) controlled by teachers with some whole view of their work, to the rise of the large school with the creation of administrative and supervisory tasks in which teaching is part of a production-line process. Head teachers moved from being *primus inter pares* and the trainers of the inexperienced, to become managers of human and technical resources. Teaching in many schools is now the endless repetition of similar data in numerous, brief encounters. There is no sense of the whole enterprise at all, and the rise of administration is a response to the need to control the complexity of the process and the movement of the deskilled unit worker.

Teaching has been intermittently altered and changed in its labour process by the steady rise of specialized or supervisory staff in the school. The slow rise through the wage scales, determined locally and then nationally, has gradually given way to 'career structures' and 'promotion ladders', all involving increased supervisory or managerial responsibility. By 1945, headteachers were paid on a separate salary scale and by 1956, the old allowances for assistants (given in large schools for advanced teaching work in or in lieu of rare head teacher promotion) were replaced by a series of graded posts, deputy headships and department heads. The comprehensive schools produced more specialist functions in the subject areas and in pastoral work. The general supervisory work of a deputy head or head of department has, over the last few years, increased in detail and specification. Deputy heads now act as public relations officers, as personnel managers, as curriculum co-ordinators or innovation leaders and with increased responsibility for timetabling – the last a new 'reskilled' job, understood by a few teachers in the schools. Heads of departments may now, through increased rationalization in schools, be organizers and integrators of complicated schemes of work they were not trained to undertake, yet they are being reskilled on the job. Faculty meetings, heads of departments cross-school meetings and top management meetings are a feature of supervisory and management work in schools.

Pastoral work is a major area of school work, concentrated now into the hands of a few 'reskilled' teachers responsible for discipline, but also a major school link with social services. Pastoral heads (heads of school 'houses') may spend a lot of time each week meeting parents, the police, the educational welfare officers, the educational psychologists, social workers, the child guidance clinic and doctors, and visiting homes or attending case conferences. School Disruptive Units are fairly common, as are youth workers/ teachers, school counsellors, careers teachers and liaison teachers (with middle/primary schools).

The specialized part of school teaching is one side of this equation, but the other is the redefinition of jobs, once recognized as accorded responsibility by age or experience, as middle or top management. The graded and promotion posts are increasingly supervisory posts not just reflecting the proliferation and integration of school functions, and they are combined especially in the present cutbacks with a full teaching load. They are there to boost productivity. As Aronowitz notes: 'The working supervisor is merely a person who performs two jobs. She is responsible for actually producing the same amount of paper herself as the subordinate; in addition, she is held responsible for the production of the subordinate as well.'[22] The new HM Inspectors' report on schools remarked that middle management in 'most schools had not been able to relate the allocations of non-teaching time to the special responsibilities which these teachers were expected to fulfil. Instead, it appears that schools could do not more than squeeze a little extra monitoring time and hope that any gaps would be filled'.[23] Responsibilities that they should be undertaking were described as, for department heads, the 'guidance, supervision and support' to department teams, and it was recognized for pastoral heads that many of their duties could only be performed 'when the pupils concerned are present'.

There is a diminishing of the quality if not the quantity of work. At the same time, it is commonly expected that many school teachers, in a period of contraction/falling rolls, should be versatile, general teachers. Redeployment within schools is often referred to as increased 'flexibility'.[24] With the rise of the reskilled staff, there is also a tendency towards deskilling staff. This is evident in maths and sciences and was remarked upon by the HM Inspectors in relation to the increased use of worksheets (more in fact than they had anticipated): 'Worksheets may be developed through shared experience of members of the department and they can be a useful support, enabling inexperienced teachers and non-mathematicians to have suitable material available.'[25] Widespread redeployment, within or between schools, can only lead to a further weakening of skill as these teachers employed as general teachers, using worksheets, programmed course or in teamwork, became more common. [. . .]

Curriculum specialists, known as curriculum co-ordinators, teacher leaders or even plain Faculty Heads, are the new specialists, the planners, in this divorce of conception from the execution of work. The qualitative aspects of teaching decline as the quantitative rate increases. This view of deskilling is similar to the recent ideas of Michael Apple,[26] but it is only a part of a wider view of labour control over the workplace, not just a relationship of knowledge or techniques. What passes as 'skill' depends on the strength of the employees in the labour process. It is not deskilling if the workers control its implementation and daily operation, combining an eclectic or pragmatic use of the materials with the creation of alternative practices. It is not the programme itself which deskills but the acts of teachers who implement the programme recognizing their loss of physical and ideological control over the work process. Teachers may in fact deliberately choose to use programmes because of the insidious position they are now in with regard to class sizes, poor capitation allowances, lack of class cover and the rise of assessment procedures: in the HM Inspectors' report, maths teachers used worksheets because of the demands made on them. But, in a changed educational climate, these programmes will be used or rejected by teacher control of the work process. The costs of retraining teachers have been, in the main, borne by teachers. It is they who spend out-of-school time on curriculum meetings, on teacher centre conferences, on in-service training.[27] The Open University provided a readily accessible opportunity for teachers to pay for their own retraining.

There has been an association between stress at work and the nature of the modern labour process; this is also related to absenteeism and high personnel turnover rates. Stress is a subjective concept and many teachers refer to stress as an element in their work. Absence from work is generally regarded as being connected to stress. As Kyriacou has noted,[28] the Department of Education and Science made special payments, since 1975, to teachers in schools designated as stressful in order to reduce high turnover. Teachers mention poor working conditions, time pressures, poor school ethos as well as 'pupil misbehaviour' as factors in stress production. Hodge (quoted in Kyriacou) notes the recent doubling of male teachers dying towards the end of their career and that the number qualifying for a breakdown pension trebled; head teachers generally seem to be retiring earlier. Stress, in a period of contraction, education cuts and redeployment, will increase: Kyriacou notes the strong correlation between a poor career structure and lower job satisfaction in causing stress. Work absenteeism, he notes, was caused by poor career structure, by too much work to do and lack of time for individual pupils, by demands for 'Efficiency of production and increased workloads, emphasising the quantitative at the expense of the qualitative aspects of work. The rise of solutions based on counselling or 'somatic' therapy are already being suggested. Work won't change but the teacher will have to.'[29]

Technology and the labour process

The process of reskilling and deskilling may be given a significant boost by the introduction of computer, microprocessor and microelectronic applications in education. Apple has argued that it involves a qualitative change in work control from simple to technical control of teachers' work.[30]

We are not discussing here the intrinsic value of microprocessors nor the creative uses to which they may be put, but the way in which they accelerate labour processes which we have described.

Computers are increasingly used in school administration, in repetitive data collection and retrieval on school rolls, details of individual pupils, their subject options, etc. Computers are a qualitative shift in the nature of work, however, and relationships alter and change. Local education authorities may now 'plug in' to this information directly and school performance may be more easily monitored. As computerization may soon be used in classroom administration (pupil records and marksheets), monitoring of pupil *and* teacher performance is easier. It has also been suggested that information may be gathered on the attendance at in-service training courses, amongst other uses.[31]

An increasing use of computers is in computer-assisted learning packages (CAL). These are usually based on American work, and are mainly in the essential, shortage subjects – maths, physics, chemistry, economics and geography. CAL enthusiasts refer to the higher-order skills, improving teaching standards and the new subjects which may be taught in this way. There is another side, related to our argument. CAL 'packages' have to be written by somebody. That person is in an increasingly specialized job. At the moment, it is suggested that to reduce costs, groups of teachers create their own 'packages'. Yet this is a complicated business, requiring time, skill and theoretical understanding – for instance, Ron Jones describes qualities needed in the CAL 'packages': 'Such skills as problem-solving, decision-making . . . divergent as well as convergent thinking skills, such as flexibility, fluency, originality, preference for the complex.'[32] The writing of the CAL packages is a problem – at the moment they are generally agreed to lack quality or be inapplicable to the United Kingdom because of their cultural specificity (made in the USA, etc.). The skills that are needed in the 'packages' can only come from experienced teachers as will the recognized capability to alter and improve the 'packages' in the school.[33]

This process appears to be an accumulation of the workers' knowledge, absorbed into the memory of the machine; it is also more than just factual knowledge – it is the experience and thought, the creative aspects of teaching which are so absorbed. The experience of teaching over many years may be built into the machine memory which can then reproduce that experience at will in many situations where the 'package' is used. The problem though is that in education, and particularly the computing education lobby, this process is not recognized – a process which could lead to the replacement of the teacher. The lack of forethought, the naïvety of statements, is exemplified by the passing reference to the fact that computers may be programmed to have 'the human attitudes of humour, warmth, criticism . . . patience and praise'.[34] Given that this high-flown enthusiasm has echoes of past, now-deceased developments in education (like programmed learning), it is still taken increasingly seriously in the way it will reskill some teachers and possibly even replace others. As the NAS/UWT recently noted, 'The time and expertise involved in writing a major educational programme for a computerized system are equivalent to the time and expertise involved in writing a textbook'.[35] In other words, most teachers will not be involved in this conception process. They will be plugging into CAL modules or perhaps fiddling new learning sequences from 'sub-routines' devised elsewhere.

Their relationship to the new technology is clear: 'no teacher is expected to have a detailed knowledge of computer technology, maintenance, operation or telecommunications systems. They and their students are expected to use the computer as a natural extension to their daily work'.[36] But as computer application in industry demonstrates, the technology appropriates skill from the worker and even worker consciousness; as Mike Cooley shows in computer-assisted design, thought on the part of the worker (in this case, the draughtsman or architect) is a positive disadvantage: 'it is a tool for silencing the common sense and creativity of the skilled worker'.[37] The machine controls the pace, content and form of the work. The worker is an append-age. Job evaluation, for instance the time necessary to complete operations, is known to the computer. The worker does not know what else the computer knows – whether or not there is a reliability of performance check, etc. It is difficult to retain those qualitative aspects of work, as Cooley notes, when faced with a controlled, quantitative output. For the reskilled, some work will be initially created in programme-making or certain specialized school applications (timetabling). Birmingham has, since 1974, had a team of computer specialist teachers who, on a peripatetic basis, train teachers in schools to operate the large investment in computerization now under way in the LEA: they attend to faults in the computer but also offer 'advice' to teachers on CAL packages or related software (books or courses). Their status to the class teacher, even the new reskilled computer teachers, is that of a specialist – knowing the system, its alternatives and functions – and controlling access to learning materials.

Within the school, the increased use of microprocessors will lead to the creation of a new management or supervisory position – providing special assistance to the teachers, scheduling equipment and giving teachers an on-the-job training.

As falling rolls and secondary reorganization continues, with the demand for shortage subjects, the claims for computer applications, es-pecially the new microprocessors, increase. Harry MacMahon explains this clearly:

> The greater the number of students, the wider the range of curricular materials, the more intensive the progress monitoring, the more widely dispersed the students, the smaller the staff/student ratio, the more heterogenous the student population, the greater the management problems and correspondingly, the greater gains to be made through computer assisted management of the learning system.[38]

Computer applications, are ideally suited to the split-site school (with mixed ability, overcrowded classes, few teachers and in-built assessment procedures) and so is the deskilled teacher. Quality control, as an LEA Inspector explained to use recently, is the job of the Inspectorate.
[. . .]

Our argument then is that the labour process in schools will increasingly resemble, as part of a continuous, historical process, work in factories and offices. Workforce flexibility, quality control, deskilling and reskilling are now, in effect, in schools.

Alongside the technological change in work, there has been a consequent reaffirmation of employer control over the labour process. Self-evaluation documents are now common in local education authority schools; job definition, from head teachers to class teachers, is becoming clearer as are supervisory duties and hierarchies. Appointment with a specified job contract. necessary for evaluation and dismissal purposes, is common.

The particular crisis and restructuring of the education service should not be studied to the exclusion of deeper, long-term processes affecting teachers. The present policies of recent governments seem to be aiming for increased teacher productivity, increased control over the work content of teaching and a movement to fixed-term contracts and job specification.

Conclusion

Our arguments centre around ways of seeing teachers' work in common with other kinds of work – as a means of survival (paid employment) and as a service. Value is created by work, but only the employer sees value in entirely financial terms.

Professionalism among teachers could be seen as an expression of service to the community, common to other kinds of work; as an expression of skill or craft or expertise; as an expression of the defence of either or both of these elements. It may also be seen as an externally created force, binding the teachers into a particular view of their work. We have suggested that each view may have a different base amongst teachers and may have had dominance in their work at different historical periods. It may indeed be losing its grip on some teachers altogether. It is neither a reactionary nor a progressive force in all its elements; different versions of it may oppose each other.

The education service has not been seen merely in terms of the imposition of employer or state demands, either implicitly or explicitly, even though these have often prevailed. It has also been seen by teachers as of value for their own purposes, expressed in terms of provision, quality or access; purposes which were often not just theirs, but an expression of a service commitment. Professionalism is, in part, an attempt socially to construct 'skill'; autonomy was, in part, the creation of a defensive space around that 'skill' by teachers.

Class we have proposed as a relational concept, involving ideological, historical and social factors, and as an historical process. We have also tried to discuss the labour process, the economic or material base of this historical process. It is obvious from our discussion that the main contradiction, for us, must always be the one between the employer and employee. During this paper, we have not referred to other contradictions in detail, but no complete historical examination of teachers could exclude the changing relations between the male/female, secondary/elementary and rural/urban teachers, amongst others. [. . .]

There are many questions this short paper has not treated directly, through lack of space. One of these would be the interesting notion of autonomy and, obviously, we would not see it as entirely state-given nor as a middle-class responsibility – we would have to include the notion of defensible space in the social construction of skill which is created in the school and in political or educational alliance. [. . .]

In this paper we have not, perhaps, countered the points made by neo-Marxist and other analyses; what we have done is suggest that there are other questions which should at least be raised and their implications explored. In stating our case we have taken on complex issues and condensed a great deal of complex material. We recognize these deficiencies in the paper, but emphasize that it is a position paper produced with the intention of provoking discussion and at least raising an alternative to what has become an orthodoxy of the right and the left. Much further careful empirical and theoretical work needs to be done.

Notes and references

1. Tropp, A. (1957) *The Schoolteachers*, Heinemann.
2. Ozga, J. and Lawn, M. (1981) *Teachers, Professionalism and Class*, Falmer Press.
3. Finn, D., Grant, N. and Jonhson, R. (1977) 'Social democracy, education and the crisis' *Working Papers on Cultural Studies* 10, '*On Ideology*', Centre for Contemporary Cultural Studies.
4. For example, Althusser, L. (1972) 'Ideology and ideological state apparatuses' in Cosin, B. (ed.) *Educational: Structure and Society*, Penguin; Poulantzas, N. (1975) *Classes in Contemporary Capitalism* New Left Books; Wright, E. O. (1978) *Class, Crisis and the State*, New Left Books.
5. See Crompton, R. and Gubbay, J. (1977) *Economy and Class Structure*, Macmillan.
6. Hunt, A. (1977) 'Theory and politics in the identification of the working class', in Hunt, A. (ed.) *Class and Class Structure*, Lawrence & Wishart.
7. Apple, M. (1981) 'Curricular form and the logic of technical control: Building the possessive individual' in Barton, L., Meighan, R. and Walker, S. (eds.) *Schooling, Ideology and Curriculum*, Falmer Press.
8. Thompson, E. P. (1979) 'Folklore, anthropology and social history', *Indian Historical Review*, Volume III, Number 2 pp. 20–21.
9. Simon, B. (1974) *The Politics of Educational Reform 1920–1940*, Lawrence & Wishart, pp. 72–4.
10. Lawn, M. A. (1982) Organized Teachers and the Labour Movement 1900–1930 unpublished PhD Thesis, Open University.
11. Crompton, R. (1976) 'Approaches to the study of white collar unionism', *Sociology*, Volume 10, Number 3.
12. Bowles, S. and Gintis, H. (1976) *Schooling in Capitalist America*, Routledge & Kegan Paul.

13. Callahan, R. (1976) *Education and the Cult of Efficiency*, New York, Free Press.
14. Percy, Lord E. (1958) *Some Memoires*, London, Eyre & Spottiswoode.
15. *Ibid.*, p. 123.
16. White, J. (1975) 'The end of the compulsory curriculum' in 'The Curriculum – The Doris Lee Lectures' 1975, University of London, *Studies in Education* 2.
17. Braverman, H. (1974) *Labour and Monopoly Capital*, Monthly Review Press.
18. A summary of part of Baverman's work in Zimbalist, A. (ed.) (1979) *Case Studies in the Labour Process*, Monthly Review Press, pp. xv, xvi.
19. An interesting discussion of this approach is in More, C. (1980) *Skill and the English Working Class 1870–1914*, Croom Helm.
20. Braverman, H. (1974) *op. cit.*, p. 305.
21. *Ibid* p. 319.
22. Aronowitz, S. (1973) *False Promises – the Shaping of the American Working Class Consciousness*, McGraw Hill, p. 301.
23. H. M. Inspectorate/DES (1980) *Aspects of Secondary Education in England*, HMSO, p. 61.
24. Evidence for 'flexibility' of teaching staff is growing especially in literature related to 'falling rolls', i.e. Briault, E. (1980) *Falling Rolls in Secondary Schools*, Slough, NFER; Shaw, K. (1977) 'Managing the curriculum in contraction' and Lightfoot, M. (1977) 'The educational consequences of falling rolls' both in Richards, C. *Power and the Curriculum*, Nafferton.
25. HM Inspectorate/DES (1980) *op. cit.*, p. 133.
26. Apple, M. (1981) *op. cit.*
27. Casey, T. (1980) Secretary of the NAS/UWT, quoted in *Times Educational Supplement* December.
28. Kyriacou, C. (1980) 'Occupational stress among schoolteachers: a research report', CORE.
29. *Ibid.*
30. Apple, M. (1981) *op. cit.*
31. Brooksbank, K. (1980) (ed.) (Society of Education Officers), *Educational Administration*, Councils and Education Press, p. 107.
32. Jones, R. (1980) 'Microcomputers; their uses in primary schools', *Cambridge Journal of Education*, Volume 10, Number 3.
33. *Ibid*, and Joiner, L. M., Silverstein, B. J. and Ross, J. D. (1980) 'Insights from a Microcomputer Centre in a Rural School District' in *Educational Technology*, Volume XX, Number 5, May.
34. Jones, R. (1980) *op. cit.*
35. NAS/UWT (1980) 'Micro-electronics: Is there a future for teachers?' NAS/UWT, December.
36. Tinsley, D. (1978) 'Educational computing facilities in Birmingham', *Trends in Education*, Volume number 2, HMSO.
37. Cooley, M. (1980) *Architect or Bee? The Human/Technology Relationship*, Hand and Brain Publishing.
38. MacMahon, H. (1978) 'Computer managed learning – the newly accessible educational technology', *Trends in Education*, Volume 2.

6

Work, class and teaching

Michael W. Apple

Proletarianization: class and gender

An examination of changes in class composition over the past two decades
points out something quite dramatically. The process of proletarianization
has had both a large and consistent effect. There has been a systematic
tendency for those positions with relatively little control over their labor
process to expand; at the same time, there has been a decline in positions with
high levels of autonomy.[1]

   This should not surprise us. In fact, it would be unusual if this did not
occur, especially now. In a time of general stagnation and of crises in
accumulation and legitimation, we should expect that there will be attempts
to further rationalize managerial structures and increase the pressure to
proletarianize the labor process. This pressure is not inconsequential to
educators, not only in regard to the kinds of positions students will find
available (or not available) after completing (or not completing) schooling,
but also in regard to the very conditions of working within education itself.
The labor of what might be called 'semi-autonomous employees' will
certainly feel the impact of this. Given the fiscal crisis of the state, this impact
will be felt more directly among state employees such as teachers. One should
expect to see a rapid growth of plans and pressures for the rationalization of
administration and labor within the state itself.[2] This is one of the times when
one's expectations will not be disappointed.

   In earlier work, I argued that teachers have been involved in a long but
now steadily increasing restructuring of their jobs. I claimed that they were
faced more and more with the prospect of being deskilled because of the
encroachment of technical control procedures into the curriculum in schools.
The integration of management systems, reductive behaviorally based

curricula, pre-specified teaching procedures and student responses, and pre-
and post-testing was leading to a loss of control and a separation of conception
from execution. In sum, the labor process of teaching was becoming
susceptible to processes similar to those that had led to the proletarianization
of many other blue, pink, and white collar jobs. I suggested that this
restructuring of teaching had important implications given the contradictory
class location of teachers.[3]

When I say that teachers have a contradictory class location, I am *not*
implying that they are by definition within the middle classes, or that they are
in an ambiguous position somehow 'between' classes. Instead, along with
Wright, I am saying that it is wise to think of them as located simultaneously
in two classes. Thus, they share the interests of both the petty bourgeoisie and
the working class.[4] Hence, when there is a fiscal crisis where many teachers
are faced with worsening working conditions, lay-offs, and even months
without being paid – as has been the case in a number of urban areas in the
United States – and when their labor is restructured so that they lose control,
it is possible that these contradictory interests will move closer to those of
other workers and people of color who have historically been faced with the
use of similar procedures by capital and the state.[5]

Yet, teachers are not only classed actors, but also gendered actors,
something that is too often neglected by many investigators. This is a
significant omission. A striking conclusion is evident from the analyses of
proletarianization. In every occupational category, *women* are more apt to be
proletarianized than men. This could be because of sexist practices of
recruitment and promotion, the general tendency to care less about the
conditions under which women labor, the way capital has historically
colonized patriarchal relations, and so on. Whatever the reason, it is clear that
a given position may be more or less proletarianized depending on its
relationship to the sexual division of labor.[6]

In the United States, it is estimated that over 90 per cent of women's
(paid) work falls into four basic categories: (1) employment in 'peripheral'
manufacturing industries and retail trades, and particularly in the expanding
but low-paid service sector of the economy; (2) clerical work; (3) health and
education; and (4) domestic service. Most women in, say, the United States
and the United Kingdom are concentrated in either the lowest-paid positions
in these areas or at the bottom of the middle pay grades when there has been
some mobility.[7] One commentator puts it both bluntly and honestly.
'The evidence of discrimination against women in the labour market is
considerable and reading it is a wearing experience.'[8]

This pattern is, of course, largely reproduced within education. Even
given the years of struggle by progressive women and men, the figures –
most of which will be quite familiar – are depressing. While the overwhelming majority of school teachers are women (a figure that becomes even higher
in the primary and elementary schools), many more men are heads or principals of primary and elementary schools, despite the proportion of women

teachers.[9] As the vertical segregation of the workforce increased, this proportion actually increased in inequality. In the United States, in 1928 women accounted for 55 per cent of the elementary school principalships. Today, with nearly 90 per cent of the teaching force in elementary schools being women, they account for only 20 per cent.[10] This pattern has strong historical roots, which cannot be separated from the larger structures of class and patriarchy outside the school.

I shall argue that unless we see the connections between these two dynamics – class and gender – we cannot understand the history of and current attempts at rationalizing education or the roots and effects of proletarianization on teaching itself. Not all teaching can be unpacked by examining it as a labor process or as a class phenomenon, though as I have tried to demonstrate in my own work much of it is made clearer when we integrate it into theories of and changes in class position and the labor process. Neither can all of teaching be understood as totally related to patriarchy, though an immense amount of why it is structured the way it is is due to the history of male dominance and gender struggles.[11] These two dynamics (with race, of course) are not reducible to each other, but intertwine, work off, and co-determine the terrain on which each operates. It is at the intersection of these two dynamics that one can begin to unravel some of the reasons why procedures for rationalizing the work of teachers have evolved. As we shall see, the ultimate effects of these procedures, with the loss of control that accompanies them, can bear in important ways on how we think about the 'reform' of teaching and curriculum and the state's role in it.

Academic knowledge and curricular control

So far I have made a number of general claims about the relationship between proletarianization and patriarchy in the constitution of teaching. I want to go on to suggest ways we can begin to see this relationship in operation. Some sense of the recent past of the state's role in sponsoring changes in curricular and teaching practice is essential here.

The fact that schools have tended to be largely organized around male leadership and female teachers is simply that, a social fact, unless one realizes that this means that educational authority relations have been formally patriarchal. Like the home and the office, male dominance is there; but teachers – like wives, mothers, and clerical workers – have carved out spheres of power and control in their long struggle to gain some autonomy. This autonomy only becomes a problem for capital and the state when what education is for needs revision.

To take one example outside education, in offices clerical work is in the process of being radically transformed with the introduction of word processing technologies, video display terminals, and so on. Traditional forms of control – usually based on the dominance of the male boss – are

being altered. Technical control, where one's work is de-skilled and inten-
sified by the 'impersonal' machinery in the office, has made significant
inroads. While certainly not eliminating patriarchal domination, it has in fact
provided a major shift in the terrain on which it operates. Capital has found
more efficient modes of control than over patriarchal authority.[12]

Similar changes have occurred in schools. In a time when the needs of
industry for technical knowledge and technically trained personnel intersect
with the growth in power of the new petty bourgeoisie and the reassertion of
academic dominance in the curriculum, pressures for curricular reform can
become quite intense. Patience over traditional forms of control will lessen.

Patriarchal relations of power, therefore, organized around the male
principal's relations to a largely female teaching staff, will not necessarily be
progressive for capital or the state. While it once served certain educational
and ideological ends, it is less efficient than what has been required recently.
Gender relations must be partly subverted to create a more efficient institution. Techniques of control drawn from industry will tend to replace older
styles which depended more on a sexual division of power and labor within
the school itself.

An example will document the long and continuing history of these
altered relationships. In the United States, for instance, during the late 1950s
and 1960s, there was rather strong pressure from academics, capital, and the
state to reinstitute academic disciplinary knowledge as the most 'legitimate'
content for schools. In the areas of mathematics and science especially, it was
feared that 'real' knowledge was not being taught. A good deal of effort was
given to producing curricular programs that were systematic, based on
rigorous academic foundations, and, in the elementary school material in
particular, teacher proof. Everything a teacher was to deal with was provided
and pre-specified. The cost of the development of such programs was
socialized by the state (that is, subsidized by tax dollars). The chances of their
being adopted by local school districts were heightened by the National
Defense Education Act, which reimbursed school districts for a large portion
of the purchase cost. That is, if a school system purchased new material of this
type and the technology which supported it, the relative cost was minimal.
The bulk of the expense was repaid by the state. Hence, it would have seemed
irrational not to buy the material – irrational in two ways: (1) the chance of
getting new curricula at low cost is clearly a rational management decision
within industrial logic, and (2) given its imprimatur of science and efficiency,
the material itself seemed rational.

All of this is no doubt familiar to anyone who lived through the early
years of this movement, and who sees the later, somewhat less powerful,
effects it had in, say, England and elsewhere. Yet this is not only the history of
increasing state sponsorship of and state intervention in teaching, curriculum
development and adoption. *It is the history of the state, in concert with capital and a
largely male academic body of consultants and developers, intervening at the level of
practice in the work of a largely female work force.* That is, ideologies of gender, of

sex appropriate knowledge, need to be seen as having possibly played a significant part. The loss of control and rationalization of one's work forms part of a state/class/gender 'couplet' that works its way out in the following ways. Mathematics and science teaching are seen as abysmal. 'We' need rapid change in our economic responsiveness and in 'our' emerging ideological and economic struggle with the Soviet Union.[13] Teachers (who just happen to be almost all women at the elementary level) are not sophisticated enough. Former ways of curricular and teaching control are neither powerful nor efficient enough for this situation. Provide both teacher proof materials and financial incentives to make certain that these sets of curricula actually reach the classroom.

One must integrate an analysis of the state, changes in the labor process of state employees, and the politics of patriarchy to comprehend the dynamics of this history of curriculum. It is not a random fact that one of the most massive attempts at rationalizing curricula and teaching had as its target a group of teachers who were largely women. I believe that one cannot separate out the fact of a sexual division of labor and the vision of who has what kinds of competence from the state's attempts to revamp and make more 'productive' its educational apparatus. In so doing, by seeing these structurally generated relationships, we can begin to open up a door to understanding part of the reasons behind what happened to these curriculum materials when they were in fact introduced.

As numerous studies have shown, when the material was introduced into many schools, it was not unusual for the 'new' math and 'new' science to be taught in much the same manner as the old math and old science. It was altered so that it would fit into both the existing regularities of the institution and the prior practices that had proven successful in teaching.[14] It is probably wise to see this as not only the result of a slow-to-change bureaucracy or a group of consistently conservative administrators and teachers. Rather, I think it may be just as helpful to think of this more structurally in labor process and gender terms. The supposed immobility of the institution, its lack of significant change in the face of the initial onslaught of such material, is at least partly tied to the resistances of a female workforce against external incursions into the practices they had evolved over years of labor. It is in fact more than a little similar to the history of ways in which other women employees in the state and industry have reacted to past attempts at altering traditional modes of control of their own labor.[15]

A note on the state

These points about the resistances of the people who actually work in the institutions, about women teachers confronted by external control, may seem straightforward. However, these basic arguments have very important implications not only about how we think about the history of curriculum reform and control, but more importantly about how many educators and political theorists have pictured the larger issue of the state's role in supporting capital. In the historical example I gave, state intervention on the side of capital and for 'defense' is in opposition to other positions within the state itself. The day-to-day interests of one occupational position (teachers) contradict the larger interests of the state in efficient production.[16] Because of instances such as this, it is probably inappropriate to see the state as a homogeneous entity, standing above day-to-day conflicts.

Since schools *are* state apparatuses, we should expect them to be under intense pressure to act in certain ways, especially in times of both fiscal and ideological crises. Even with this said, though, this does not mean that people employed in them are passive followers of policies laid down from above. As Roger Dale has noted:

> Teachers are not merely 'state functionaries' but do have some degree of autonomy, and [this] autonomy will not necessarily be used to further the proclaimed ends of the state apparatus. Rather than those who work there fitting themselves to the requirements of the institutions, there are a number of very important ways in which the institution has to take account of the interests of the employees and fit itself to them. It is here, for instance, that we may begin to look for the sources of the alleged inertia of educational systems and schools, that is to say what appears as inertia is not some immutable characteristic of bureaucracies but is due to various groups within them having more immediate interests than the pursuit of the organization's goals.[17]

Thus the 'mere' fact that the state wishes to find 'more efficient' ways to organize teaching does not guarantee this will be acted upon by teachers who have a long history of work practices and self-organization once the doors to their rooms are closed. However, the fact that these are primarily women employees who have faced these forms of rationalization has meant that the actual outcomes of these attempts to retain control of one's pedagogic work can lead to rather contradictory ideological results.

Legitimating intervention

While these initial attempts to rationalize teaching and curricula did not always produce the results that were anticipated by their academic, industrial, and governmental proponents, they did other things that were, and are, of considerable import. The situation is actually quite similar to the effects of the use of Tayloristic management strategies in industry. As a management technology for deskilling workers and separating conception from execution, Taylorism was less than fully successful. It often generated slowdowns and strikes, exacerbated tensions, and created new forms of overt and covert resistance. Yet, its ultimate effect was to legitimate a particular ideology of management and control both to the public and to employers and workers.[18] Even though it did not succeed as a set of techniques, it ushered in and finally brought acceptance of a larger body of ideological practices to deskill pink-, white-, and blue-collar workers and to rationalize and intensify their labor.

This too was one of the lasting consequences of these earlier curriculum 'reform' movements. While they did not completely transform the practice of teaching, while patriarchal relations of authority which gave teachers some measure of freedom were not totally replaced by more efficient forms of organizing and controlling their day-to-day activity, they legitimated both new forms of control and greater state intervention using industrial and technical models and brought about a new generation of more sophisticated attempts at overcoming teacher 'resistance'. Thus this new generation of techniques – from systematic integration of testing, behavioral goals and curriculum, competency based instruction and pre-packaged curricula to management by objectives, and so forth – has not sprung out of nowhere, but (like the history of Taylorism) has grown out of the failures, partial successes, and resistances that accompanied the earlier approaches to control. This is not only the history of the control of state employees to bring about efficient teaching, but a rearticulation of the dynamics of patriarchy and class in one site, the school.

Intensification and teaching

Having paid particular attention to the historical dynamics operating in the schools, I shall now focus on more current outgrowths of this earlier history of rationalization and control.

The earlier attempts by state bureaucrats, industry and others to gain greater control of day-to-day classroom operation and its 'output' did not die. They have had more than a decade to grow, experiment, and become more sophisticated. While gender will be less visible in the current strategies (in much the same way that the growth of management strategies in industry slowly covered the real basis of power in factories and offices), it will be present in important ways once we look at changes in the labor process of teaching, how some teachers respond to current strategies, and how they interpret their own work.

In previous work I have focussed on a number of elements through which curricula and teaching are controlled (aspects of deskilling and reskilling of labor and the separation of conception from execution in teachers' work); here I shall concentrate on something which accompanies these historically evolving processes: what I shall call *intensification*.

Intensification 'represents one of the most tangible ways in which the work privileges of educational workers are eroded.' It has many symptoms from the trivial to the more complex – from no time at all to even go to the bathroom, have a cup of coffee or relax, to having a total absence of time to keep up with one's field. We can see intensification most visibly in mental labour in the chronic sense of work overload that has escalated over time.[19]

[. . .]

Intensification also acts to destroy the sociability of non-manual workers. Leisure and self-direction tend to be lost. Community tends to be redefined around the needs of the labor process. And, since both time and interaction are at a premium, the risk of isolation grows.[20]

Intensification by itself 'does not necessarily reduce the range of skills applied or possessed by educated workers.' It may, in fact, cause them to 'cut corners' by eliminating what seems to be inconsequential to the task at hand. This has occurred with doctors, for instance, where many examinations now concentrate only on what seems critical. The chronic work overload has also caused some non-manual workers to learn or relearn skills. The financial crisis has led to shortages of personnel in a number of areas. Thus, a more diverse array of jobs must be done that used to be covered by other people, people who simply no longer exist within the institution.[21]

While this leads to a broader range of skills having to be learned or relearned, it can lead to something mentioned earlier – the loss of time to keep up with one's field. That is, what might be called 'skill diversification' has contradictions built into it. It is also part of a dynamic of intellectual deskilling[22] in which mental workers are cut off from their own fields and again must rely even more heavily on ideas and processes provided by 'experts.'

While these effects are important, one of the most significant impacts of intensification may be in reducing the *quality*, not the quantity, of service provided to people. While traditionally 'human service professionals' have equated doing good work with the interests of their clients or students, intensification tends to contradict the traditional interest in work well done, in both a quality product and process.[23] *Getting* done becomes more important than what was done or how one got there.

Some of these aspects of intensification are increasingly found in teaching, especially in schools dominated by behaviorally pre-specified curricula, repeated testing, and strict and reductive accountability systems. To make this clear, I shall draw on data from recent research on the effects of these procedures on the structure of teachers' work.

I have argued here and elsewhere that there has been a rapid growth in curricular 'systems' in the United States, one that is now spreading to other countries.[24] These curricula have goals, strategies, tests, textbooks, work-sheets, appropriate student response, etc. integrated together. In schools where this is taken seriously,[25] what impact has this been having? We have sufficient evidence from ethnographic studies of the labor process of teaching to be able to begin to point to what is going on. For example, in one school where the curriculum was heavily based on a sequential list of behaviorally defined objectives, multiple worksheets on skills which the students were to complete, with pre-tests to measure 'readiness' and 'skill level' and post-tests to measure 'achievement' that were given often and regularly, the intensification of teacher work is quite visible.

In this school, such curricular practice required that teachers spend a large portion of their time evaluating student 'mastery' of each of the various objectives and recording the results of these multiple evaluations for later discussions with parents or decisions on whether or not the student could 'go on' to another set of skill-based worksheets. The recording and evaluation made it imperative that a significant amount of time be spent on administrative arrangements for giving tests, and then grading them, organizing lessons (which were quite often pre-packaged), and so on. One also found teachers busy with these tasks before and after school and, very often, during their lunch hour. Teachers began to come in at 7.15 in the morning and leave at 4.30 in the afternoon. Two hours more work at home each night were not unusual. [26]

Here too getting done became the norm. There is so much to do that simply accomplishing what is specified requires nearly all of one's efforts. 'The challenge of the work day (or week) was to accomplish the required number of objectives.' As one teacher put it, 'I just want to get this done. I don't have time to be creative or imaginative.'[27] We should not blame the teacher here. In mathematics, for example, teachers typically had to spend nearly half of the allotted time correcting and recording the worksheets the students completed each day. [28] The situation seemed to continually push up the work load of these teachers. Thus, even though they tended to complain at times about the long hours, the intensification and the time spent on technical tasks such as grading and record keeping, the amount of time spent doing these things grew inexorably. [29]

Few of the teachers were passive in the face of this. Even though the elements of curricular control were effective in structuring major aspects of their practice, teachers often responded in a variety of ways. They subtly changed the pre-specified objectives at times, thereby attempting to overcome the separation of conception from execution. They sometimes simply informally refused to teach certain objectives because they could not see their relevance. They tried to resist the intensification as well: first, by trying to find some space during the day for doing slower paced activities; and second, by actually calling a halt temporarily to the frequent pre- and post-tests, worksheets and the like and merely having 'relaxed discussions with students on topics of their own choosing'. [30]

This, of course, is quite contradictory. While these examples document the active role of teachers in attempting to win back some time, to resist the loss of control of their own work, and to slow down the pace at which students and they were to proceed, the way this is done is not necessarily very powerful. In these instances, time was fought for simply to relax, if only for a few minutes. The process of control, the increasing technicization and intensification of the teaching act, the proletarianization of their work – all of this was an absent presence. It was misrecognized as a symbol of their increased *professionalism*.

Profession and gender

We cannot understand why teachers interpreted what was happening to them as the professionalization of their jobs unless we see how the ideology of professionalism works as part of both a class and gender dynamic in education. For example, while reliance on 'experts' to create curricular and teaching goals and procedures grew in this kind of situation, a wider range of technical skills had to be mastered by these teachers. Becoming adept at grading all those tests and worksheets quickly, deciding on which specific skill group to put a student in, learning how to 'efficiently manage' the many different groups based on the tests, and more, all became important skills. As responsibility for designing one's own curricula and one's own teaching decreased, responsibility over technical and management concerns came to the fore.

Professionalism and increased responsibility tend to go hand in hand here. The situation is more than a little paradoxical. There is so much responsibility placed on teachers for technical decisions that they actually work harder. They feel that since they constantly make decisions based on the outcomes of these multiple pre- and post-tests, the longer hours are evidence of their enlarged professional status:

> One reason the work is harder is we have a lot of responsibility in decision-making. There's no reason not to work hard, because you want to be darn sure that those decisions you made are something that might be helpful. . . . So you work hard to be successful at these decisions so you look like a good decision maker.[31]

It is here that the concept of professionalism seemed to have one of its major impacts. Since the teachers thought of themselves as being more professional to the extent that they employed technical criteria and tests, they also basically accepted the longer hours and the intensification of their work that accompanied the program. To do a 'good job', you needed to be as 'rational' as possible.[32]

We should not scoff at these perceptions on the part of the teachers. First, the very notion of professionalization has been important not only to teachers in general but to women in particular. It has provided a contradictory yet powerful barrier against interference by the state; and just as critically, in the struggle over male dominance, it has been part of a complex attempt to win equal treatment, pay, and control over the day-to-day work of a largely female labor force.[33]

Second, while we need to remember that professionalism as a social goal grew at the same time and was justified by the 'project and practice of the market professions during the liberal phase of capitalism',[34] the strategy of professionalism has historically been used to set up 'effective defenses against proletarianization.'[35] Given that I said earlier about the strong relationship between the sexual division of labor and proletarianization, it would be not only ahistorical but perhaps even a bit sexist as well to wholly blame teachers for employing a professional strategy.

Hence, the emphasis on increasing professionalism by learning new management skills and so on and its partial acceptance by elementary school teachers can best be understood not only as an attempt by state bureaucrats to deskill and reskill teachers, but also as part of a much larger historical dynamic in which gender politics have played a significant role.

Yet the acceptance of certain aspects of intensification is not only due to the history of how professionalism has worked in class and gender struggles. It is heightened by a number of internal factors, as well. For example, in the school referred to earlier, while a number of teachers believed that the rigorous specification of objectives and teaching procedures actually helped free them to become more creative, it was clear that subtle pressures existed to meet the priorities established by the specified objectives. Even though in some subject areas they had a choice of how they were to meet the objectives, the objectives themselves usually remained unchallenged. The perceived interests of parents and the establishment of routines helped assure this. Here is one teacher's assessment of how this occurs:

> Occasionally you're looking at the end of the book at what the unit is going to be, these are the goals that you have to obtain, that the children are going to be tested on. That may affect your teaching in some way in that you may by-pass other learning experiences simply to obtain the goal. These goals are going home to parents. It's a terrible thing to do but parents like to see 90's and 100's rather than 60's on skills.[36]

In discussing the use of the skills program, another teacher points out the other element that was mentioned. 'It's got a manual and you follow the manual and the kids know the directions and it gets to be routine.'[37]

Coupled with perceived parental pressure and the sheer power of routine is something else, the employment practices surrounding teaching. In many schools, one of the main criteria for the hiring of teachers is their agreement with the overall curricular, pedagogic, and evaluative framework which organizes the day-to-day practice. Such was the case in this study. Beyond this, even though some investigators have found that people who tend to react negatively to these pre-packaged and systematized curricular forms often leave teaching,[38] given the depressed market for new teachers, and the conscious decision by school districts to hire fewer teachers and increase class size, fewer jobs are available. The option of leaving or even protesting seems romantic.

Gendered resistance

To return to a claim I made earlier, teachers have not stood by and accepted all this. In fact, our perception that they have been and are passive in the face of these pressures may reflect our own tacit beliefs in the relative passivity of women workers. This would be an unfortunate characterization. Historically, for example, in Britian and the United States, the picture of women teachers as non-militant and middle-class in orientation is not wholly accurate. There have been periods of exceptional militancy and clear political commitment.[39] However, militancy and political commitment are but one set of ways in which control is contested. It is also fought for on the job itself in subtle and even 'unconscious' (one might say 'cultural') ways, ways which will be contradictory as we shall now see. Once again, gender is of prime import.

In my own interviews with teachers it has become clear that many of them feel rather uncomfortable with their role as managers. Many others are less than happy with the emphasis on programs which they feel often 'lock them into a rigid system'. Here the resistance to rationalization and the loss of historically important forms of self-control of one's labor has very contradictory outcomes, partly as a result of sexual divisions in society. Thus, a teacher using a curricular program in reading and language arts that is very highly structured and test based states: 'While it's really important for the children to learn these skills, right now it's more important for them to learn to feel good about themselves. That's my role, getting them to feel good. That's more important than tests right now.' Another primary grade teacher, confronted by a rationalized curriculum program where students move from classroom to classroom for 'skill groups', put it this way: 'Kids are too young to travel between classrooms all the time. They need someone there that they can always go to, who's close to them. Anyway, subjects are less important than their feelings.'

In these quotes, resistance to the administrative design is certainly evident. There is a clear sense that something is being lost. Yet the discomfort with the process is coded around the traditional distinctions that organize the sexual division of labor both within the family and the larger society. The *woman's* sphere is that of providing emotional security, caring for feelings, and so on.

Do not misconstrue my points here. Teachers should care for the feelings and emotional security of their students. However, while these teachers fight on a cultural level against what they perceive to be the ill effects of their loss of control and both the division and intensification of their labor, they do so at the expense of reinstituting categories that partly reproduce other divisions that have historically grown out of patriarchal relations.[40]

This raises a significant point. Much of the recent literature on the role of the school in the reproduction of class, sex, and race domination has directed our attention to the existence of resistances. This realization was not inconsequential and was certainly needed to enable us to go further than the overly deterministic models of explanation that had been employed to unpack what schools do. However, at the same time, this literature has run the risk of romanticizing such resistances. The fact that they exist does not guarantee that they will necessarily be progressive at each and every moment. Only by uncovering the contradictions within and between the dynamics of the labor process *and* gender can we begin to see what effects such resistances may actually have.

Labor, gender and teaching

I have paid particular attention here to the effects of the restructuring of teachers' work in the school. I have claimed that we simply cannot understand what is happening to teaching and curriculum without placing it in a framework which integrates class (and its accompanying process of proletarianization) and gender. The impact of deskilling and intensification occurs on a terrain and in an institution that is populated primarily by women teachers and male administrators, a fact that needs to be recognized as being historically articulated with both the social and sexual divisions of labor, knowledge, and power in our society.

Yet, since teachers are primarily women, we must also look beyond the school to get a fuller comprehension of the impact of these changes and the responses of teachers to them. We need to remember that women teachers often work in *two* sites – the school and then the home. Given the modification of patriarchal relations and the intensification of labor in teaching, what impact might this have outside the school? If so much time is spent on technical tasks at school and home, it is possible that less time may be available for domestic labor in the home? Other people in the family may have to take up the slack, thereby partly challenging the sexual division of household labor. On the other hand, the intensification of teachers' work, and the work overload that may result from it, may have exactly the opposite effect. It may increase the exploitation of unpaid work in the home by merely adding more to do without initially altering conditions in the family. In either case, such conditions will lead to changes, tensions, and conflicts outside the sphere where women engage in paid work.[41] It is worth thinking very carefully about the effects that working in one site will have on the other. The fact that this dual exploitation exists is quite consequential in another way. It opens up possible new avenues for political intervention by socialist feminists. Showing the relationship between the home and the job, and the intensification growing in both, may provide for a way of demonstrating the ties between both of these spheres and between class and gender.

Thinking about such issues has actually provided the organizing framework for my analysis. The key to my investigation has been reflecting about changes in *how* work is organized over time and, just as significantly, *who* is doing the work. A clearer sense of both of these – how and who – can enable us to see similarities and differences between the world of work in our factories and offices and that of semi-autonomous state employees such as teachers.

What does this mean? Historically the major struggles labor engaged in at the beginning of the use of systematic management concerned resistance to speedups.[42] That is, the intensification of production, the pressure to produce more work in a given period, led to all kinds of interesting responses. Craft workers, for example, often simply refused to do more. Pressure was put on co-workers who went too fast (or too slow). Breaks were extended. Tools and machines suddenly developed 'problems'.

Teachers – given their contradictory class location, their relationship to the history of patriarchal control and the sexual division of labor, and the actual conditions of their work – will find it difficult to respond in the same way. They are usually isolated during their work, and perhaps more so now given the intensification of their labor. Further, machinery and tools in the usual sense of these terms are not visible. And just as importantly, the perception of oneself as professional means that the pressures of intensification and the loss of control will be coded and dealt with in ways that are specific to that workplace and its own history. The ultimate effects will be very contradictory.

In essence, therefore, while similar labor processes may be working through institutions within industry and the state which have a major impact on women's paid work, these processes will be responded to differently by different classes and class segments. The ideology of professional discretion will lead to a partial acceptance of, say, intensification by teachers on one level, and will generate a different kind of resistance, one specific to the actual work circumstances in which they have historically found themselves. The fact that these changes in the labor process of teaching occur on a terrain that has been a site of patriarchal relations plays a major part.

I do not want to suggest that once you have realized the place of teaching in the sexual division of labor, you have thoroughly understood deskilling and reskilling, intensification and loss of control, or the countervailing pressures of professionalism and proletarianization in teachers' work. Obviously, this is a very complex issue in which the internal histories of bureaucracies, the larger role of the state in a time of economic and ideological crisis,[43] and the local political economy and power relations of each school play a part. What I do want to argue quite strongly, however, is the utter import of gendered labor as a constitutive aspect of the way management and the state have approached teaching and curricular control. It is the absent presence behind all of our work.

Notes and references

1. Wright, E. O. and Singelmann, J. (1981) 'The proletarianization of work in American capitalism,' University of Wisconsin-Madison Institute for Research on Poverty, *Discussion Paper* 647–81, p. 38.
2. *Ibid.*, p. 43. See also Apple, M. W. (1981) 'State, bureaucracy and curriculum control,' *Curriculum Inquiry* 11, 4, pp. 379–88. For a discussion that rejects part of the argument about proletarianization, see Kelly, M. (1980) *White Collar Proletariat*, Routledge & Kegan Paul.
3. Apple, M. W. (1981) 'Curricular form and the logic of technical control,' in Barton, L., Meighan, R. and Walker, S. (eds), *Schooling, Ideology and the Curriculum*, Falmer Press, pp. 11–27. This argument is expanded considerably in Apple, M. W. (1982) *Education and Power*, Routledge & Kegan Paul.
4. Wright, E. J. (1980) 'Class and occupation,' *Theory and Society* 9, 2, pp. 182–3.
5. Apple, M. W. (1982) *op. cit.* (Note 2).
6. Wright, E. J. (1980) *op. cit.*, p. 188 (Note 4). Clearly, race plays an important part here too. See Reich, M. (1981) *Racial Inequality*, Princeton University Press and Barrera, M. (1979) *Race and Class in the Southwest: A Theory of Racial Inequality*, Notre Dame Press.
7. Holland, J. (1980) 'Women's occupational choice: The impact of sexual divisions in society,' Stockholm Institute of Education, Department of Educational Research, *Reports on Education and Psychology*, p. 7.
8. *Ibid.*, p. 27.
9. *Ibid.*, p. 45.
10. Kelly, G. and Nihlen, A. (1982) 'Schooling and the reproduction of patriarchy,' in Apple, M. W. (ed.), *Cultural and Economic Reproduction in Education: Essays on Class, Ideology and the State*, Routledge & Kegan Paul, pp. 167–8. One cannot fully understand the history of the relationship between women and teaching without tracing the complex connections among the family, domesticity, child care, and the policies of and employment within the state. See especially David, M. (1980) *The State, the Family and Education*, Routledge & Kegan Paul.
11. For an interesting history of the relationship among class, gender, and teaching, see Purvis, J. (1981) 'Women and teaching in the nineteenth century,' in Dale, R., Esland, G., Fergusson, R. and MacDonald, M. (eds), *Education and the State Vol. 2: Politics, Patriarchy and Practice*, Falmer Press, pp. 359–75. I am wary of using a concept such as patriarchy since its very status is problematic. As Rowbotham notes, 'patriarchy suggests a fatalistic submission which allows no space for the complexities of women's defiance.' Quoted in Davis, T. (1981) 'Stand by your men? Feminism and socialism in the eighties,' in Bridges, G. and Brunt, R. (eds), *Silver Linings: Some Strategies for the Eighties*, Lawrence & Wishart, p. 14. A history of women's day-to-day struggles falsifies any such theory of 'fatalistic submission'.
12. Barker, J. and Downing, H. (1981) 'Word processing and the transformation of the patriarchal relations of control in the office,' in Dale, R., Esland, G., Fergusson, R. and MacDonald, M. (eds), *Education and the State Vol. 1: Schooling and the National Interest*, Falmer Press, pp. 229–56. See also the discussion 'of deskilling in Edwards, R. (1979) *Contested Terrain*, Basic Books.
13. For an analysis of how such language has been employed by the state, see Apple, M. W. (1982) *op. cit.* (Note 3), Apple, M. W., in press, 'Common curriculum and

state control,' *Discourse*, and Donald, J. (1979) 'Green paper: Noise of a crisis', *Screen Education* 30 (Spring).

14. See, for example, Sarason, S. (1971) *The Culture of the School and the Problem of Change*, Allyn & Bacon.

15. Apple, M. W. (1982) *op. cit.* (Note 3), Benson, S. P. (1978) 'The clerking sisterhood: Rationalization and the work culture of saleswomen in American department stores,' *Radical America* 12, (March/April), pp. 41–5.

16. Roger Dale's discussion of contradictions between elements within the state is quite interesting in this regard. See Dale, R. (1981) 'The State and education: Some theoretical approaches,' in *The State and the Politics of Education*, The Open University Press, E 353, Block 1, Part 2, Units 3–4, and Dale, R. (1982) 'Education and the capitalist State: Contributions and contradictions,' in Apple, M. W. (ed.), *Cultural and Economic Reproduction in Education: Essays on Class, Ideology and the State*, Routledge & Kegan Paul, pp. 127–61.

17. Dale, R. (1981) *op. cit.* (Note 16), p. 13.

18. I have examined this in greater detail in Apple, M. W. (1982) *op. cit.* (Note 3). See also Edwards, R. (1979) *op. cit.* (Note 12), and Clawson, D. (1980) *Bureaucracy and the Labor Process*, Monthly Review Press.

19. Larson, M. (1980) 'Proletarianization and educated labor,' *Theory and Society* 2, p. 166.

20. *Ibid.* Larson points out that these problems related to intensification are often central grievances even among doctors.

21. *Ibid.*, p. 168.

22. *Ibid.*, p. 169.

23. *Ibid.*, p. 167.

24. Apple, M. W. (1982) *op. cit.* (Note 3). See also Buswell, C. (1980) 'Pedagogic change and social change,' *British Journal of Sociology of Education* 3, pp. 293–306.

25. The question of just how seriously schools take this, the variability of their response, is not unimportant. As Popkewitz, Tabachnick and Wehlage demonstrate in their interesting ethnographic study of school reform, not all schools use materials of this sort alike. See Popkewitz, T., Tabachnick, B. R. and Wehlage, G. (1982) *The Myth of Educational Reform*, University of Wisconsin Press.

26. The section of my analysis is based largely on research carried out by Andrew Gitlin. See Gitlin, A. (1980) 'Understanding the work of teachers,' unpublished PhD thesis University of Wisconsin, Madison.

27. *Ibid.*, p. 208.

28. *Ibid.*

29. *Ibid.*, p. 197.

30. *Ibid.*, p. 237.

31. *Ibid.*, p. 125.

32. *Ibid.*, p. 197.

33. This is similar to the use of liberal discourse by popular classes to struggle for person rights against established property rights over the past 100 years. See Gintis, H. (1980) 'Communication and politics,' *Socialist Review* 10, 2/3 pp. 189–232.

34. Larson, M. (1981) 'Monopolies of competence and bourgeois ideology,' in Dale, R., Esland, G., Fergusson, R. and MacDonald, M. (eds), *Education and the State Volume 2: Politics, Patriarchy and Practice*, Falmer Press, p. 332.

35. Larson, M. (1980) *op. cit.* (Note 19), p. 152.

36. Gitlin, A. (1980) *op. cit.* (Note 26), p. 128.
37. *Ibid.*
38. Lawn, M. A. and Ozga, J. T. (1981) 'Teachers: Professionalism, class and proletarianization,' unpublished paper, p. 15 in mimeo.
39. Ozga, J. T. (1981) 'The politics of the teaching profession,' in *The Politics of Schools and Teaching*, The Open University Press, E 353, Block 6, Units 14–15, p. 24.
40. We need to be very careful here, of course. Certainly, not all teachers will respond in this way. That some will not points to the partial and important fracturing of dominant gender and class ideologies in ways that signal significant alterations in the consciousness of teachers. Whether these alterations are always progressive is an interesting question.
41. While I have focused here on the possible impacts in the school and the home on women teachers, a similar analysis needs to be done on men. What changes, conflicts, and tensions will evolve, say, in the patriarchal authority structures of the home, given the intensification of men's labor? I would like to thank Sandra Acker for raising this critically important point.
42. Clawson, D. (1980) *op. cit.* (Note 18), pp. 152–3.
43. Apple, M. W. (1981) *op. cit.* (Note 2).

Section III

Deskilling at work

7
Pedagogic change and social change

Carol Buswell

One of the important changes in schools in recent years has been the growth of the curriculum 'package' where the content may be externally determined (SMP Mathematics, SRA English) or written by teachers within the school (some humanities and social science schemes). Pupils working at their own pace through the programme is often a feature of such schemes, and this aspect is also likely to be adopted by schools if they organize the pupils in 'mixed ability' groups. The self-pacing feature of the curricular schemes involves teachers in a different pedagogic style, and if Durkheim's[1] contention – that pedagogic change is related to social change and can only be understood in that context – is correct, then these developments may signify more than simply a change in classroom practice.

The new curriculum packaging involves not only a predetermined content but may, therefore, also contain a predetermined pedagogy, where the manner of transmission is also laid down. This would suggest that Braverman's[2] claim that there is an increased deskilling of mass middle-level occupations such as teaching might have some basis – a point also discussed by Apple.[3] Carchedi[4] similarly maintains that in the present stage of capitalism the non-manual worker is placed in a more contradictory position with the job becoming more proletarianized at the same time as the worker is expected to subscribe to an ideology based on a lost position.[5] The loss of privilege is, Carchedi suggests, symbolized in all kinds of ways including more surveillance and control – which is, as will be illustrated, also a feature of the new curricular schemes which not only represent an aspect of deskilling but also contain within themselves a new form of control over both teachers and pupils. As far as teachers are concerned any loss of autonomy and control may, of course, only be relative to the recent past because, as Whiteside and

Bernbaum[6] point out, the 1950s and 1960s represented a 'high point' for the freedom of teachers.

If, however, deskilling is occurring for some teachers there is a parallel reskilling in extra-classroom activities for others. The development of this tendency is likely to be important for future social relations within schools and between schools and outside agencies. Olin Wright,[7] in defining social classes in terms of their location within the social relations of production, maintains that non-correspondence between the dimensions of production relations generates a series of contradictory class relations – one of which he defines as 'semi autonomous employees' who, although employees, retain aspects of control over what they produce. Olin Wright suggests that most broad occupational categories have hetereogenous class compositions and, on the basis of American survey data, divides teachers roughly into half as 'semi autonomous employees' and half as 'workers' who have little control. Any increase, therefore, in the proportion of workers within the occupation will not only affect relationships between groups of teachers but between classroom teachers (workers) and pupils. Olin Wright further maintains that in every occupational category women are more proletarianized than men, which was beginning to be apparent in this school, and thus there is likely in future to be more – not fewer – discrepancies between the jobs of male and female teachers which, in turn, may well affect the education of boys and girls.

If changes in the control of teachers over their jobs is related to broader economic factors so, too, are the innovatory aspects of curriculum developments. Gorz in discussing the economic purpose of technological innovation, points out that in a virtually saturated market the problem of monopolies is not to increase production but to escalate demand for consumer goods which are increasingly made absolete.[8] Some of the curriculum packages are produced by the publishing companies of corporate concerns, and Apple has pointed out how lucrative a market the schemes represent in America.[9] At least one firm is now 'operating' (i.e. selling, training, consciousness-raising among teachers) in Britain,[10] and if the materials are not only disposable but also based on 'relevance' they have to be 'updated' frequently. Where packages are produced by schools themselves, however, they are cheaper than books which might be an important consideration in times of 'fiscal crisis.'

The effects of such curricular schemes are also related to the economic structure in as much as, in legitimating underachievement, they prevent the oversupply of qualified individuals at a time of economic recession but, at the same time, place responsibility for lack of achievement more firmly on the individuals themselves. It is, however, important not to oversimplify the 'correspondence'[11] between the economy and education but to be aware of the ways in which the outcomes are 'created'[12] in the day-to-day processes of the school. Although the new curriculum and pedagogic changes act as a different form of control over both teachers and pupils, and alter the social relations between them, individuals and groups modify and recreate the intentions of such changes and there are some examples, in this school, of 'resistances'.[13]

The research

A term was spent in the school, which was a large (1500 pupils and 100 staff) urban comprehensive in the north of England with a predominantly work-ing-class intake. In the first three years the pupils were organized in 'mixed ability' groups, and there were ten classes in each year.

The research started with no hypothesis or particular aspect of the curriculum as the main concern – that was intended to emerge from what was happening in the school, and the problem focused on was to determine the methods used after the initial observation. Initially, therefore, at least a day's teaching in each department, and across all years, was observed – and also informal participation and attendance at meetings took place. The lower school curriculum had been changed during the previous eighteen months, with the introduction of 'humanities' to replace geography, history and religious education, and the head regarded the lower school curriculum as now 'fixed' with future changes envisaged for the upper school. The subjects taught in the lower school represented a range of content packaging and pedagogic styles across subjects.

At one end of the spectrum mathematics represented an externally written, self-pacing programme that was sophisticated and supplemented by teacher additions and regular testing of pupil performance. The SMP scheme had been introduced by the head of department seven years previously and pupils worked through the books at their own pace for three years – marking their own completed class work, doing the built-in tests when they occurred and completing teacher-designed homework sheets appropriate to each exercise. Supplementary work cards were being produced for pupils considered to be in need of more practice in particular exercises. Arithmetic testing had been added to the scheme and this took place every six weeks.[14]

The humanities scheme which had been introduced by the head, with the agreement and cooperation of some staff, consisted of 'units' which had been written by the teachers (of history, geography and RE), the topics of which had been jointly decided.[15] Each unit contained five books of increas-ing 'difficulty' through which the pupils worked at their own pace. The scheme was not as linear as mathematics, as each class moved on to a new unit at the end of a month, with all pupils starting on Book 1. The staff, however, were in the process of discussing the possibility of pupils starting new units at different levels depending on their past performance. The units consisted of text, pictures and diagrams with pupil tasks (exercises) interspersed. Teachers taught one class for a year, and there were monthly meetings to discuss the units. The expressed aim of humanities was to teach pupils 'how to learn' rather than to be concerned with content, but staff were beginning to be concerned about whether there was any learning and pupil testing was being introduced. For one topic outside material had been used, and there was discussion about using more.

French was taught by using an external package which was very 'loose' in the sense that the intention was for the booklets to be supplemented by teachers. Class teaching, however, operated and at least one teacher had ceased using the package at all. The science department also operated class teaching for the second- and third-year pupils, although a tight lesson-by-lesson syllabus operated and each science teacher taught all three sciences to one class for a year. The syllabus and lesson plans had been produced by the appropriate specialist in that subject.

English represented the other end of the spectrum compared with mathematics. Not only did class teaching operate, but there did not seem to be a syllabus. One teacher had introduced the SRA comprehension scheme, which was self-pacing and self-marking, and most of the other teachers had started to use it for one lesson a week. This, therefore, was being introduced from the 'bottom', rather than the top, of the hierarchy.

It was decided to focus on these five subjects as they operated in the second year of the school, a year which was regarded by teachers as less problematic than either the first year (pupils newly arrived from different kinds of primary schools) or the third year (no remedial class so pupils who could not read or write were in groups with those that could). Thirty different teachers taught these five subjects to the second year and one-half of a term was spent observing each of them teaching at least two different lessons to the year. The second-year pupils were also observed in subjects other than these five, and two of the second-year classes were followed for a whole day. During this time informal staffroom participation occurred as well as meeting attendance and interviews with senior staff, but it was deliberately decided to leave the arranged interviews of the thirty teachers until the second half of the term by which time there might be more trust and the observations would allow more relevant discussion relating to actual practice. The record cards and test marks of second-year pupils were also collected.

The thirty teachers were interviewed privately, in a relatively unstructured way with discussion of the particular lessons and classes observed, the curriculum being taught, besides more general topics. As it was impossible, because of time constraints, to interview all the second-year pupils – there was a problem of sampling in order to obtain a representative group in terms of school rated ability and behaviour. Discussions with teachers indicated considerable agreement about individuals considered to be 'able', but less agreement over who was 'average' or 'weak'. All the pupils in the two classes that had been followed for a day were, therefore, interviewed and eight or ten pupils from the other eight classes were picked as representative from record cards and subject marks. This gave a total of 188 pupils, balanced equally also by sex, which was almost one-half of the total second-year group. The pupils were interviewed in pairs, for their own comfort, and shown flash cards which contained the name of each of the five subjects and they were asked to talk about the subject and the way of working, besides more general questions.

The implementation of changes

The Head, on arrival five years previously, had introduced several curriculum changes, of which the Humanities scheme had been the latest. Regarding the curriculum, in general, he said,

> I believe it's no good building a house on sand, so the first three years have to be right. I believe in a common curriculum taking into account the children's background. So I set down a broad framework for that lower school. I introduced some changes in spite of the staff. I broke the rules and didn't wait for staff to be in favour, or we'd still be waiting. When I came to the school most staff weren't 'curriculum aware'. I am trying to implement the ideas of Hirst and Lawton, and to have a balanced curriculum.

Concerning Humanities, he went on to point out,

> I wanted to minimise the effect of weak and lazy teachers, and to give all pupils access to good material. At the time I introduced it about a third of the staff agreed with me, a third were opposed and a third didn't care.

Thus the introduction of the scheme was a deliberate attempt to unify the classroom practice of a hetereogenous group of staff and to exert more control over the 'weak and lazy'. Control was further being increased by the fact that all departments had produced 'Aims' (broad) and were being requested to produce 'Objectives'[16] (measurable) which would clearly be a further check on, not only pupil, but also teacher performance. The senior staff felt this was necessary for pupils to obtain a 'fair deal' but decreasing teacher autonomy may increase their alienation which in turn, leads to more loss of control.

Pedagogic change and the deskilling of teachers

Initial observation did not make obvious which teachers in humanities might have been opposed to the scheme and pedagogy. Apart from one lesson, classroom practice was strikingly similar – pupils working, teacher sitting at the front, pupils going out with problems; occasionally a teacher might perambulate round the room, or call particular pupils out.[17] A teacher's greatest autonomy is conceived of as being inside the classroom yet curriculum changes which had altered their pedagogy, within the previous eighteen months, did not seem to have given rise to different ways of dealing with this,[18] even though there were some teachers who did not agree with the changes. Teachers do, of course, have little power as individuals in an institutional context if a head decides to implement a change which decreases their autonomy, and there might be a reluctance to use even the channels that are open to them because of the importance of the head – not only over career prospects – but also over the day-to-day life of the teachers. The head may also use the existence of new and scaled posts to appoint/promote individuals whose job specification includes implementing or administering the changes which diminish other teachers' autonomy.

Given a large and heterogeneous staff, curriculum packaging allied to individualized pedagogy can be a more coercive form of control than reliance on a unified belief system or assumed homogeneity.[19] The standardized and increased testing of pupils which is part of most of these schemes, ostensibly to test pupil learning, is also a way of monitoring teacher behaviour and making it possible to identify individuals whose practice differs from requirements thus making it difficult for teachers to do otherwise. Young has pointed out that the Schools' Council sponsorship of curriculum packages perpetuates the teacher as a 'transmitter of prepackaged materials'[20] but if the package also contains the method of transmission they are even more limited. One humanities teacher, in describing the scheme, said, 'we're just glorified clerks now'. The growth and adoption of such schemes can therefore be seen as an aspect of deskilling with a new form of control.

Teachers' lack of power in an institutional context is not, however, the only reason for their apparent acceptance of an erosion of classroom autonomy; cultural assumptions are also important. The separation of content, pedagogy and assessment to different groups of specialists is well advanced, and teachers may not be immune to the more general social assumption that 'experts' are always someone else. As Gleeson indicates, the hierarchical conception of curriculum development 'not only assumes a split between "experts" and classroom teachers, but also implies a clear ascendancy of curriculum "theory" over classroom "practice"'.[21] This was illustrated in the school by the fact that there was a senior teacher/curriculum advisor whose job was described as being 'to bring forward to the management and staff ideas about change, and to be aware of current thinking in the Universities etc. about the curriculum' – In other words, the task of 'thinking' about the curriculum had been institutionalized into one organizational position filled by an individual as the 'local expert.' This had an effect on staff as several commented that they did not 'know' anything about the curriculum, and one pointedly said 'He's the only one who knows, he's our think-tank'.

The growth of internally written and assessed examinations such as CSE Mode 3 might be cited as increased teacher control over content and assessment. Whitty, in describing the waning enthusiasm for this examination, says 'It is as if teacher control can only be tolerated for those pupils who have already been defined as "failures" anyway'.[22] Broadfoot also makes the point, 'As the qualification concerned becomes progressively devalued and thus less significant in the allocation of life chances, so it can more safely be left to the informal, more personal responsibility of the teacher.'[23] But it is not only a question of teachers being 'allowed' (or not allowed) to have control, many have internalized and operate traditional notions of 'standards' which they themselves maintain are not as 'high' in, for example, Mode 3. In the school one department had voluntarily gone back to Mode 1 assessment not only for this reason but because 'Mode 3 isn't equivalent to externally assessed exams'. At the same time, therefore, as the teachers were increasing their control over the curriculum of the 'less able' they were also accepting outside control over the assessment of *increasing* numbers of pupils who were being entered for external examination. This process might pave the way for accepting that earlier and earlier in a pupil's school career the content and way of working are legitimately decided elsewhere.

Teachers' responses to deskilling

(a) *Acquiescence*

To explain teachers' acquiescence in terms of structural and cultural constraints is not itself, however, adequate. They way that both structural and cultural assumptions are mediated by individuals and groups, and the mechanisms by which the changes are legitimated, are also important. Account has to be taken of the fact that some teachers embraced the schemes enthusiastically, and one scheme was introduced by teachers themselves.

Mixed ability grouping highlights the heterogeneity of pupils, and some teachers have difficulty in 'controlling' classes in the traditional way of treating them as a homogeneous group. In this context, individualized work schemes can act as a different form of control over pupils. Classroom observations illustrated contrasts between classes where some teachers struggled to maintain dominance in order to 'class teach' and classes in which individualized work predominated and pupil behaviour was often much less of a problem. In the latter kind of lesson teachers only related infrequently to the group as a whole, with most of the interactions being on a one-to-one basis.[24] Of fourteen individualized lessons observed – seven only had group instructions at the beginning and the end, five had these instructions plus four or five commands (all to do with noise), one lesson had a short question and answer session in the middle, and the one unusual humanities lesson mentioned earlier. By minimizing the group aspect of the class through individualized pedagogy it would seem that, for some teachers, control is facilitiated and thus the schemes represent a 'solution' to problems in their day-to-day practice.

Observations suggested that some teachers who had no problems of control in class-taught lessons were also favourable to the schemes. One such teacher, who expressed concern about 'giving the majority of pupils a fair deal', in explaining his enthusiasm for humanities stressed that the teachers who were opposed to it mainly had 'traditional educational ideas, and are nostalgic for the past'. The scheme seemed, therefore, to represent to him a 'progressive' method which would be adopted and implemented by those with progressive ideas. The opposite also pertained, teachers who were not in favour of the schemes felt it labelled them as traditional. For example, a mathematics teacher explained, 'I don't like SMP much – I suppose I'm old fashioned', and a science teacher commented, 'I'm a traditionalist, I don't like individualized work'.

Adoption of such schemes also solved a contradiction of teachers, which was brought about by mixed ability grouping, in a context in which assumptions about 'ability' had not changed. A typical remark from a humanities teacher illustrates this: 'You can't teach mixed ability classes without mixed ability materials. It's OK talking to them, but when you come to give them work to do – it's a problem without an individualized scheme.

This particular teacher was strongly opposed to labelling pupils through streaming, but the label of 'mixed ability' clearly signalled to him that the pupils *were* mixed ability in terms of the traditional labels of 'bright', 'slow learners', etc. The adoption of the scheme therefore enabled this teacher to maintain his opposition to labelling pupils at the same time as allowing him to utilize those labels within the class, where the schemes allowed the pupils themselves to demonstrate which 'category' they were in.

(b) *Ambivalence*

Among many of the teachers who, in theory, agreed with the schemes there was an ambivalence regarding their operation in practice: 'With humanities it's good to know that you've got good materials, and it's good to know the children are getting the benefit of that. It makes life easy for the teacher once it's prepared. But perhaps that creates a loophole for lazy teaching, which does happen.' And one of the teachers who was instrumental in setting up the scheme said:

> In theory, learning should take place by pupils working through the material – but, in practice, I'm not sure if it works like that. I don't think they're learning very well. Our aim is to teach them to learn rather than to teach them content, but it's easier to test content. Ideally, we should assess whether the skills of learning are being acquired and I don't know how to do that.

This ambivalence was leading to increased testing of pupils[25] and a tightening up of the operation of the schemes, as the failure of pupils to learn was considered to be due to inadequate procedures rather than a weakness in the procedures themselves.

(c) *Modification and resistance*

The humanities lesson which had appeared different from the others was taught by a person who was ambivalent towards it, but was not sure what was best for the pupils. In this lesson pupils' individual work was punctuated by teacher requests for named individuals to stand up and 'tell the class what you've found out'. When the teacher was asked a question, the answer was generally addressed to the whole group. The teacher was fulfilling the requirements of the scheme and, at the same time, treating the class as a group and minimizing the individual aspect of the work. Another teacher who was extremely opposed to the scheme, but whose lessons followed the required pattern, confessed that he started all the pupils on Books 2, 3, etc. *together*, because he maintained that pupils lagged behind more because of absenteeism than lack of ability. A mathematics teacher who had reservations about individualized work sometimes gave 'class lessons' if a number of pupils had difficulty with something, and he also ran a lunch–time mathematics club so that he could 'relate to the pupils in a different way'. These are examples of teachers making individual modifications to schemes that had the adherence of most of their colleagues.

The most striking example of resistance was by a whole department of five staff who had been requested to use an external, individualized package and had resisted on the grounds that the language and the level were not right. They were requested to write their own, but never 'got round' to it – however the search was on for a more suitable scheme, which has now been introduced. This group of teachers formed a strong reference group inside the school, and they articulated their dissatisfactions in terms of the management of the organization and their increasing lack of control over their teaching. Three of the staff were actively attempting to leave teaching altogether, and their resistance would eventually take the form (opportunities permitting) of leaving the scene. [. . .]

An appropriate working-class education?

Carter, in discussing the correspondence between schooling and work, maintains that in schools: 'Basic cognitive and analytic skills are imparted, but their use is confined to increasing ability to digest information, understand complex instructions, budget time and the like.'[26]

The humanities units illustrated this vividly. The text directed pupils to books and information kept elsewhere, which was part of the aim of teaching them to 'learn'. But a 'particular answer' was still required, and finding it became a complicated orienteering exercise conducted through the printed word whereby acquiring any content was made more difficult. The emphasis in all the units was on following precise instructions and replicating what someone else had produced, very little creativity was required.[27] This seems to represent an extreme form of the 'banking model' that Freire describes.[28] With regard to mathematics, the teachers explained 'we teach an understanding of maths, not simple arithmetic', and 'we teach concepts, not methods'. The use of flow diagrams to explain equations was cited as an example of this, as pupils were not given an arithmetic formula to work out the answer. Yet flow diagrams can be seen as a visual, rather than arithmetic, method and not necessarily as 'concept formation'. The pupils still had to acquire the 'right answer' and for some of them this was made more difficult.

Several teachers described the majority of pupils as coming from backgrounds 'without books' – yet in humanities they might only handle books if they reached the highest book in a unit, which was usually a library project. Books that were necessary for other tasks were kept at the front of the classroom, or in the library, but most of the work was done with the units – which were bits of paper stapled together. The content of the units had been 'copied' from books, but presented to pupils in a less attractive form. A unit which has been in the pocket for a couple of weeks is far less attractive in visual and tactile terms than a book. Pupils were increasingly, therefore, not being offered at school what it was considered they were not offered at home.

The school had a language programme to extend pupils' vocabulary and literacy skills, but it was operated mainly through the medium of the 'work sheet' – they were actually beginning to *talk* to the pupils less. This concern with the content of language rather than with its use and acquisition is paralleled by the concern with the content and organizational operation of the other curricular schemes at the expense of considering how they are 'received' and operated by pupils. The introduction of individualized work in several subject areas can mean, in practice, that pupils could spend up to one-half of a day with minimal oral and social contact with teachers in the classroom.

The most striking feature of individualized work in the school was not the extent to which it recognized pupils' differences and allowed them to 'progress' at their own pace, but the extent to which it resembled routine occupational work – most people working on a similar, but not identical, process with supervision and monitoring and the worker controlling the 'work rate'. Work of this kind minimized social and oral activities, which may facilitate control over pupils, but does not aid them in developing these skills. Professional occupations usually require a combination of literate, social and oral facilities and if the latter two are not developed in school the importance of a pupil's home background in terms of their previous possession of what Bordieu calls 'cultural capital'[29] becomes even more crucial for their success. At the same time the schemes provide justification for failure[30] as the assumptions embodied in them presume that the able will achieve and this becomes more dependent on pupil action than on teacher intervention. This, too, relieves teachers of the problems associated with previous criticisms concerning underachievement through labelling[31] and teacher expectations[32] – with these schemes the pupils label themselves.

Conclusion

In considering the relationship between the curriculum and social relations, Bernstein maintains that 'Power and control are made substantive in that classification and framing procedures which, in turn, create particular contexts and forms of educational practice which constitute the particular acts of social relations of the school.'[33]

In considering the move towards a stronger 'collection code'[34] that these schemes represent it is important to consider the relationship of these to social relations with the school. It has been suggested that the deskilling of some classroom teachers is paralleled with the reskilling of others into extra-classroom activities (pastoral, administration, curriculum development). Carchedi observes that 'The process of devaluation of labour power splits the stratum of employees into two parts, the largest of which is pushed towards the bottom of the organisational chart.'[35]

Of fourteen teachers in the school who were involved in individualized schemes, four could clearly be identified as 'reskillers' and ten as the majority of future deskilled. The women and non-graduate men seemed to be beginning to comprise the latter category.[36] An important consideration then becomes the extent to which all teachers want to maintain autonomy for, as Freire points out, a pedagogy based on 'banking' creates dependent relations through which *teachers* and pupils come to rely on external factors.[37]

Contradictions in the teacher's position stem from the fact that their own knowledge, skill and expertise have been devalued and yet they are expected to represent the embodiment of knowledge and expertise to pupils in schools and classrooms with hierarchical teaching relationships. If 'alienation' can be inferred from low morale and lack of commitment to the organization, then the deskilled teachers exhibited and reported this – which, in turn, led senior staff to attempt to exert more control, thus escalating the problem.

Eggleston and Gleeson suggest that contradiction in teachers' and pupils' work may 'provide the conditions through which alternative theory and radical consciousness may emerge' and they go on to consider that 'critical alternatives may only be conceived within the interrelationship of teachers and children alienating realities and contradictions'.[38] But dissatisfaction of teachers in this school was not interpreted by the majority of them in terms of structural or institutional contradictions but interpreted at their level of practice, and they 'explained' their problems in terms of 'the kind of pupils we get in this school'. In other words, they articulated their alienation, not with reference to groups above them in the hierarchy, but in terms of the group below. It was the deskilled teachers who interacted less with pupils and stereotyped them more, which would suggest that they would be likely to develop more stringent controls over them than act with pupils to produce 'critical alternatives'.

Dale argues that the central function of schooling – 'to produce a constant flow of workers attuned attitudinally and cognitively to the requirements of the wage labour system' – is achieved primarily through the form rather than the content of schooling.[39] It has been suggested that the form of the packages teaches skills rather than content, and often makes it harder for the pupils to discover what the content is. The importance of a pupil's cultural capital in providing them with the characteristics that the school is not teaching ensures that there will not be an abundant oversupply of qualified labour power at the same time as legitimating the outcome in terms of individual responsibility.

Larsen, in describing the overtraining and under employment of teachers in the United States, refers to them as a 'reserve army' of labour whose occupational position is likely to worsen: 'With their new role in the labour force of advanced capitalist societies, most educated workers also acquire a corresponding vulnerability to their society's contradictions and crises.'[40]

Falling rolls and fiscal crisis not only suggest that increasing control over the majority of teachers will be exercised, but demands that their 'professional duties' be written into their contracts perhaps indicates that this has become an issue, as increased alienation lessens their commitment to the organization and perhaps, ultimately, to the pupils.

Notes and references

1. Durkheim, E. (1977) On education and society, in: Karabel, J. and Halsey, A. H. (eds) *Power and Ideology in Education* (Oxford, Oxford University Press).
2. Braveman, H. (1974) *Labor and Monopoly Capital* (New York, Monthly Review Press).
3. Apple, M. (1980) Curricular form and the logic of technical control: building the possessive individual, in Barton, L., Meighan, R. and Walker, S. (eds) *Schooling, Ideology, and Curriculum Change* (Lewes, Falmer Press).
4. Carchedi, G. (1980) The proletarianisation of employees, in Nichols, T. (ed.) *Capital and Labour* (London, Fontana).
5. See also Habermas, J. *Towards a Rational Society* (London, Heinemann).
6. Whitside, T. and Bernbaum, G. (1979) Growth and decline: dilemmas of a profession, in: Bernbaum, G. (ed.) *Schooling in Decline* (London, Macmillan).
7. Olin Wright, E. (1980) Class and occupation, *Theory and Society* 9, pp. 177–214.
8. Gorz, A. (1977) Technical intelligence and the capitalist division of labour, in: Young, M. and Whitty, G. (eds) *Society, State and Schooling* (Lewes, Falmer Press).
9. *Op. cit.*
10. The publishers of the SRA schemes hold 'conferences' for teachers and advisors

who use, or show an interest in, the product. The teachers are introduced to new packages within the schemes and 'trained' in their use. This raises the problem of the control of both content and form by groups outside education altogether.

11. Bowles, S. and Gintis, H. (1976) *Schooling in Capitalist America* (London, Routledge & Kegan Paul).

12. Apple, M. (1979) *Ideology and Curriculum* (London, Routledge & Kegan Paul).

13. Willis, P. (1978) *Learning in Labour* (Farnborough, Saxon House).

14. Largely, I suspect, because of local and employer concern – articulated through the local press – about school leavers' 'inability to do simple sums'.

15. The concern of this paper is with curriculum form, rather than content, but it is interesting to note that the topics of the units largely consisted of a new way of presenting the topics that were previously taught except for the units produced by the staff who were instrumental in setting up the scheme – their units crossed subject 'boundaries' much more.

16. For discussion on the problematic aspects of education objectives see Inglis, F. (1975) Ideology and the curriculum, in: Inglis, F. (ed.) *Ideology and the Imagination* (Cambridge, Cambridge University Press).

17. The uniformity in mathematics classes was even more marked, although the staff were an extremely hereogeneous group in terms of age, qualifications and experience.

18. I attempted to check how 'usual' the lessons I had observed were, by eliciting other teachers' and pupils' descriptions of the practices of individual teachers, and I did further observation if there seemed to be a chance that the lessons I had observed were special performances for my benefit.

19. Bernstein, B. (1971) Open schools – open society? in Cosin, B. (ed.) *School and Society* (London, Routledge & Kegan Paul).

20. Young, M. (1976) The rhetoric of curriculum development, in Whitty, G. and Young, M. (eds) *Explorations in the Politics of School Knowledge* (Driffield, Nafferton Books).

21. Gleeson, D. (1978) Curriculum development and social change: towards a reappraisal of teacher action, *Journal of Further and Higher Education* 2, pp. 41–51.

22. Whitty, G. (1976) Teachers and examiners, in: Whitty, G. and Young, M. (eds) *Explorations in the Politics of School Knowledge* (Driffield, Nafferton Books).

23. Broadfoot, P. (1979) *Assessment, Schools and Society* (London, Methuen).

24. See also Edwards, A. and Furlong, V. (1978) *The Language of Teaching* (London, Heinemann).

25. See Karier, C. (1976) Testing for order and control in the corporate liberal state, in Dale, R. *et al.* (eds) *Schooling and Capitalism* (London, Routledge & Kegan Paul).

26. Carter, M. (1976) Contradiction and correspondence: analysis of the relation of schooling to work, in: Carnoy, M. and Levin, H. (eds) *The Limits of Educational Reform* (London, Longman).

27. In one fairly typical Unit, the tasks involved the following:
    (a) reading sixteen named pages in a particular book;
    (b) working out a calculation;
    (c) copying three pictures from a book;
    (d) drawing a comic strip of a named story;
    (e) joining up numbers to form a diagram;
    (f) finding four words, on named pages, to fit into spaces, in sentences.

28. Freire, P. (1972) *Pedagogy of the Oppressed* (Harmondsworth, Penguin).
29. Bourdieu, P. (1973) Cultural reproduction and social reproduction, in Brown, R. (ed.) *Knowledge, Education and Cultural Change* (London, Tavistock).
30. See Bowles, S. (1976) Unequal education and the reproduction of the social division of labour, in: Dale, R. *et al.* (eds) *Schooling and Capitalism* (London, Routledge & Kegan Paul).
31. Hargreaves, D. (1967) *Social Relations in a Secondary School* (London, Routledge & Kegan Paul).
32. Rosenthal, R. and Jacobson, L. (1968) *Pygmalion in the Classroom* (London, Holt, Rinehart & Winston).
33. Bernstein, B. (1975) Relations between education and production, in: Bernstein, B. (ed.) *Class, Codes and Control. Vol. 3* (London, Routledge & Kegan Paul).
34. Bernstein, B. (1975) On the classification and framing of educational knowledge, in Bernstein, B. (ed.) *Class, Codes and Control, Vol. 3* (London, Routledge & Kegan Paul).
35. *Op. cit.*
36. Research, on a part-time basis, is still continuing and developments of this aspect will be noted.
37. *Op. cit.*
38. Eggleston, J. and Gleeson, D. (1977) Curriculum innovation and the context of the school, in: Gleeson, D. (ed.) *Identity and Structure: Issues in the Sociology of Education* (Driffield, Nafferton Books).
39. Dale, R. (1977) Implications of the rediscovery of the hidden curriculum for the sociology of teaching, in Gleeson, D. (ed.) *Identity and Structure: Issues in the Sociology of Education* (Driffield, Nafferton Books).
40. Larson, M. (1980) Proletarianization and educated labour, *Theory and Society* 9, pp. 131–71.

8

Teacher 'burnout' and institutional stress

Sara Freedman

'Deskilling' is a term recently coined to explain a new type of work situation. From its traditional base in factories and filing pools, this process of deskilling or 'proletarianization' has been observed spreading to the professions, particularly ones that are female-saturated or are now more hospitable to women joining their ranks. In all of these professions we now see women and minorities ghettoized into the less lucrative, lower paying and routinized areas while white men continue to dominate the remunerative and powerful sectors.

In addition, new positions within these fields are being created. Even though all nurses, lawyers, engineers and social workers share the same title, a portion of them now manage the others. In female-saturated occupations some are recruited into those professions with the express purpose of having them fill those new positions. The two key proposals of the Commissions on Excellence – the creation of a 'master teacher' slot and the allocation of merit pay – reflect attempts to restructure teaching along similar lines in the belief that these incentives will recruit and retain better teachers.

It is important to note that the deskilling of the labour force isn't just happening to workers 'out there', or to the students in the classrooms. A part of the workforce also labours in schools, and the deskilling of that labour force – teachers – is occurring in ways that affect that particular group of workers as well as those they train.

> When I was a kid in the fifties I went to a strict, traditional school. The teachers were thirty- and forty-year veterans. They never varied from plans written many years ago. In September the same pictures were posted on the blackboard. The construction paper borders were replaced each year but the paper faded early in November and was a dull sheen by March. I loved those teachers. They conformed to many of the

stereotypes of longtime women schoolmarms – stern, swift in justice, unimaginative, inflexible, sure of their methods. They praised the docile, hard-working, quick-to-grasp pupil and were alternately punishing or neglectful of the silent majority. The wicked were quickly subdued.

In fifth grade a spate of male teachers arrived, returning GIs straight out of college, who had a fertile field in the burgeoning school industry. They were different – young, creative, with lots of energy. They introduced SCIENCE!, giant papier-mâché animals, and new seating patterns. We all wanted to be in their classrooms. Most of them soon moved to other positions in the quickly expanding system – principal, science co-ordinator, creative arts department. The children were left with the old women teachers – and with a disdain of old women teachers.

When I began teaching ten years ago, I had a clear image of the kind of teacher I wanted to be – Mr Williams, the fifth grade teacher who had introduced the most daring educational experiments and who worked tirelessly, coming to school on Saturday. He was the closest person I actually knew to the figures portrayed by Jonathan Kozol, Herb Kohl and John Holt in those books coming out of the sixties. And I managed. I worked tirelessly, tried all kinds of experiments, came in on Saturdays. It was exhilarating – for the first few years. But as the years wore on and on, I began to notice that the drive was being replaced by myriad frustrations. Many teachers who arrived with me on the crest of the sixties' waves, felt tethered in place. We became less experimental, angrier, more isolated. I was turning into my present perception of one of them – those female teachers of long ago who worked year after year in a closed space, each class merging into the next, stale ideas, frayed construction paper.[1]

'Burnout' is the term now popular to describe the phenomenon. The term has begun to appear regularly in the magazines directed to the teaching profession to explain widespread feelings among teachers of inadequacy, listlessness and decreased dedication to teaching. It is important to question the implications of using such a term to explain teacher frustration. 'Burnout' implies that at some point a finite amount of energy has been consumed. The number of articles and workshops that explore the issue of teacher burnout has greatly increased during the past few years. This is occurring at the same time in which many teachers face layoffs and a shrinking job market. The coining of the term 'burnout' at the same time that teachers are threatened with the loss of their jobs serves to direct the focus of each teacher's growing anger away from a critical analysis of schools as institutions to a preoccupation with her own failure.

No one changes from a dynamic teacher into a conservative pedagogue for mysterious personal reasons. Schools as institutions create contradictory feelings and demand contradictory actions from teachers. The rhetoric surrounding the institution of public education often proves to be in direct conflict with the function a teacher finds herself required to perform. The dissonance between the goals teachers presume they are striving for and the realities they encounter may be more or less pronounced depending on where they teach, but the contradictory requirements of schools have always existed. Attempts to improve schools offered today, as in the past, do not address the contradictions – the inherent barriers to the growth of teachers within the structure of schools. Rather the solutions buttress the 'blame the victim' approach. This approach defines the problem as an aggregate of disaffected or incapable teachers whose deficiencies are seen as personal rather than as a reflection of the failure of the educational system to grapple with and confront these contradictory demands. Examples of the main conflicts inherent in public education are:

Teachers work in an institution which supposedly prepares its clients for adulthood, but which views those entrusted with this task, the teachers themselves, as incapable of mature judgement:

> When our principal is talking to a first, or second, or third grade teacher, . . . I find that she's repeating directions one, two, or three times, almost as you would to a first-, second-, or third-grader. When you get higher up, fourth, fifth, and sixth, the directions are not repeated as much, but they're more done in like an outline form as you would give to kids who are a little bit older. (AA, 1980)[2]

When the teachers' work has created a major programme their contribution appears publicly as negligible and secondary. Their isolation from each other and the need to funnel any request and information up through the levels of the hierarchy and back down again rather than directly to each other has not allowed them to use their unique knowledge, of classroom life, which they alone possess, as a basis for determining system-wide, or even school-wide policies.

> After working for months on the fourth grade reading curriculum, we brought it up to the Assistant Superintendent. We had put a blanket statement at the beginning stating that we would assume that the teachers would be responsible by consulting the textbooks and other resource materials and their expertise and so on and so forth. . . . He made it quite clear that he didn't think they were capable of going over anything by themselves, finding the materials, using them appropriately. . . . We're smart enough to do all the busy work but not smart enough to carry it out. (D, 1980).

Professional development courses for teachers are frequently planned by others in the school hierarchy and dictated to the teacher whose concerns and opinions are disregarded. Faculty meetings, which could provide a forum for issues and ideas, a place where group discussion and decision-making might be encouraged, are more likely to be organized for the presentation of previously made decisions to the assembled teaching staff.

> Every Tuesday is a half day for faculty meeting. The boss does all the talking. They are just sit-and-listen types of things. . . . If he asks for suggestions on things, it usually is put like this, 'Now this is what I have planned. If there's anybody who wishes to disagree or there's anybody who doesn't care to go along with that. . . .' That might not be his exact words, but he really doesn't care to open anything to discussion. People sit there with a deadpan look because they don't want to commit themselves, you know, get themselves into any kind of hot water, a little afraid sometimes, depends on who the principal is. (E, 1979)
> [. . .]

Education is an institution which holds that questioning and debating, risk and error develop one's thinking ability. But learning situations are structured to lead to one right answer, and both teachers and students are evaluated in ways that emphasize only quantifiable results.

> The principal was a marvelous person for handling the paper work, organizing the building, but when it came right down to the individual child, I think sometimes he missed the point a little. Once I remember he came into the classroom and said, 'Look at that, and that, and that'. He was pointing to the reading scores of three children. And these children were so, so unbelievably slow. I thought they were doing beautifully. They really sustained their interest to the end of the year and slow children don't *do* that. And I was enthusiastic. I was pushing a new program in reading for all it was worth. I can remember feeling awful, just awful when he said that. I felt I had been put down, a terrible put-down. I used to work like a son of a gun, always that push to do your best. And I felt awful. I don't think I dwelt on it forever, but I can remember getting feelings of like what a thankless job, you know. Really (E, 1980)

A teacher who works day by day alongside a youngster knows which words a child will more likely stumble over, which words must be introduced in several different contexts and which stories excite interest or increase the shuffling of feet and emergency trips to the bathroom.

> I can learn something by the papers that a kid turns in but I learn more by watching them do it, and that's particularly useful with kids. . . . When kids really know something, I know it. They have a confidence about it. When they do it, they make the comment, 'Oh, boy, I love doing it', or 'this is easy'. . . . I have to hear that or see that. (B, 1979)

Parents, school committee members, researchers and future employers would like to have the same information the teacher has without spending six hours every day in the classroom reading stories and learning times tables. If the teacher's own description of the child's progress is dismissed as too biased and personal, the only way to communicate what a child knows to those outside the classroom is to abstract that experience by quantifying the results.

A couple of years ago they developed a reading checklist in this district. Each year you are supposed to check off what the child has accomplished during that year in your classroom. They developed a math checklist, and we have to give what is called a test of essential skills in reading, and that's supposed to measure their progress. Then we enter all the stuff on the checklist. And they have these little punch cards that during the year you're supposed to punch out each time they've learned something in math, and then you fill out the little checklist at the end of the year. I piloted one in writing last year, and writing is too subjective to evaluate in that way. All of these things are absolute killers for teachers, and personally, I don't think they are valid. (Y, 1981)

Once she has entered the child's progress into her book or on the blackboard, both the teacher and her pupils are easily understood and evaluated. The desire to nurture and support students, a major reason for many to enter teaching, is transformed into the drive to keep each student on a predetermined grade level.

My principal gets upset because he doesn't see enough low science and social studies marks that should correlate well with reading. . . . He complains about this in general . . . if they don't read well, how could they be doing well in science and social studies. He's also the same person who told us that . . . if they're in the eighth or ninth stanine that means they're an A or B student and their report card marks should reflect this. (C, 1980)

The teacher, under attack for failing to help children reach arbitrary grade level goals, accedes to the greater wisdom of the commercial test makers and the research academics. Once started on the road to quantification, the method becomes addictive, even for attributes other than achievement.

I went to a very exciting convention about learning style. They have been doing a lot of research on it and finally validated a reliable test so that you can give it to kids so that you can determine learning style. . . . It's a multiple choice test of a hundred questions, just very simple questions. . . . It's like the Stanford Diagnostic that tells you exactiy what you need to know about a kid and all. Even if you did it yourself you wouldn't really figure it out – what the computer can do, put all the little things together. (F, 1979)

Principals and school board members then use the same types of evaluation created by the researcher to evaluate the teachers. The new 'objective' type of teacher evaluations that have recently been introduced into the schools are examples of such quantitative methods. They take great pains to code and enumerate the type, number and direction of the interactions of the teacher with her pupils within the classroom. She is not evaluated outside the classroom because presumably these contributions to the school as a whole, enhancing the sense of community of the school, are not properly considered her responsibility or more strongly, not really 'her business'.

When she helps a teacher reorganize her classroom, when she 'takes in' a difficult child so that teacher and child can have a rest from each other, she is simply being nice. She is not being 'professional' and no professional benefits will accrue.

What is left for the evaluator to write down are the concrete manifestations of the interactions of the teacher with her pupils that can be observed by the examiner himself. Only those moments become part of the meticulously documented, seemingly exhaustive evaluation of the teacher. It seems as though the examiner is riveted to the teacher, but it is actually the teacher who, in a more important way, is focused on the principal. What the principal does not see or is not done for his eyes becomes irrelevant, even counterproductive.

> My principal says, you know, he could look in the room and in one second he knows everything that's going on. Well, yeah, he might get an idea of what's going on, but that doesn't mean it's the right idea, and you know, sometimes it's not . . . One day . . . I came back to my room after dittoing off papers, and there I am sorting out my papers out on the table, and all of a sudden I realize there's a presence in my room – all my kids are all at art or music or something. And I look up, and there's the principal sitting in my room, with an evaluation sheet . . . writing down – he's looking at the questions on the board, he's looking at the bulletin boards I've got up, he's looking at everything around and he wrote me up a detailed evaluation based on what he saw in my classroom when my kids weren't there and I wasn't there. (C, 1980)

The more quantitative measures and national exams are used to evaluate the teacher, the more she will feel the need to use such quantitative methods to judge her students and other teachers. She is now the in-class representative of the national norms and country-wide bell curves. Once she has entered the child's progress into her books or on the blackboard, both she and her pupils are assured to be easily understood and evaluated.

The schools have the responsibility of developing the whole child. But the structure of the institution constricts the types of behaviour acceptable in teachers and pupils.

Teachers, especially those in less affluent districts, often feel that they and their colleagues are encouraged to show only a few facets of their personalities within the confines of school.

> I don't think that there are people who are really close. I can just not picture one teacher going to another one in tears. I really can't. There's no one to run to. Not just for me. People really just don't get that close. And I think part of it is working in an impersonal system. You do what the boss tells you. You don't have choices. You file at 10:10, whether you like it or not. . . . Everything is impersonally handled – time, bells. (A, 1979)

The message quickly gets across that order and quiet are the primary goals, leaving teachers to stifle, in themselves and their students, any activities that might be disruptive.

Teachers of working-class children are not surrounded by the many signs of their pupils' affluence – and probable future success – that bolster the teachers' and the students' sense of worth. It is difficult for such a teacher to justify 'developing the whole child' when the local paper publishes yearly standardized test scores. The teacher's ability to identify with her job and with her students is threatened.

> When I changed from kindergarten to first grade teaching, it was a whole new scene. I just seemed to take on a first grade personality. I think you just become a different type of person because you're more instructor and you don't have time to develop their personalities. The whole point in kindergarten was to develop this child so he's happy and likes school. If he's uncomfortable about something in his life, you try to make him loved. You get to first grade, forget it. I haven't got time for you. You've got to learn to read. You've got to finish that book before the second grade teacher sees you. . . . Somebody raises their hand, in the kindergarten you would listen. You're hoping to develop their language, and you listen. . . . You get to first grade, it was 'Put your hand down. That's all the stories for now. Pay attention. Sit up.' And they go to talk to you, 'I don't want to hear your story. We're lining up. You have to go out. The clock doesn't wait for anybody. Be quiet. Be quiet. We have to leave the room.' A whole new emphasis. (E, 1980)

The definition of 'skills for life' varies according to the social class of the school and the teacher. A teacher in a working-class school:

> In my school it's a luxury to think about those things – inter-personal relationships, how to encourage spontaneity – we have to teach the basic skills for life. Basic skills, that's the most important thing I teach them. Reading and math because those are the tools to succeed in life, you know, to help you in life. (H, 1980)

[. . .]

Ironically, these teachers who want to provide 'enrichment activities' – creative writing, improvization dramatics – must increase the pace and pressure of the classroom in order to cover the real work already established by the basal reader. The extras can be added only by a furious winding-up of prescribed work.

Education is charted with the social task of providing equal opportunity for the school-age population of a pluralistic, multi-level society. But the structure of schools emphasizes comparative worth and increases competition not only among the pupils but also among parents, teachers, and administrators.

> We never had any administrative encouragement to work together. There was never any time, there was never any made, there were very few group decisions. It's a very individual thing, if you found someone you wanted to share materials with, you did it on your own. No, nobody has ever encouraged that route. . . . It only comes from the individual teachers in our building. None of it is encouraged by the principal. (D, 1979)

[. . .]

For teachers caught up in the demands of school, there is no time to think about the divisions among the staff and how these divisions often undermine the school's atmosphere and educational effectiveness. Resentment and competition can split teachers along many lines – older vs younger, traditional vs innovative, classroom teacher vs specialist, those whose jobs are 'safe' vs those threatened by lay-offs, those teachers requested by parents vs those who are not, those who are given aides vs those who aren't.

> We have to have kids till the last day of school. Why doesn't everybody have to have kids? Now people who are specialists in tutoring kids have to do a lot of testing and writing of reports. We have to write reports four times a year. We have report cards. I have to write my core. I have three of those to write. I realized I was really pissed. (B, 1979)

The competition among children in the classroom and among teachers in the school building is often echoed in the antagonistic feelings fostered among schools in the district.

> The superintendent made it very clear that the quote-unquote more aggressive schools would get funding and materials for the programs they wanted. . . . He said, 'The more aggressive buildings will get the money. If there's something you want to do in your building and you can give us a good reason for it, then we may be able to make it available to you.' Some schools took advantage of that, like the _____ School. They have a lot of parents who know how to write proposals and they always get their way. (W, 1981)

Public education is charged with upholding democracy by developing an electorate capable of critical thinking and the intelligent balancing of alternatives; but teachers are required to pursue this goal by increasingly mechanical, technical means.

> The principal started another programme in kindergarten that he wanted to adopt, working with small groups, using electronic equipment like head sets and things, very carefully planned individualized instruction with the children. He was structuring, planning fifteen minute segments. He wanted to try something new. We would have a half-hour of concentrated teaching in small groups. . . . So you worked on listening to sounds or you worked on your workbooks in small groups and then after fifteen minutes it was [clap hands] change groups. And no matter what, you had to stop at that point. There was one little girl, who had had kidney surgery, in my room who wasn't learning and had a lot of problems and I felt I couldn't sit and do the work like that. And I remember one day when I said, 'You know, she just had kidney surgery', he said, 'I'm tired of hearing about her kidney surgery. I'm tired of hearing emotional things blamed for reading problems.' (H, 1981)

In poorer and working-class schools, where standardized test scores provide the major indicator of how much a pupil has learnt, the teaching of discrete mechanical skills takes on primary importance. Expertise is seen to lie in the books, not in the teacher. These tools are seen as the crucial determining factor in the education or miseducation of the child. If the teacher adheres strictly to the text, the child should learn.

> We can't use any supplementary materials until we've finished all the textbook work. . . . I can show you the memo. [The memo read: 'Teachers are reminded that only materials found in the adopted textbooks can be duplicated. Supplementary materials are not to be stenciled and duplicated. It is the feeling of the administration that materials in the textbooks are adequate and must be completed before other materials are to be introduced in the curriculum.'] Even the kids who are repeating go back through the same materials. . . . Last week I was teaching a reading lesson and the story was about Galileo. Now I have a wonderful ditto about Galileo and telescopes. But it's from the science unit, so I couldn't use it. The administrator's aide controls the ditto machine and files all the dittos that are run off. If we have any supplementary dittos, they have to be cleared first.[3]

[. . .]
Retaining teachers then becomes a question of choosing the person who will most strictly adhere to that mechanical solution, rather than the one who will weigh and discuss, choose and implement.

> I'm realizing that the other third grade teacher who is my colleague, with whom I exchange children for reading, has what is presumably the

middle group. I have presumably the top and bottom group. I find out that her top group is almost where my top group is, and we've been on our book since the beginning of the year, and she didn't start it until just two months ago. It makes me feel that maybe I'm holding these kids back, but consensus is that these books are pretty hard. They've got some rather intriguing stories, ones that are not just run of the mill ordinary kinds of stories, with a lot of metaphorical language and different kinds of fiction and fantasy. We do a lot with that sort of thing. I just feel really that I don't know if I'm doing the right thing in spending all that time on each story and having the children do a lot of things with each story. She's obviously bombing through the book. A story a day, I guess. It makes me nervous that somebody is going to say I'm not a very good teacher. I really feel as though my kids are getting a great deal out of their reading. But it's one of those things that doesn't look good on paper. (Y, 1980)

The roots of these conflicts have never been addressed within the context of analysing classroom issues. Rather, critics have focused teachers' attention on the failure of the individual – the teacher, the student, and the student's parent – and his or her inability to adjust to the established system. Understanding how life inside the classroom is crucially affected by the structure of the school system as a whole is considered counter-productive to a teacher's career.

Many teachers are hired to do their thing in the classroom, but that's as far as they're supposed to go. They're not really part of policy or curriculum in very meaningful ways. I think that's what a lot of the isolation is about. I certainly have the feeling – I know I'm not alone in this – there's a lot of futility in that and frustration. (B, 1979)

If every teacher would only be perfect – responding fairly, efficiently, and effectively with infinite wisdom and tact to every child and exigency – we would have the perfect system. Teachers know that they are incapable of such persistent perfection. They often react in ways that increase their sense of isolation and reinforce their powerlessness in the institution. When confronted with stereotyped choices that deny or obscure the conflicting demands placed on teachers, teachers frequently lash out in angry denial while internalizing the negative message. They are told, and have come to believe, they have 'burnt out'.

I had found that toward the middle of last year I was beginning to feel – dead. And I was beginning to feel frustrated and I was beginning to feel sort of like this was a drudgery. And I had never felt like that before – I mean, classroom teaching was my thing. I really loved it. Then this year coming into the situation and getting such a difficult class, I started off the year with a tremendous sense of frustration. I thought, 'My God, what am I going to do with these kids?' I kept thinking, 'I'm not really, really happy with what's happening in this class and I wonder how much of it is my own fault'. (W, 1981)

The present-day discovery of teacher dissatisfaction as a recently recognized phenomenon obscures the fact that the basic contradictory demands on teachers have been present since the doors of the brick grammar school first closed behind a staff of schoolmarms, a male principal and a rush of youngsters.

The modern concept of 'burnout' is the natural result of the new ideology of professionalism which encourages teachers to see themselves as more powerful than they actually are and, therefore, more responsible alone to correct complex societal and institutional dilemmas. What has been labelled 'burnout' is, in fact, anger and frustration. Today, the more publicized 'burnt-out' teacher has come to represent the 'true identity' of all dedicated teachers. The concept encompasses even those who haven't burnt out. If burnout is the natural end to a dedicated teacher, those who have managed to survive are seen as callous and self-serving.

The two labels of 'burnout' and 'deadwood' further divide the teaching workforce. Younger teachers or those still with other career options are told they have worked too hard and have therefore 'burnt out'. Older teachers are told they aren't working hard enough and have become 'deadwood'. The fact that both are demoralized points to similar concerns, but the labels obscure the commonalities.

'Burnout', however, does not come from overtaxing one's intellectual and mental capacities. Burnout comes from not being able to use those abilities to handle difficult emotional and managerial problems. These problems are often the result of administrators' analysis of a situation far removed from their personal and immediate responsibility. The establishment of the master teacher position which would remove teachers from classrooms to oversee other teachers would add another level of managers who are separated from the rank and file.

> In short, the paradox that to become increasingly professional in teaching means increasingly subjugating personal values and interests to system maintenance functions tends not to be confronted except in isolation. With rare exception, professional organizations that have followed the American labor union model for organization and action continue to ignore quality of life issues.[4]

The reward offered to master teachers – removal from the classroom and a chance to participate in curriculum development, supervision, and decision-making or institutional concerns – confirms the true confinement of being inside the classroom and the dearth of possibilities for classroom teachers to influence the more content and structurally oriented areas.

In contrast, those who exhibit managerial, that is distant, 'objective' relationships with colleagues and students, would have the edge in being chosen master teacher, much as they now have the edge on being chosen principal.

> You have to make yourself very well known to get any recognition in this system. I've decided that. You have to belong to the teachers' union and the negotiating team and negotiate with these people. Then I think they get a feeling for your strengths and weaknesses and get to know you. . . . I was just thinking the other day, 'Who are the busy little bees that do all the dirty work, put together minimum competency standards and tests, do all the background work for curriculum decisions? Women. Who's on the negotiating team? Men.' And I think if you don't do those things there is no other way they get to know you because they certainly don't go in classrooms. No one would ever recognize you for that. And that's what I've done all my life and I don't think they know me from a hole in the wall. Or if they did, it doesn't really count.

These reports also deplore the level of intelligence of teachers, particularly those presently entering the field. They do not investigate the absence within teaching of opportunities for exhibiting this characteristic. This critique of teachers is not new, despite the nostalgic assertion of the majority of these reports that teachers just aren't what they used to be. It may be that intelligent women were lured into teaching as these reports contend, but it wasn't their intelligence and the promise of being able to use it that was seen as an effective hook. To the teachers themselves, their now much vaunted intelligence was never mentioned. What was emphasized was their 'natural' ability for working with children, a trait that earned teaching the label 'women's true profession'. The emphasis on the nurturing qualities of good teaching – empathy, patience – made irrelevant any discussion of the intellectual abilities of teachers.

Intelligence is only the latest in a string of attributes reported to be lacking – each attribute having been seen at the time of its exposure as part of the essential make-up of a good teacher. Rather than investigating how the system often deadens teachers, these reports concentrate on the individual, who alone in her classroom creates the soft pockets of civilization. Focusing criticism on the individual person, who – for different reasons at different moments in history – 'just shouldn't teach' or is not of master teacher quality, perpetuates the idea that it is the individual alone who must make a difference, or that by being the right kind of person a teacher will be exempt from the failures others have experienced. There is no recognition within these reports of the structural barriers to enhancing educational potential for either student or teacher and no incentive to look at how the institutional framework of schools frequently creates stagnation while punishing attempts to challenge and improve bad school practices.

Notes and references

1. Freedman, S. (1979) Personal journal.
2. Letters are used to indicate specific teachers interviewed by the Boston Women's Teachers' Group. Single letters indicate teachers interviewed bi-weekly over a year's teaching schedule. Double letters indicate teachers interviewed bi-monthly over a school year calendar.
3. McCutcheon, G. (1980) 'How Do Elementary School Teachers Plan?' in *The Elementary School Journal* 8: 27.
4. Bullough, Jr, R. (1982) 'Paradox and Professionalism', in *The Educational Forum*, Winter, p. 208.

9

Subject teachers under stress

Bede Redican

Introduction

Much of the debate about educational arrangements, like the policy decisions that eventually determine to some extent how schooling is experienced, are carried out at a distance from the process itself. Armchair rhetoric about the distribution of educational opportunity and more recently about the assessment of both pupil and teacher performance, a rhetoric that has emerged in contrasting perceptions of the economic climate, has questioned the simple assumption that education is a good thing in itself and criticized our inept management of the process. It has largely ignored the lived experience of those teachers daily involved in the schooling process. The purpose here is to explore beyond the secret garden of the curriculum, beyond the externally imposed parameters of school size and resource allocation, and to examine 'the back room of school administrative procedures'. The focus is the career and workplace perceptions of teachers as individuals or as groups with similar conditions of service, and the internal dynamics of the school as perceived and sustained by them. How do they see the reality of schooling from the inside, 'the back region', and what tactics do they employ to chance or sustain procedures that they regard as worthwhile, despite the external parameters determined by economists, politicians or armchair theorists? Such tactics may have important consequences for both educational distribution and standards of performance. An examination of this kind requires form and this is sought by adopting ethnography as an appropriate research method[1] and by seeking to operationalize some aspects of a social theory proposed by Giddens.[2]

The data on which this chapter is based is drawn from an ethnographic study of two large comprehensive schools. Ethnography is selected as the research method because it involves participation in the lived experience of those under study. It asks the researcher to recognize the reflexive character of the research and it involves the watching, listening and recording activities required to collect data. The definition of ethnography, preferred here, is the broader definition that includes a wide range of sources of information – in fact collects whatever data are available to throw light upon the issues involved.[3] This study includes both interviews and participant observation, and it explicitly recognizes that all social research has a reflexive character. We can neither escape the world in order to study it nor avoid having an effect upon it in the study process. No data may be regarded as 'pure' data, and consequently a more realistic aim, adopted here, is to seek to interpret the data obtained, acknowledging the foreshadowed problems, anxieties and biases, the surrounding developing theory and the limitations implicit in the interview interactions and in the recording of observed episodes of situated interaction.

As suggested by Giddens,[4] the concept of 'region', Goffman's front and back regions, is pertinent to small-scale institutional analysis of the kind employed here. The researcher must be aware that the setting of encounters (in the front room) may be purposively arranged to hide the potentially compromising or dangerous features of such encounters. The penetration of such time/space setting is a fundamental part of the analysis. Foreshadowed problems, those issues anticipated on the basis of reading and experience, may emerge as real issues or as merely part of a carefully sustained legend. The objective here is neither to collect relevant data to test a hypothesis, nor to confirm assumptions by imposing ideas on the data, but to seek to remain anthropologically strange. This is sought by acknowledging aspects of the reflexive character of the research while searching for that penetrating collaboration or contradiction, the issues that emerge substantiated during the process. [. . .]

The ethnographic context

Two Midland comprehensive schools were selected for the collection of ethnographic data. Both schools were comprehensive schools, created by the amalgamation of grammar and secondary modern schools and had accepted a comprehensive school intake for seven years at the time of this research in 1981–3. They were mixed with approximately 1,100 pupils and fifty-six staff in each school at the start of the two-year research period. Access was negotiated through the head teacher, and the programme of interviews and observation periods through the deputy heads responsible for timetabling. All staff interviews took place in the spring terms, during staff free periods. While this may be initially seen as an imposition upon the scarce free time staff have available for planning and marking, it did guarantee that they would not have to 'cover' for absent teachers during that period. There were two clearly defined objectives. On the one hand, staff were to be interviewed formally and informally and, on the other, I was to observe and record incidents of situated interaction. In almost every case, teachers welcomed an opportunity to discuss their problems in a situation where confidentially and trust had been established, where no consequences for future conditions of work or promotion prospects were involved and where a sympathetic but informed ear was available. Confidentiality was stressed and the interview always took place in a private office, prep-room or work area. The object was to ensure that teachers felt relaxed on their own territory and safe from intrusion. Throughout, an attempt was made to minimize the inhibitors of communication, in particular, the competing time demands, ego threatening or embarrassing questions or traumatic incidents.[5] Initial questions and reactions throughout the interview sought to allow the interviewee to search for meaning in his or her own experience and to see the exercise as valuable for the future of the profession and the quality of the education available to children.

My second objective was to observe, record and analyse a selection of routine or unusual incidents of situated social interaction. This process has three distinct parts, registering, interpreting and recording. The actual recording inevitably takes place retrospectively. In this significant time gap – normally three hours or more, the observer recreates the event and assesses the various participant attitudes and behaviours. There is the search for collaborative evidence, the checking of his own perceptions with those of others. The final account for analysis is consequently a collection of what was registered and what became more apparent during the interpretation and recording process.[6] We therefore only reach an approximate 'reality', the event is potentially distorted and misinterpreted. The presence of the observer means that movements are made and orientations are developed towards him which would not otherwise have occurred.[7] The challenge is to be fully aware of reflexivity, to share the lived experience of staff, but to observe and record their behaviour as objectively as possible.

The emergent problem

As the fieldwork progressed, the evidence from both interviews and participant observations indicated that teachers were aware of the reality of so-called pastoral staff activities, of the increasing power and influence of such post holders and of their drift into supervisory staff roles. The legend may be that so-called pastoral posts are filled by staff who are more concerned with teaching in the broadest sense, but in reality their occupants drift from petty administration, discipline and control, to the supervision of both pupils and staff in the pursuit of overall school objectives. The challenge was to present sufficient evidence to substantiate this teacher knowledgeability and to propose how the supervisory staff used communication, power and sanction to bring about and sustain this superiority. Sufficient evidence would include a demonstration that the split between those teachers who 'manage' and those who 'do' is not only a teacher perception but also a teachers' representation of how things actually are embedded in the normal rules and procedures of the school. Teachers both anticipate that this is the reality of the backroom and that they have to contend with and actually behave in recognition of it. Necessarily, the interview data [. . .] must show that those who hold pastoral posts actually carry out traditional management tasks and use management strategies. Managers in any organization plan, organize, arrange staffing, direct staff, coordinate, report and budget.[8] Managers take precautions to distance themselves from accountability for 'doing', taking steps to separate conception from execution. They seek to interact with staff in a manner that promotes their superiority, that consolidates their position as capable of legitimately telling others what to do, even or especially, in areas where they obviously can do it themselves and in an occupation where the autonomy of the teacher of the classroom is high.

The interview data and the implications emerging from it

This section sets out the evidence on which the drift into two career ladders is claimed to have moved from a foreshadowed problem to a substantiated emerging issue in these two large schools. First, teachers are demonstrated to be aware of the fact of promotion opportunities for supervisory positions and to be aware that such positions are supervisory and designed to assist the head with the administration of the school on a day-to-day basis. Second, it is sought to demonstrate that supervisory staff actually use management strategies in their daily interactions with relatively powerless classroom subject staff.

(a) Promotion for 'pastoral' staff
It is obviously important to know the teaching background of pastoral staff even though it is seven years since the schools became comprehensive and made the initial appointments to fit staff from grammar and secondary modern schools to the new larger institutions. During the two years 1981–3 covered by the field research in those two schools, there were fifteen internal promotions and six appointments from external applicants. Thirteen of these internal promotions were attached to pastoral and administrative responsibilities. Ten of the total staff promotions and appointments were restricted to staff who already held administrative staff posts and five were for young staff making their initial move from scale one. Only five staff were appointed and one promoted for classroom subject teaching. One of the staff described the reason for his decision to apply for a year tutor's post:

I did grab a pastoral post because I really needed to have a scale two, but it meant that I teach my subject less well. To some extent I haven't time to do justice to my pastoral job either. A lot of it is routine administration. The really interesting problems do not conveniently arise when I have my free periods.

Not only did his promotion lead to a perceived reduction in his teaching effectiveness but there is a hint that the two 'jobs' are incompatible and that you need more 'free periods' to cope. It is apparent also that it is not the type of pastoral care that Marland considers an integral part of teaching that is perceived as the new role requirement but the much more extra-curricular counselling, guidance and supervision.[9] The reluctance to leave the real job of teaching was further emphasized by another new year tutor: 'I enjoy my teaching . . . but to get on here, you have to sell your soul to the administration . . . I don't think I would have got any promotion unless I had accepted an administration job.' Senior staff, too, were aware of the need to 'sell your soul' to the administration. 'It is a pity scale four or sometimes senior teacher is the limit for a teacher who really wants to make the connection, subject knowledge – pupil talent – psychic reward' (Head of Department, scale 4). Even a deputy head stated that to get beyond a scale four, a subject teacher must offer to take on some administrative task. However, it may well be too late for a scale four head to switch career ladders. There may simply be too few subject specialists left or more likely the 'pastoral staff' career ladder may have already been colonized by teachers who lack good subject knowledge qualifications. At one of the schools only two of the seven senior administrative staff had graduate qualifications in the curriculum subject areas and all seven had teachers certificates plus additional education degree qualifications. In addition, four of the five young staff making their initial move from scale one were teachers without graduate qualifications of any kind. Rewarding the qualified subject teacher did not appear to be a major feature of either the salary structure or the promotion procedures at either school. Good administrators, not good teachers, were the models.[10] The system encouraged low, short-term commitment to classroom teaching.

(b) Pastoral staff are rarely qualified to teach 'real' subjects but possess delegated headteacher authority
Staffing procedures and comments made by staff lend support to the proposition that the rise in supervisory staff numbers was a response to the need to control the complexity of the process.[11] Size and demands for accountability appeared crucial in legitimizing the process, but if those promoted were those who had been less well qualified to inspire pupil learning, classroom failures could be found supervising the work of classroom successes. As the fieldwork progressed I became increasingly aware that classroom staff perceived supervisory staff as both unqualified to do 'real' subject teaching

and required to carry out delegated headteacher activities. One head of subject for example, asked:

> How can you respect those who are supposed to be superior but who can't do anything real? It is not as if they were all really good classroom teachers either. Some of them, I know, couldn't control pupils when they had them in a classroom, so how are they going to do it now?

A subject teacher with a scale three post echoed these sentiments:

> So-called pastoral staff have the right to call in pupils' books and staff record books for inspection, but they could not do the job themselves, they don't know how to do it. They are not qualified in any subject . . . do they just call them in to prove that they can do it? . . . just trying to see if I'm giving homework and marking it?

Such supervision was seen as worse than no supervision at all. It provided no opportunity for constructive help, allowed really good work to pass unacknowledged and emphasized conformity to routine requirements rather than the creative, spontaneous and innovative aspects of real learning. There was evidence in both schools, despite the derisory comments made about pastoral staff competence in subject areas, that some pastoral staff had been successful subject teachers. It may be argued, as John did,[12] that teaching 'real' subject courses is now as much the protected preserve of the classroom teacher as pastoral care is of the supervisory staff. Supervision by the head of subject department was not perceived as a realistic alternative.

If the qualifications held by some staff disqualified them for actually doing many of the structured and progressive courses on the curriculum, what can they actually do? Their main teaching commitment was with non-examination classes. To be seen to teach lower-status classes may encourage them to glorify the demands of such remedial and non-examination work. It may lead to their search for recognition in extra curricular drama, music and sporting activities. However, the adoption of certain delegated headteacher administrative and supervisory activities may have most appeal. A preoccupation with 'control' may be discerned as the traditional paternalistic attitudes of the English headteacher.[13] Heads identify with their schools and overemphasize their responsibility for all that goes on in them. Heads in smaller schools were able to control the activities of teachers in a manner more appropriate to workers performing routine skills, than to relatively autonomous professionals.[14] There is a way in which heads were expected to manage a school. They alone embodied its aims, determined the curriculum, controlled the timetable, distributed finance, selected staff and dominated the communication networks, or in industrial management terms, they directed, controlled, planned, coordinated and evaluated activities. The head did not actually teach, except in emergency situations. The dichotomy between controlling and executing was maintained by distancing himself from the classroom work, by directing and by inspecting the work of the staff. As this authority was delegated to various grades of pastoral/administrative staff, such staff received management trappings: more periods free from actual teaching, more access to confidential information and a private or shared office to deal with pupils and parents as professional clients. All thirteen senior administrative staff in these two schools had their own private offices and some year tutors had found a private space where such consultation would be facilitated. A brief look at the principles of scientific management suggests some useful comparisons. Managers (headteachers and their delegates):

(a)   give all 'teachers' only partial processes to perform – teaching mere subjects while they retain responsibility for the total education of the child,

(b)   concentrate information exclusively in the hands of the management group – only members of senior conference and pastoral staff have access to the full range of confidential information about pupils,

(c)   use their monopoly of resources to control privileges, promotion and working conditions.[15]

A newly appointed head of year was pleased to point out that, 'promotion to my current head of year post has meant that I am now told more confidential information, information not even given to my head of subject . . . about kids generally'. Such access to confidential information, plus attendance at the senior management meetings where 'problems' are sorted out, in part of a whole nexus of strategies designed to consolidate the supervisory staff groups' dominant position. An analysis of how they normally deal with their subject colleagues and how they seek to devalue the classroom subject teachers role is now attempted.

(c) Supervisory staff interactions with other teachers are predominantly of a 'commanding nature' and rarely involve 'consultation'
Martin suggests that 'contacts with subordinates' are most likely to have the following flavour.[16] They are rarely of a collegial nature in which work problems are discussed, mutual input into the decision making process encouraged, or long-range strategic plans generated. They are occasionally for the purpose of evaluating the performance of the subordinate and frequently to give orders or instructions, or to reprimand the subordinate for some deficiency or delinquency in carrying out past directives. Martin quotes some evidence supporting this position, claiming that they found managers' contacts with subordinates were largely for the purpose of making requests, sending or receiving information and occasionally strategy making.[17] During a period of two months I noted every interaction between supervisory staff (the thirteen senior administrative staff) and the teaching staff that occurred where I could observe it, in the staff room, corridors, and classroom. I noted thirty-seven such interactions in a random way. Sixteen of

these were clearly 'one way' interactions, giving instructions about new arrangements for class movements and about duties that needed doing, including leaving the staff room promptly when the bell goes. Twelve were eliciting information about required petty administrative tasks such as collecting money, completing reports, collecting permission slips, and relatively public announcements about 'school-wide' activities, plays and exhibitions. The other nine were significant because they were accompanied by either the giving out of typed forms which required some action by the teacher or they involved interactions of a humorous kind that accompanied the posting of substitution lists or revised duty rotas on the staff room notice board. The contents of these duty lists could dramatically effect a teacher's plans for the day. He could find himself losing preparation or marking periods, doing duties in his lunch break or covering for absent colleagues. The humour, somewhat 'in group', was only addressed to certain members of staff, and referred to activities outside of school, for example, local soccer team results, holiday plans, car problems, incidents at staff socials and so on. There was also a large quantity of instructions or commands that appeared in writing: memos, notes, weekly events, newsletters and general information. Staff also spent some time talking to supervisory staff in private offices. When I asked about these private meetings I was told that when such interviews were held at the request of supervisory staff they were regularly intended for the discussion of individual pupil problems. When they were requested by classroom staff they were more frequently to resolve conflicts between staff or between staff and pupils. By far the majority of staff interactions in private offices took place between those who had private offices themselves. They were places, away from the staff room and out of the corridor, where discussions regarding planning, staffing, organizing and budgeting, administrative staff 'doing' activities, could take place. Those I did obtain access to were predominantly about circumventing tension or anticipating opposition to plans they intended to introduce. Coffee and tea were frequently available and such encounters could be described as 'places of association' where supervisory staff belonged and others definitely did not. They were not as open as other 'hideaways' such as the science prep-rooms, CDT offices and HE kitchens, where other staff associated in cliques, away from the isolation of the classroom and the crowded staff room.

Although supervisory staff were rarely qualified to advise on subject matters (schemes, plans, resources required, etc.), it is clear that to have sought advice from subject staff would also have risked the exposure of some inadequacy. No member of the subject classroom staff could remember when their opinion had been sought. One head of subject, for example, put it this way:

> Career is 'fame' not 'fortune' – fame from being 'worthy to be consulted' instead of being consulted merely because of your position. If the head would only consult us, he would reduce that craving to get

promoted so that someone listens to you. To have a say is to be respected.

This lack of consultation was a major insult to the pride and integrity of those classroom subject teachers who were doing a good job. Lack of consultation was perceived as lack of respect, appreciation and positive criticism. 'Teachers', said one head of subject, 'are frustrated by having to work in conditions where they see how classes could be better arranged, but do not have access to the decision-making that could bring about these changes'. 'We are unable', added another experienced subject teacher, 'to persuade management of our priorities – they never ask – if we raise it they refuse to listen to complaints'.

(d) Supervisory staff take steps to devalue the subject department heads and the work they coordinate and carry out
The delegation of traditional headteacher authority to a group of senior administrative staff has not occurred without struggle, and it is a situation that has to be continually sustained. While the head's authority may be sufficiently acknowledged, so that it is not vulnerable to threat from simple association with staff, supervisory staff generally have to employ strategies to limit the power of the major opposition group, the heads of subjects and their power base, their subject knowledge and their autonomy in the classroom.

The heads of subjects may be regarded as the only group that seriously challenges supervisory staff positions. They are normally experienced and well qualified in their subjects. Twenty-four of the thirty-four subject heads in the two schools held first degrees in their subject and a further nine were heads of subjects where degree qualifications were not available until recently (i.e. PE, HE, CDT). Only one head of subject was only a certificated teacher in a subject area where graduate qualifications would normally have been available. Heads of subject may thus be perceived as the leaders of the 'doers'. They have the capacity to provide academic leadership rather than adminis-trative management. There was no evidence that any steps were taken in either school to support or to promote the influence of these leaders. The lack of innovation and the poor examination results were more popular super-visory staff comments. Meanwhile, the isolation and lack of support was echoed by all the heads of subject interviewed.

Heads of subject, like myself, are not consulted about appointments or about the promotions of our own subject staff. Members of my department are given points of responsibility for administrative reasons and it is not clear for what and to whom they are now really responsible. Scale promotions and appointments reduce my 'hold' over staff. Why should they listen to me? Doing a little 'leg' work for the administration brightens their career prospects while working for me gets them nowhere.

If supervisory staff had set out deliberately to reduce the power of heads of subject, their success was overwhelming. Heads of subjects were denied office space, indeed any secure working area, timetabled in excess of the junior staff in their own subject areas who had year tutor posts and scheduled to perform the general duties from which supervisory staff on lower grades were exempt. In addition, they were regularly called upon to cover for absent colleagues in their own subject areas because lower-grade supervisory staff were not qualified enough to teach pupils. Even a probationary teacher had noticed that 'heads of subject do not have a room of their own – they must leave their classroom and go to the staff room during their free periods, just as we do, because their rooms are timetabled for the use of other members of staff'.

To consolidate the decline in status of the head of subject it appears that the supervisory staff had to devalue subject knowledge itself and to reduce psychic rewards gained from classroom success for those teachers. In the latter case it was better to risk poorer results than to have classroom subject teachers with a powerful base recognized by pupils and parents alike. The 'comprehensive intake' appeared to imply that much of the subject-based expertise and concentration upon examinations was irrelevant. Many pupils were suited to alternative courses. However, there was little evidence that staff, resources and finance were provided to create and sustain alternative courses. Those teachers who did initiate new courses were quickly promoted out of the classroom and often out of the school itself. Once external supporting agencies left the schools to carry on with innovations, after the initial injection of resources, the programmes faded. In place of sustained efforts to create viable alternative courses, we discern the labelling of former grammar school subject staff as too narrowly subject-orientated to cope, while former secondary modern school staff fled the classroom. The grammar school ethos, that link between the challenging subject, the talented pupil and highly appreciated achievement, was rejected *tout court*. On the contrary, it was claimed that education was a process of personal education through the medium of subject knowledge rather than a glorification of the acquisition of subject knowledge. The task of the new comprehensive school was much bigger than mere subject knowledge and beyond the resources providers were prepared to lavish upon it. A senior teacher said that 'ex-grammar-school staff have been sensitive to a decline in privilege. We began by being sensitive about élitism but soon gathered from what new staff were saying that we were somehow not appropriate, not needed by the new school – many who could do so, left, of course.' Another head of subject referred to the perceived decline of standards: 'Doing really well by hard work is not appreciated, not even expected by upper echelons of staff. To get promoted you need to get out of your subject.'

Lortie argues that what makes a good day for teachers is when psychic rewards gained in the classroom situation are high.[18] 'Good things' are always linked to classroom matters. Negative events include any incursions on teaching time for petty administrative or clerical tasks. They resent interruptions. Programmed lessons should take priority over other activities.

'I regret', said one subject teacher, 'any interruptions of the classroom lesson, however important. The sanctity of the lesson is interrupted too easily and eroded daily.' A head of subject identified a relationship between examination failures and the number of interruptions: 'When I was asked why there had been so many examination failures, I replied at length, stating how many lessons had been missed or cancelled without request or advanced notice'. Supervisory staff in both schools appear to have established, by practice, the right to interrupt lessons to give non-essential messages, to withdraw pupils for trips, drama, sport or religious activities that are rarely timetabled in advance – just reported in weekly newsletters. A subject teacher on a scale 2 summarized by claiming that 'little priority is given to loss of lesson time . . . pupils are withdrawn, lessons are cancelled at the drop of a hat'.

Weekly newsletters are just one example of the exploding quantity of paperwork. Keeping classroom subject staff at a distance and increasing their inert time may be helped by producing and demanding paperwork. 'There is no doubt', claimed one member of staff, 'that more administrative work is created by having special people with responsibility for it. This is because they create work for others rather than serve the teachers working at the chalk face.' Both the larger school and the allocation of responsibility for certain delegated administrative jobs is recognized as a cause of the paperwork explosion, but some question the depersonalization and distancing effects of this. Subject staff commented that 'as paper work explodes, personal contacts die'. Another said, 'there is too much bureaucracy – even staff are given numbers. The paperwork reduces you to a cog in a wheel and divides you from the people you are working with. The personal touch is missing.' Many staff considered the required administrative tasks menial and a serious distraction from the real job. A head of year admitted that 'staff are asked to do too many menial tasks, a great deal of paperwork should be done by a good secretary or teachers' assistant. I don't need all the training I have had to do these tasks.' A newly qualified teacher observed that 'paperwork is just one more way of misusing teacher time . . . others include doing extra detentions, missing lunch breaks, searching for trouble makers, collecting absence slips, registers, etc.' [. . .]

Conclusion

On the evidence that emerged from the analysis of the interviews [. . .] it is claimed that the distinction between relatively classroom-based subject teaching staff and relatively non-classroom-based supervisory staff is upheld. The teachers perceive it as such and act in recognition of the existence of this division. Those in dominant supervisory posts act to reproduce this distinction. The unintended consequence is that the quality, disposition and status of the teacher programmed to interact with pupils in the classroom is devalued.

But management has no other purpose than to facilitate the creation of the most effective teaching/learning situations.[19] Such a purpose may have become more difficult as schools have become larger, their precise objectives less clear, their resources restricted and their internal dynamics devoid of adequate consultations. However, the evidence presented here substantiates to some extent how one group of teachers who began in a less favoured position academically, were able to exploit the pastoral care legend, and now continue to have the major say about how things will normally be done in schools. Tactics used to retain their right to the dominant decision-making processes, have eclipsed their care for establishing effective teaching/learning situations and promoting the self-esteem and disposition to their task of those teachers who interact with pupils in classroom situations.

References

1. Hammersley, M. and Atkinson, P. (1983) *Ethnography:* Principles in Practice, Tavistock, London.
2. Giddens, A. (1979) *Central Problems in Social Theory: Action, Structure and Contradiction in Social Analysis*, Macmillan Press, London.
3. Hammesley, M. and Atkinson, P. (1983) *op. cit.* p. 2.
4. Giddens, *op. cit.*, p. 210.
5. Gordon, R. L. (1975) *Interviewing, Strategy, Techniques and Tactics*, Dorsey Press, Chicago, Illinois.
6. Schwartz, M. A. and Schwartz, C. G. (1955) 'Problems in participant observation', *American Journal of Sociology* 60, 343–53.
7. *Ibid.*
8. Martin, S. (1983) *Managing Without Managers*, Sage Library of Social Research, SAGE, London.
9. Marland, M. (1974) *Pastoral Care*, Heinemann, London.
10. Richardson, E. (1973) *The Teacher, the School and the Task of Management*, Heinemann, London; and Richardson, E. (1975) *Authority and Organisation in the Secondary School*, Macmillan, London.
11. Ozga, J. and Lawn, M. (1981) *Teachers, Professionalism and Class: a study of organised teachers*, Falmer Press, Lewes.
12. John, D. (1980) *Leadership in Schools*, Heinemann Educational Books, London.
13. Coulson, A. A. (1976) 'The role of the primary head', in R. S. Peters (ed.), *The Role of the Head*, Routledge & Kegan Paul, London, pp. 92–108; Caspari, I.E. (1976) 'Roles and responsibilities of head teacher and teaching staff in primary schools' in Peters, R. S. (1976) *The Role of The Head*, Routledge & Kegan Paul, London.
14. Hoyle, E. (1969) 'Professional stratification and anomie in the teaching profession', *Paedegogica Europaea* 5, pp. 60–71.
15. Braveman quoted in Martin (1983), *op. cit.*

16. *Ibid.*
17. *Ibid.*
18. Lortie, D. C. (1975) *School Teacher: A Sociological Study*, University of Chicago Press, Chicago.
19. Gray, H. L. (1982) *The Management of Educational Institutions: Their Research and Consultancy*, Falmer Press, Lewes.

Section IV

The social construction of teachers' work

10

Skill in schoolwork: work relations in the primary school

Martin Lawn

In recent years research on teachers in schools has been strengthened by ideas drawn from labour process theories which draw analogies between teaching and other kinds of work. The potential of this approach has yet to be realized, but it is already apparent in the work on the deskilling process in teaching. The case for this approach has been made by reference to new developments in the control and content of schooling in the United States, most notably by Apple.[1] These developments include the move towards the competency-testing of pupils and teachers, the standardization of the curriculum and the rise of a mass-produced commercial curriculum. Elements of these North American developments have surfaced in Britain, and in 1987, strong, central direction in the detailed content of a national curriculum and the regular appraisal of the teachers who will operate it, is very evident.

At different periods in our educational history, the mode of control of teacher's work has altered, varying from detailed regulations on the curriculum and the training of teachers to the near invisibility of central direction and the emphasis on local control and partnership with teachers.[2] The idea of the 'good teacher' – or, to put it another way, the qualities and skills that a teacher or worker should have – has been variously defined according to the needs of the state and the degree of centralized control exercised at any one time. In a period of relative consensus, for example, there would be no detailed specification of the 'good teacher', but there was a particular version of the 'good teacher' produced within the discourse of the state emphasizing service and duty. Skill is now to be defined, emphasized in teacher contracts and regularly appraised. In this paper I will use the Department of Education and Science's *Better Schools*[3] policy statement and Her Majesty's Inspectorate's *Education Observed 3: Good Teachers*[4] to discuss the proposed reorganization of teacher's work, the specification of the teacher's skills and the structure of management and supervision which become necessary to control and appraise teachers.

Within a different context to North America, it is possible to show how the *necessity to specify* teacher's skills and the *actual specified skills* are an attempt to control the nature of teacher's work and, in so doing, deskilling it and them. It is also possible to see in the specification that, in teaching, skills are not necessarily knowledge or process-based but have a substantial personal qualitative base which then *becomes* technical. Cooperativeness will no longer be a possible quality a teacher may embody but a necessary technical requirement in the term-based teaching and management of the curriculum proposed for schoolwork.

There is a further issue in the debate about skill in schoolwork which needs to be explored and which is described in the substantive part of this essay. It is possible to discuss skill and the good teacher with respect to particular periods in the relations between teachers and the state and to market and other factors which alter teachers' work, but what is lacking so far is the actual working out of these tendencies in the schoolwork of teachers. How is skill mediated and negotiated in the day-to-day work relations of the school? Apple has discussed the possible courses of action for teachers faced with a pre-specified curriculum, which include changing parts of it, refusing ('informally') to teach parts of it or resisting its order and pace. He discusses the problems teachers have in altering or resisting this process because of their own history of work, gender and class:

> the intensification of production, the pressure to produce more work in a given period, led to all kinds of interesting responses. Craft workers, for example, often simply refused to do more. Pressure was put on co-workers who went too fast (or too slow). Breaks were extended. Tools and machines suddenly developed 'problems'. Teachers . . . will find it difficult to respond in the same way.[5]

The difficulty lies, Apple says, in their isolation from each other at work, the fact that there are no 'machinery and tools' to stop and that, being professionals, working in 'a site with patriarchal relations' might even lead them to partial acceptance of these changes. At the same time he does allow the possibility of a specific kind of resistance occurring. It is the contention of this paper, based upon accounts drawn mainly from women teachers in the primary schools, that there is a mediation and resistance to the patriarchal management of schoolwork by teachers, and this is an attempt to socially construct and defend skill in their daily work relations. The accounts drawn upon in this paper were made by eight women primary-school teachers (5–11 age range) and a woman middle-school teacher (8–13 age range), over a period of a year; they had all taught for between fifteen and twenty years.

The paper is organized in three parts. First, I discuss the development of work and the management of work in primary schools in the post-war period and the new official proposals to alter it, and relate this context to the question of skill and the management of skill in schoolwork. Second, I discuss, through the interview data, the way in which primary teachers deal with management, and I identify three responses which I term 'individual strategies', 'tacit understandings' (for group or individual actions) and 'collective acts' (the teachers as a whole). Third, I focus on the problem of understanding teachers in work and, with the use of a case study of a Midlands primary school, show how teachers require a work problem (of the classroom or 'production') to be *solved* if they are to cooperate in meeting management changes in the work process. The overall objective of the paper is to try to move the discussion of deskilling on to the question of the social construction of skill and how this operates through the work relations of the school and the contesting, by heads and teachers, of control over work.

Changes in educational work in the primary school

Teachers' work in the primary school has changed over the last forty years. The look of the classroom, especially its physical organization has altered, and the curriculum is now less likely to be school-grown and more likely to be a product of a commercial educational publisher. One aspect of their work has remained constant, though its form has changed, and that is headteacher control of the work environment and its practices. Up to the early 1960s (and later for many schools) the headteacher used the old *Handbook of Suggestions for Teachers* and its successor, *Primary Education*,[6] to organize the school timetables, produce syllabuses and determine curriculum activity. Since the forerunner of the headteacher had been seen as *the* certified teacher and everybody else a form of assistant, the tradition had been established in which the head controlled the teacher's work. The only leeway for a class teacher was to be viewed as highly competent by the head and so allowed to alter the activities if not the syllabus. By the mid-1950s, although the work relations between the head and the class teacher remained the same, the form began to change. A new group of assistant headteachers was created. These were class teachers – unlike the headteacher who was losing more and more teaching time to administration – but they had a management function of one type or another. Scale posts had arrived and a system of distributing them in school had to be produced.[7] For the next two decades, the function of the scale postholder was unclear or even irrelevant to the school organization as the posts were often given to teachers on the basis of seniority. The teachers were all seen as generalists, although the rise of primary-school specialists was mentioned officially in the late 1950s. It was seen as unlikely in the primary school, but if teachers had 'specialist knowledge or skills', for instance as 'naturalists . . . musicians . . . lovers of English',[8] then the headteacher was encouraged to make use of them and help them work with other teachers. The 1960s and early 1970s were characterized by the continuing function of the headteacher as the leader of school but the staff were viewed as a 'team' of people who were in close touch with each other and with other school-teachers and were trusted with the gradual evolution of the school curriculum. The head did not control the school by determining the pace, content and form of the work so much as by the introduction of changes and encouraging staff to learn about them and going on the new education courses available locally. The head became the manager of the team, encouraging and initiating the process of review.

The different strands of this account, such as the rise of scale posts, the new administrative and specialist functions of the class teacher and the changing role of management still did not challenge the headteacher's function as the manager of the school. As the school altered, so did the form of that management.

However, within the last few years, and especially during and since the first wave of teachers' action, the proposed management of the primary school has been reorganized. Work and the teacher have been redefined. It is possible to review these proposals and create a relatively coherent model of the work relations in the primary school proposed for future decades. It is to this I now turn.

In the 'Better Schools' paper, the formalization of the early tack, of specialists in the primary school, has taken place. Now every primary teacher has to have a specialist role as well as a generalist one:

> each new primary school teacher should be equipped to take on a particular responsibility for one aspect of the curriculum (such as science, mathematics or music), to act as a consultant to colleagues on that aspect and to teach it to classes on his [sic] own.[9]

The idea of specialist knowledge as unlikely to be in the primary school and then only as a 'talent' has been overturned. It is now a requirement. It is also an additional function for the class teachers who will teach their own class and also the classes of other teachers. As scale post functions are revised, they are seen as specialist curriculum posts, and they now have a supervisory function never envisaged when they were first created. Consultancy is moving already to supervisory responsibility. Management functions in the school appear to be spread wider than in the old headteacher's role. Team work, especially between those with posts of curriculum responsibility (described as 'delegated responsibilities' in *Good Teachers*, p. 12), is now to be part of the new work relations. It may have existed before, but now it is to be part of the formal organization of schoolwork and described as the 'corporate development' of the school (*Better Schools*, p. 44).

Specialist functions and supervisory teams are only one part of the same new package of government proposals for teachers and their work. The context of schooling policy has altered considerably from one in which the teachers were seen as a body of trusted servants who acted with little direction and yet responded to new demands upon them by changing the emphasis and scope of their work,[10] to one where they are seen as managed, appraised and checked in a standard work process:

> the Government welcomes the sustained efforts made by many parties to negotiate a new salary structure for primary and secondary teachers, embracing new pay scales, a new contractual definition of teachers' duties and responsibilities and the introduction of systematic performance appraisal, designed to bring about a better relationship between pay, responsibilities and performance, especially teaching performance in the classroom.[11]

Productivity, pay and performance are to be the new features of work, and they centre upon the management and control of the teacher's skill.

A reading of 'Better Schools' suggests three main elements present in the 'good teacher'; these are duties, responsibilities and performance. The meanings given to these elements may have changed over the years. For example, in the 1950s they were defined by the headteacher within a context of evolutionary change and professional control; in the 1980s they are now to be redefined nationally, in a contract and by appraisal, within a context of severely reduced education expenditure and a return to differentiated schooling.

Good Teachers explains in some detail the new job requirements of the teacher. The document reflects both the new structuring of school management and some rather older traditions of the teacher as exemplar of moral behaviour and so on, but it serves as an ideal-type model of the new skills required of the teacher. Duties, responsibilities and performance are here defined, and so, presumably, will sometime be made contractual and appraised. The performance or the technical skill of teaching is discussed in terms of the use of different teaching strategies in lessons, differentiating methods according to pupil needs, planning schemes of work for individuals and groups, marking and recording progress of pupils and so on. This is a codified description of the 'progressive' primary-school teacher of the 1960s and the new assessment emphasis of the 1970s made into a comprehensive listing of technical skills. Again, the managing of teachers has always been the head's area of interest, but here it is defined as matching their experience and training to particular tasks – and with a responsibility to obtain their commitment and professionalism in that task. Teachers are to be managed, no longer to be left alone in their classrooms and in their generalist teaching. There is also a significant new way in which that 'managing' has to take place and that is in teams which identify goals for every aspect of the school. The school is no longer defined as the head's area of policy but that of the team of teachers. So, paradoxically, heads assume a new tightened-up role of selecting and organizing teachers to perform defined tasks and of keeping them effective, and yet they lose the control over the whole school as their domain and become instead workers in a team of teachers sharing with them the definition and execution of collective school goals. Managing work has been redefined, as has work itself; it is now a task with a complex, technical aspect and operated in an interdependent way with the tasks of others, for increased efficiency. Professionalism in the primary school has moved on from being classroom-based, usually in isolation from other teachers, fairly well defined by the head, but in a context of responsibility and autonomy, to a collective, schoolwide job, based on narrowly defined though complex tasks within a context of shared management functions and tight areas of responsibility, clearly defined and appraised.

To be a good teacher, however, is not reducible to the technical knowledge skills described earlier. Throughout *Good Teachers* other qualities are outlined. There is a strong reference to the qualities a teacher must have – curiosity, sense of purpose, calm attitude, character, reliability and punctuality. One of these qualities, 'cooperativeness', is vital to the new role of the teacher in the team – developing school discipline policies, agreeing a whole school policy and so on. So strong are these references to teacher qualities that they cease to be ideal characteristics of the good teacher and become part of a job specification for that teacher. To appear to have these qualities is in itself a new skill requirement of teaching. Without appearing to be cooperative, there will be no secure job. The definition of the teacher has subtly altered – no longer the classroom generalist, they will be part of a team, a professional team; for professionalism is here defined as a collective matter in teaching.

In each significant period of the contemporary history of education, professionalism, defined by teachers or the state, has been of importance in the relations between them. The state as the effective employer of the teacher has encouraged, through a professional ideology, a broad view of its teaching workforce. Today, this view is much more specific. Professionalism is defined as taking the state's description of teaching as your own, working in teams with headteacher leadership, working in the day and evening (in private study or in-service training) and working in extracurricular activities. In contrast to the recent past, it is not classroom but school-based work which defines professionalism; not autonomy but team work on task; not the achievement of a national consensus on educational policy issues with a recognized place for teachers but a decentralized professionalism centred on the school. Removed from the national area where it has been replaced by centralization of finance, curriculum, pay and appraisal, professionalism is now seen to be reducible to a way of working with others, of working longer hours and of being cooperative.

This presents a problem for the teacher in the school because the head tries to determine the content of the pedagogy or the resources or the environment. Even when the determination of work was strong in terms of curriculum content and timetable, the teacher (especially the 'good teacher') was often allowed the privacy of the classroom as an uninterrupted place of work. However, there is a transition occurring in schools as they gradually shift to a system of delegated management functions, as scale postholders take on job descriptions which make them supervisors of other staff.

Headteachers will no longer be sole managers of the school; in turn they will become a kind of middle manager not creating but enforcing policy in a more directed way. The classroom will no longer be a refuge.

Teachers will find that teamwork or collegiality really means the spread of management and supervision and its fragmentation so that an element of it is now included in their job description. Teachers' qualities constitute, with other technical skills, a new way of judging the 'good teacher', these are also to be placed in the job description.

How did teachers cope with this determination of their work in the past and what effect will this new means of managing them have on their individual and collective strategies in the future? It is to this question I now turn.

Contesting schoolwork

Some years ago, while supervising an oral history of primary-school teaching based on one school, I was told a story about dealing with headteachers.[12] During the short period of time when one head retired and a new head was appointed, a member of staff hid the small, portable language laboratory. It was hidden, effectively lost, from that moment on. It had been keenly supported by the former head and the teacher was not risking its continued use under the new regime. Why was this curriculum innovation of its day buried? For the same reason computers and their trolleys are cursed in many primary schools – they are seen as a disruptive of the natural order of the classroom and they are avoided because of the difficulty in moving them around the school, up and down stairs, etc. This was one of a number of stories illustrating the power of the headteacher in that school and the ways that teachers contested that power. While the individual heads differed in their policies, organization and style (one extremely formal, one informal and so on), they were significant controllers of teachers' work, and teachers had to find ways of dealing with them. Reasserting control of their work, at the expense of a small capital asset, the language lab, was a necessity. An interesting aspect of the story was the fact that it was one of only three or four instances given of a member of staff acting alone but with the tacit support of the rest of the staff, for all of them knew it had been 'lost'. Most of the stories involved individual strategies for coping with the head. This one involved tacit understandings between all the teachers; there was no example of an open collective act of resistance to the head. With different groups of in-service teachers I have followed up this element of their work relations – something which is barely mentioned in primary-school research. These examples are drawn, in the main, from the primary schools of the West and South Midlands.

Individual strategies for dealing with heads and their school policies were always known to the other teachers. One infant teacher used to hide in her stockroom, a small room off her classroom, during her free periods to avoid taking the classes of absent teachers in the junior school. Another teacher would always consult her diary before making comments on possible new teaching commitments; this is not the simple act it appears, for this strategy was remarked upon by other teachers as being very effective in defending free time from the head and acted as a clear sign of independence; this is an extreme example of the individual teacher avoiding the demands of the head:

> The head had a habit of waiting for staff outside the staffroom during break and lunch periods and taking them to his room for 'private talks'. One staff member regularly avoided him by climbing through the cloakroom windows, walking across the roof and climbing into her own classroom. (A)[13]

In each case, these teachers were dealing with management in ways which would, in a different place of work, be seen as 'skiving' or 'being cheeky' and so on. Each act is a recognition of the head's position as the 'boss' and also of the limitations of their own position and of the limitations of 'formal' opposition – which may well reflect patriarchy. A simple refusal to talk or to cover was not possible and so a subterfuge was used.

One of the key ways in which heads evaluate their teachers is through the quality and quantity of their 'displays'. While these may be ostensibly to do with the exhibition of children's work and the lesson content, they are seen by primary teachers as a means by which heads raised their productivity, recognized signs of teacher quality and differentiated them from each other. It was not uncommon for teachers I talked to to mention their difficulties in doing displays, usually it was a question of time and the pace of work, sometimes a question of skill. Teachers mentioned ripping down their displays when they saw the superiority of another's display. In schools with large wall surfaces and a keen head, displays seem to become the major aspects of work, only rivalled by class teaching:

> We have to change corridor and main area displays each half term. The first half-term display has to go up within a fortnight of the term starting. With falling rolls and staff cuts, this had become an exercise in instant display from the children during the first two weeks, with enormous expenses to cover. Staff had been trying for some time to negotiate [with the head], through scale three [postholders] and then the deputy head, to have a gradual building up of display throughout the term with display remaining up over the holidays until about three weeks into the term, when it would be slowly changed. This was agreed to during one particularly short term – but *only* for that one term. (B)

Although the strategy of negotiation, carefully operated through in the senior postholders, failed to reduce the problem, the teacher went on to say that 'staff were still searching for a suitable alternative policy'. They needed to control the head's definition of 'work as displays', nearly all, of course, organized, pinned and framed in the teacher's non–class contact time (breaks, lunch hours, after school). If a school didn't have this kind of half-termly schedule, then the head might pass a memo around the classrooms, carried by a child, to say that 'the boards haven't been changed for a while, could we have some new pictures up?' (C). Either way, displays are a problem of work.

There is a problem for teachers in deciding how to influence head-teachers without risk. When there is no sense of collectivity, and competition between teachers is encouraged, then difficult compromises have to be made: 'One strategy of teachers to increase their autonomy is to form alliances for or against those not necessarily highest with hierarchy known to have the "ear" of the head'. (D) Sometimes a thought would be expressed to others if a judgement had already been made that it would not be passed on to the head. If, for example, the staffroom clock was to be turned back to extend the break, then this action had to be protected by a tacit understanding between them all.

Action against a new management policy can occasionally move from being an act of a teacher in the classroom or an action based on tacit agreement between teachers into covert but active opposition. Not surprisingly, in the two examples here, it becomes an active opposition when school resources are affected. Resources are collected and used in classrooms or departments and become an expression of privilege between groups of teachers. This is, in part, a reflection of the older emphasis on the generalist, classroom teacher and a continuing reflection of the difficulties which occur in work when resources are shared. A new deputy head, in a middle school, tried to centralize the school's audio and duplicating equipment and was supported by the headteacher and the departments with few resources:

> departments and staff who had good resources were against *their* equipment going out of *their* control. They saw what was, in fact, school property as their own possessions, paid for out of the depart-mental capitation. [They] resisted all attempts to group the audio/duplicating equipment into a common area – they reported on the form [assessing their resources] that equipment was damaged, or stolen when it was not; they changed the locks on their stockrooms; made deals with other well-resourced departments to share equipment and made a case to the deputy head about equipment in constant use. (G)

In the latent culture of classroom or departmental autonomy, the private nature of resources was the basis for these teachers' opposition, but the degree to which they used oppositional and group strategies was dependent on the strength of the management intervention.

In another middle school, a new scale-two post for head of resources was given to an internal candidate who had been 'boasting' about a plan to change staff access to the centralized resources areas. In the last week of the term, a new stock of paper for duplicators and overhead projectors had just arrived, as the scale post was appointed:

> At the end of the school day, teachers in the staff room (about two-thirds of the whole staff) decided to distribute this stock around the classrooms as an exercise in taking 'the wind out of his sails'. They gave him one day to worry, sweat and *panic* and then returned the stuff outside the resources area door at the end of the day. At this point the postholder began to realize the limitations! (A)

Again, in opposition to a new management policy, staff had to bring another teacher into line. When management functions become delegated, as they often do to scale postholders, then the contradictory aspects of the job, for management and teacher, are revealed. Usually this might be revealed to the postholder by staff 'hostility' (Campbell 1985: 69) or by a silent resistance, such as, 'Avoiding those areas [of the school] where "informal" discussions were taking place, "distancing" themselves which enabled them to "carry on as before".' (D) Yet the idea of taking collective action to continue work norms and rational organization, as they saw it, and to discipline or control a 'manager' for stepping out of line are actions not usually associated with schoolwork, it is much more likely to be associated with craft and skilled work in industry (and with male rather than female employees).

The contest for control of schoolwork, between head and staff, is clearly seen when a new head is appointed. The ethnography of classrooms reveals the 'critical encounters' between teachers and pupils as important in defining their continued relations, and so it is with schoolwork. The teacher who 'lost' the language lab was using an important moment to gain a little more control of the work situation in terms of what is defined as work and what skill is associated with it. A key member of staff in another primary school used that moment to try to isolate a new head who had used PTA money to buy some new, expensive science kits for the school. This had been done without consultation with the staff and so she organized them, demanding of those who wished to use the kits, 'whose side are you on?' (J). In other words, if there was to be no consultation about schoolwork then the head's version was to be opposed, *regardless* of whether it was a good idea or not. However, the very same science kits, bought by the head without consultation in another school were not opposed by the staff as they recognized an unspoken agreement between management and staff that they were bought as an 'insurance policy' against an inspector's visit and there would be no pressure to use them.

If a male head was aggressive or shouted a lot at the teachers, then women teachers seemed to have a number of ways in which to avoid him or to avoid arguments. A group of women teachers decided they had had enough of being shouted at, so they developed a strategy, over some time, which really altered him – saying things like 'cool down, I'm not one of the children' or 'calm down, now what's the problem?' (B). In the nature of work relations in a primary school, which are generally gender-biased, with a male head and mainly female staff, then those phrases could have been quite electrifyingly effective. Management theories of headteacher roles are gender-biased and assume a noisy, bossy, unreflective leadership, dressed in an androgynous theorizing, in which the women teachers are seen as deficient, often lacking initiative and accepting of head's decisions. The use of an authoritative tone of voice in response to the head, together with a sharp or subtly insulting phrase, is not discussed in leadership case studies and is probably more fundamentally oppositional and overt than even the most sophisticated understanding between staff to forestall management plans.

A retiring head was openly provoked by staff, who asked him for stories at assemblies which he repeated time and again. The pleasure this gave the staff can't be guessed at by the outsider unless the patriarchal and daily oppression by the head of their working lives was understood. Staff have even been known, in local primary schools, to send their head to 'Coventry', employing the deputy as the effective head in 'his' place. Hargreaves describes a situation in a middle school where a headteacher and staff held a series of regular curriculum decision-making meetings to develop a new curriculum for the following year.[14] These meetings took place in the summer term and moved near a deadline which made the inconclusiveness of the discussions a matter of unease for staff and head. Hargreaves describes these discussions, borrowing from Keast and Carr,[15] as exhibiting a 'pooled ignorance' of experiential-based talk which was almost bound to be exhausting and time-consuming and lead, as it did, to the intervention of the head, who then acted alone and produced the curriculum himself. This is described by Hargreaves as the staff dissociating themselves from 'the collective affairs of school-life' and a failure of 'democratic staff involvement'[16] and he argues that this failure was due to the limited base of classroom experience which teachers drew upon, as opposed to, say, educational theory. This may be so, but alternative analysis could be made drawn from the work relations of schooling which would suggest that the staff enthusiasm and their consequent confusion and depressed morale might have been due to the regular interventions of the head to 'close off' discussion, the exhaustion of regular meetings taking place over and above regular working hours and the constant necessity of trying to work out what the head wanted. 'Uncertainty' and 'inconclusiveness'[17] were, to an extent, created by the headteacher asking for 'ideas'. Many questions are begged in this account by reference to the democratic process of school and its collectiveness when neither factor has ever been strongly associated with schooling (although the concept of collegiality, delegation and teamwork may be seen as the future of school work relations). More useful would be the work relations perspective which would see the middle-school staff wanting to take control over aspects of their work yet not being able to, not through the inadequacy of their theorizing but because the head opened and closed off discussion, operated without a clear agenda and did not make clear his own preferences. This took place within the context of a very ambitious goal, a shortage of time and discussions operating over and above classroom and school commitments.

The difficulty of moving from individual strategies, covert group strategies and tacit understandings to a collective decision-making process – the new collegiality – is not just a question of numbers of staff but a major shift in the power relations of work at school.[18] Resistance would have to be replaced by collective decision-making and action. When teachers have tried to develop collective decision-making procedures, usually in secondary schools, then evidence suggests that the headteacher finds ways to circumvent them. Burgess, when discussing a reorganization of pastoral care systems in a secondary school, talks of the way in which the head tried to avoid the staff as a collective by using questionnaires, making private deals with some staff, co-opting others into his plans, controlling meetings and controlling information so as to eliminate opposition and 'pick-off' individuals.[19] No question there of the teachers having an inappropriate conceptual framework for creating change nor of them avoiding 'democratic staff involvement'. This was, in my opinion, a case study about the determination of work in school.

Solving problems in the work process

As schoolwork is determined by the head, and strategies to create some 'leeway' or relative autonomy can involve risk, how do teachers manage to cope with school management in other ways? One way, suggested by the following case study, is to work with the head's policy in a way which also suits the teacher's working needs.[20]

A primary school in the Midlands had a new head appointed who, within a period of eighteen months, changed both the maths and reading schemes in the lower school. Her strategy was to change the reception and first-year infants' practice first and so develop the work in the school as the class moved up. The change was necessary, in her view, because the maths scheme was unimaginative and the reading scheme was too graded and developed poor reading habits. The first bargain struck, implicitly perhaps, was that if change was going to come, and the head said it was, then the clear strategy of changing one year group at a time was approved by the teachers and so was the understanding that the school would use the new maths scheme in its own way 'with our children and within the school philosophy'. Given that the head had said 'I want' (Y) this to happen, then the promise of a pragmatic usage bound to 'these children', not some ideal model, was a good negotiating point accepted by the teachers. The old maths scheme had one major flaw: it was worksheet-based. Although this was cheap, and the worksheets could be endlessly reproduced, the scheme involved a great deal of management. The recently appointed maths postholder had just spend two terms sorting, filing and labelling all the worksheets for use by the infant department and she was the only one who really understood its organization. Yet the worksheets were a useful way of solving another of the teacher's problems, which was the large class in the reception/first-year infant area, numbering sixty-eight pupils. The worksheets could be used by everyone. They covered the 'ability range' and they were cheap to produce. They solved a work problem in the classroom. The head had to solve this work problem with her new scheme otherwise there would be some form of teacher resistance. The head had made contact with the publishers of a new scheme who welcomed this interest as they wanted trial schools which they could use to develop their product. The school would get cheaper maths resources for the trial period, the head would get some kudos for the school and an in-service programme for staff (the trial period), and the teachers would have the chance to change and alter the scheme, not only within the school but nationally – they could use their experience and skill to alter the product, which is what they did. But the scheme still had to pass the major work test, the large number of children and be easy to organize. It also had to be seen as an improvement over the old scheme in terms of its presentation and its ability to interest 'their children'. The teachers liked the new scheme – it worked. It had a big teacher's book which could be upstanding so a group of children could see it and work from it with the teacher; there were three printed workbooks for each child per year, and these could be supplemented by worksheets if necessary. So, it reduced the organization of resources problem, the quality of its presentation was high and the children's work was contained within neat workbooks. It did, however, create more work for the teachers who now had to develop a rotational group work system, but they were pleased because the number work was now interactive (which the worksheets weren't) and the children's work was better. It also solved a further problem. A supply teacher could look at the teacher's book and continue the work straightaway without the difficulties experienced previously.

Again, the head said 'I want . . .' when suggesting a new reading policy. The previous head had allowed the teachers to use a combination of a number of schemes, based on graded reading books and tests, because it paid off in high reading scores in the school and pleased parents. In this case the teachers were worried by the change of policy which might threaten their success and their freedom of decision. The new policy was not dependent on a newer reading scheme but, almost paradoxically, on the reverse. There would be no scheme but an approach to reading based on reading books, not readers, and developing critical reading skills not racing through graded tests. The scale postholder was worried about this move but had to 'put on a face' when talking to other staff, that is try to carry out the new policy of the head's and lead her team, regardless of her own worries. Money was found to buy a lot of new books which were chosen because of their interesting narratives and their lack of sex-stereotyping and so on. The immediate advantage of this approach, whatever the misgivings, lay in the abandonment of the graded readers. Parents and children were always asking about the books, about the stages and their progress, and it was very boring for a reception teacher to have to keep reading, over and over again, the first stages of the scheme. (Special meetings to explain the new policy to the parents probably brought the teachers together as there was some hostility to or confusion about the non-scheme.) There was another advantage, the new critical reading approach, based on asking questions, sharing views with other children and discussing their writing based on a teacher-scribe system, was connected to the early years policy on language use as a major activity in the classroom. It followed the approach the teachers felt they had, or should have, in their oral work. The consequence of this policy was the development of staff teams, sharing practice on developing reading and in a regular discourse on the value of the approach and the new books arising.

In both cases, the headteacher created the policy and a clear strategy for its implementation, including the use of postholders. Policies which appear to be irreconcilable in terms of the debate about deskilling and the use of a 'packaged' curriculum, that is adopting a newly published maths scheme and abolishing the reading schemes, each worked because of the advantages to be gained from the teacher's view of schoolwork. One way or another the head would get her way, so the choice lay in covert individual strategies or tacit agreements to ignore the development – both difficult in shared classrooms and with a determined head – or in open resistance. The latter was never likely, for in each case there was a real advantage for the teachers in solving a problem of the work process. In one case, the difficulties of organizing and running the worksheet and loose file-based scheme was outweighed by a scheme solving that problem and offering other advantages as well. In the other case (a more threatening development), another problem of the work process, the graded readers, was solved by a more active and yet still organized approach to reading, congruent with their approach to language use, which allowed them a flexibility in work organization.

This case may be seen as the 'partial acceptance' that Apple identifies, yet it had clear, concrete features which suggest it was not lack of will which led to acceptance. In each case, in their view of the work process, the changes that occurred, which they could not stop but could erode or individually contest, were agreed with because the innovations solved a pressing problem in their daily work. In their judgement, based on pressing problems in the classroom with a large number of children and a sense of what should be happening (as opposed to what was), the innovations were right. In all sorts of ways, discussed in the previous section, they could have chosen, individually or as a group, to bring the innovation to a halt.

Conclusion

The control and definition of schoolwork is contested by management and by teachers. This is true of the immediate past as it is of the present. The proposed emphasis on supervision, specialization and teamwork alters the mode of control but not its essential contestation.[21] Yet the form of individual, tacit or collective resistance to a management function which is now to be dispersed among groups of teachers is not to be resolved here.

The idea of the social construction of skill could be as fruitful a research tool on work in teaching as it has been in other areas of work, notably engineering and printing.[22] This paper has tried to show how the informal culture of the school is built around 'dealing with the head', solving problems in the organization and curriculum of the classroom and using strategies which are individual, tacit or collective. In periods of tight labour markets or teacher shortage the informal culture of the school may be on the offensive as it was in some primary schools during the teachers' action of 1985–6. Another element of the 'social construction' argument is the influence of the employer in defining 'the good teacher' not just by adding or subtracting 'technical' skills but by defining personal qualities in such a way that they become necessary job skills, blurring the boundary between 'technical' and 'non-technical' skills. In fact, Mainwaring and Wood have argued that 'non-technical' skills become the technical requirements of particular jobs, as has been argued here.[23]

The women primary teachers discussed in this paper have found a number of ways to contest the patriarchal management of their schools and in so doing, individually or in groups, have tried to protect their definition of 'the good teacher' and so of their skill. This leads, at times, to actions that may appear to be irrational from the point of view of management or outside observers (such as curriculum developers), yet it is necessary, given the imbalance of power in school and the limited ways in which they can creatively intervene in the organization of schoolwork. At other times, if the teachers feel that problems in their work are being solved, they can accept management intervention.

If the definition of the 'good teacher' is, in part, the construction of the state, or, in school, the head, then as it alters, according to the needs of the state and the degree of central control, so may the strategies open to the teachers. The most common individual and group actions may be altered, in future years, as teachers deal with the new teacher contracts and regular appraisal.

Notes and references

1. Apple, M. (1982) *Education and Power*, London, Routledge & Kegan Paul; and Apple, M. (1983) 'Work, Class and Teaching' in Barton, L. and Walker, S. *Gender, Class and Education*, Lewes, Falmer Press.

2. Lawn, M. and Ozga, J. (1986) 'Unequal Partners: Teachers under Indirect Rule', *British Journal of the Sociology of Education*, Vol. 7, No. 2.
3. Department of Education and Science/Welsh Office (1985) *Better Schools*, London, HMSO.
4. Her Majesty's Inspectorate (1985) *Education Observed 3: Good Teachers*, London, HMSO.
5. Apple, M. (1983) *op. cit.*, p. 64.
6. Board of Education (1904 edn) *Handbook of Suggestions for Teachers*, London, HMSO; DES (1959 edn) *Primary Education: Suggestions for the Consideration of Teachers and Others Concerned with the Work of Primary Schools*, London, HMSO.
7. Wallace, M. (1986) 'The Rise of Scale Posts as a Management Hierarchy in Schools', *Educational Management and Administration*, Vol. 14.
8. DES (1959 edn), *op. cit.*, p. 93.
9. DES (1985) *op. cit.*, p. 51.
10. DES (1959 edn) *op. cit.*, pp. 114–15.
11. DES (1985) *op. cit.*, pp. 55–6.
12. Wise, L. (1982) 'Curriculum Change in a Primary School: An Oral History', BEd dissertation, Westhill College.
13. Letters are used to indicate specific teachers interviewed.
14. Hargreaves, A. (1984) 'Experience Counts, Theory Doesn't: how teachers talk about their work', *Sociology of Education*, Vol. 57.
15. Keast, D. and Carr, W. (1978) 'School-based INSET – Interim Evaluation', *British Journal of In-Service Education*, Vol. 5.
16. Hargreaves, A. (1984) *op. cit.*, p. 252.
17. Hargreaves, A. (1984) *op. cit.*, p. 251.
18. The problems of work relations in the primary school which are discussed in this paper are significant in relation to discussions about participative decision-making or collegiality in schools – in so far as this is a realistic idea at all. See Alexander, R. (1984) *Primary Teaching*, Eastbourne, Holt Rhinehart & Winston. Coulson, A. (1978) 'Power and Decision-Making in the Primary School', in Richards, C. (ed.) *Power and the Curriculum*, Driffield, Nafferton.
19. Burgess, R. (1987) 'The Politics of Pastoral Care'. Paper given at the West-hill International Sociology of Education Conference, Westhill College, Birmingham.
20. The following section is based on a number of interviews with teachers denoted as (A) or (B) etc. after the direct quotation.
21. Salaman, G. (1986) *Working*, Chichester, Ellis Horwood, p. 29.
22. More, C. (1980) *Skill and the English Working Class, 1840–1914*, London, Croom Helm. Cockburn, C. (1983) *Brothers–Male Dominance and Technological Change*, London, Pluto Press.
23. Mainwaring, I. and Wood, S. (1985) 'The Ghost in the Labour Process', in Knight, D., Wilmott, H. and Collinson, D. (eds) *Job Redesign*, Aldershot, Gower.

11

Supplying the demand? : contract, mobility and institutional location in the changing world of the supply teacher

Mark Loveys

The research

In September 1984 unemployment appeared imminent. After five years of full-time teaching followed by a years' full-time degree course at a college of higher education, an extra year of part-time study meant remaining in or around the area, a large city, for that year at least. With education cuts and redeployment policies in the city education authority (CEA) a temporary full-time post was not a realistic option, so I applied to become one of the team of part-time daily-rate supply teachers offering to work anywhere within the city for the duration of my college course. Although qualified as a teacher of the middle years, I offered, and was accepted, to teach any age range in order to ensure that as much work as possible might come my way, and after several weeks of constantly haranguing the city supply office, I was eventually offered a day's work at a junior school. Although the opportunity has arisen since to undertake the occasional day of supply teaching, the majority of data used in this paper was collected during that period 1984–5 and is concerned with supply-teaching experiences in *primary* schools. This is important to note, for although many of the experiences of supply teachers working in secondary schools may be very similar to those of their counterparts in the primary sector, experience of the differences in school organization and staff/school cultures forces me to distinguish between the two groups.

A substantial proportion of the college course involved a piece of action research. It quickly became apparent that a career in supply teaching would more than adequately support a research project involving a remarkably under-investigated area, and in the spirit of Glaser and Strauss's (1967) technique of Grounded Theory whereby 'the analyst jointly collects, codes and analyses his data and decides what data to collect next and where to find them', a research diary was initiated within which day-to-day activities were carefully recorded in order that analysis of significant interaction and phenomena could be undertaken and, if necessary, new directions established. On the one hand, as an ethnographic researcher, traditional problems associated with participant observation were almost totally transcended and I was privileged to be able to witness pupil response to a supply teacher in its purest form. Access to the teaching situation and the adverse reactivity which so often cause problems in such research became central to the project, for once accepted onto the supply-teaching register, access to the teaching situation was ensured and any consequent problems were absolutely central to the ongoing analysis. On the other hand, however, there arose the real problem of achieving objectivity, for how far could I go as full-participant towards observing from an outsider's viewpoint a scene which I was central in creating? After much deliberation, experimentation with electronic recording devices and consultation with tutors, the central data collection technique remained in the form of the research diary with salient features of interaction being frequently, and privately, jotted down at each available moment. On top of the everyday, often 'off the cuff', work involved in supply teaching, this made for an increasingly hectic working day on my part. Later on in the research, interviews were arranged with headteachers and teachers whose schools I had worked in and, where possible, other supply teachers who I'd met out on the circuit. This along with conversations and comments from other parties such as parents, school secretaries and, of course, the pupils, formed the basis of my methodology.

This paper is deliberately narrative, for all research is unavoidably structured through biographical and situational constraints, and since such constraints are fundamental to any methodology, they must be made explicit, (Smith 1978; Lawn and Barton 1985). This is not always easy, however, for to observe one's own actions in a critical light is in itself a difficult undertaking, yet to discover and admit to motives underlying reactions to specific periods of critical interaction and *then* to render those motives explicit and public is, potentially at least, a dangerous exercise.

Supply and demand

LEA provision for supply teachers appears to vary between local education authorities (LEAs) according to demand. Earley (1986) has discovered that whereas particular LEAs may benefit from a surfeit of supply teachers, others experience tremendous difficulties in attracting any qualified and experienced personnel whatsoever. Primary school supply teaching in middle-class areas appears to be most popular amongst teachers, whilst inner-city secondary sectors experience very considerable difficulties in attracting supply staff. As a consequence, local demand for supply cover directly influences local policies regarding the employment of supply teachers, so basic economic laws of supply and demand dictate access, opportunities and conditions of work for teachers within an LEA. For example, during 1984–5 in the CEA, a member of staff was required to have been absent for at least two days before a supply teacher was provided, whereas evidence from a personal survey of twenty LEAs in England and Wales revealed that elsewhere that period of time varied from a week to less than a day. Furthermore, qualification requirements in LEAs appeared to vary according to the contemporaneous state of supply and demand. For instance, the more plentiful primary-school supply applicants were required to have successfully completed a probationary year, whereas in the less popular secondary sector one needed to have a basic teaching qualification only.

It would of course be misleading to regard supply teachers as an homogenous group of workers. A variety of factors influence the conditions of work that any one supply teacher is likely to experience. For example, two types of contract existed in the CEA. The vast majority of supply teachers were employed on a casual part-time basis paid no higher than Burnham scale one regardless of qualifications and previous experience. They did not enjoy the full working rights of their full-time counterparts, were employed on a half-daily basis, did not benefit from paid sick-leave and were paid up to two months in arrears. On the other hand, there existed a small pool of 'permanent supplies' who were employed on a full-time Burnham scale-two contract. These were teachers who for some reason had been displaced from the system and were awaiting redeployment and were sent into schools to cover periods of long-term absence by other teachers, ranging from a half term to a whole year. Although they shared many experiences of supply work with their part-time colleagues, continuing employment was not an occupational hazard for them since they enjoyed the same contractual conditions as normal full-time teachers.

Gender

When considering the motivations of teachers who take up supply work it must be emphasized that the vast majority of supply teachers in the CEA primary sector, (approximately 92 per cent), were women. Of the three male teachers other than myself on the register, two had left teaching to start up their own businesses and were using supply teaching merely as a safety net, and the other was seeking alternative work. Since it is a claim of this paper that LEA supply-teaching pools have traditionally served to provide a surplus of poorly rewarded labour devoid of normal teachers' working rights, the issue of the position of such sections of the workforce within the wide LEA framework in any discussion of part-time teachers and their work, is a central one. Furthermore, the fact that this reserve labour force is almost entirely comprised of women is crucial to any consideration of teacher's work, particularly if we take into account Apple's (1983) claim that 'women are more apt to be proletarianized than men . . . [for] whatever reason, it is clear that a given position may be more or less proletarianized depending on its relationship to the sexual division of labour'.

The majority of supply teachers interviewed were undertaking the work in order to 'keep in touch' with teaching with a view towards hopefully re-entering the classroom on a full-time basis at a later date. Many were mothers who had broken off their careers in order to raise a family, while others had left teaching with a view of pursuing alternative careers and were supply-teaching in order to keep their options more widely open. For those whose eventual intention was to take up a full-time post, supply-teaching provided them with a convenient vehicle for playing the field a little prior to applying for jobs in local schools. As will be pointed out later, it also assisted heads and teachers in 'knowing' certain supply teachers who might apply for jobs at their schools. For these teachers, then, supply teaching functioned very much as a second probationary period whereby teachers could sample schools and *vice versa* without the interference of any formal contractual obligations on either side. Just as schools could terminate a supply teacher's placement without reason, so the supply teacher could leave a school at very short notice and similarly without reason, although as will be later pointed out, this involved far more potential risk on the part of the teacher than that of the school.

From my own experience in schools, it quickly became apparent that supply teaching was regarded as a woman's job, and being a male in a normally female role attracted a large degree of curiosity and suspicion. Without exception I was probed by heads and teachers as to why I was supply teaching and not engaged in the traditional struggle for promotion within the system. When my reasons became clear, my role became accepted since I was then regarded as sensibly investing in my future as teacher through the sacrifice of a year's full-time work. Female supply teachers appeared to experience no such expectations.

It could be argued that commonly held assumptions regarding traditional female roles in relation to 'The Family' serve to legitimate the inferior working conditions and limited career opportunities which they are forced to accept. This is patently clear in the case of teaching where, if a woman wishes to bring up a family, then she is likely to need to sacrifice her career in order to do so. It is a 'price one must pay', but one that is not generally expected to be paid by men. Returning to teaching as a supply teacher on a casual hire-or-fire basis and with constant pressure to demonstrate competence in a multiplicity of teaching situations with little, if any, support has become an occupational reality for numerous women teachers who may well need to prove themselves under such conditions in order to commence their full-time teaching career again.

Schools and character

Obviously, just as it would be mistaken to refer to 'supply teachers' as an homogenous entity, it would be equally wrong to similarly talk of 'schools'. It is readily apparent to teachers, parents, pupils and particularly politicians, that even schools which are geographically in close proximity to one another and are controlled by the same LEA may differ widely in philosophy, practice and reputation. That schools can be identified in terms of individual character may be regarded as stating the obvious, but the reasons why are perhaps not so readily apparent. For example, I spent successive half-terms with the same age range (9–10 years olds) at CEA junior schools in virtually identical catchment areas. Both were the same size and age, and both were combined with infant departments under the one headteacher, but beyond these similarities there existed a variety of salient contrasts between the two schools. For instance, the head of Lakeside School was regarded by his staff as 'very demanding' and put particular emphasis upon a 'sensible mix of traditional and progressive methods'. Weekly staff-meetings occurred without fail, and weekly as well as half-termly forecasts were expected from all members of staff, myself included. A great deal of effort was expended upon display work over which regular meetings were held to coordinate projects across the entire school, from reception to top juniors. As well as everyday teaching, I experienced considerable pressure right from the outset to renew children's display work both in the corridor, hall and the classroom. Each member of staff, including me, was expected to contribute to the running of at least one extracurricular activity after school.

Moss Lane was very different. Although the head and teachers also proided themselves upon having achieved a 'realistic mix of traditional and progressive teaching methods', the contrast in expectations for both myself and the regular teaching staff was distinctly marked. During my six weeks there, there was no staff meeting, display work was still on the walls from the previous class of eight months before, and the corridor walls were practically bare. Out of nine classes, six were taught in rows. Unlike Lakeside, regular assessment through the use of standardized tests was a feature of classroom life, and a prominent house 'merit and demerit' system provided the backbone of school discipline, which was regarded locally as being 'good'. Here were two junior schools which were regularly visited by local inspectors and advisors and which were subject to the same overall local policies and yet operating in significantly different ways. So what is it that gives a school 'character'?

Research would suggest (Lortie 1975; Denscombe 1982; Nias 1984) that there exists among teachers a conventional wisdom of schooling which they acquire through their experiences of schools, both inside and outside of institutions and which, despite the best efforts of teacher-training establishments, remains relatively untouched. This wisdom, then, is both biographically and experientially determined. So if a teaching staff contributes no more than a collection of personal views of schooling each operating independently of one another, how do cohesive school policies come to be formulated which might distinguish that school from any other?

The very nature of the workings of schools as institutions generates a variety of constraints which members of that institution at all levels may commonly experience. Becker and Geer (1971) proposed that amongst any group of individuals confronted with similar problems there develops a set of 'group perspectives', and that when and if these group perspectives achieve some degree of cohesion and consistency, this leads to the formation of a 'subculture'. Clearly, within the school situation this not only applies to teachers but to any group which is faced with similar exigencies and which forms a degree of solidarity in an attempt to overcome or at least come to terms with them. This would apply to groups of parents, non-teaching staff and pupils as well as teachers, in fact any group involved in the overall educational enterprise. Becker further points out that culture should not imply consensus, and that any dominant, 'manifest' subculture is continually in interaction with a number of differing and competing 'latent' subcultures. Neither do subcultures hold equal amounts of power, for although the overall school culture may be the product of the competing interests and expectations of a variety of subcultures, the group within the school with the *formal* power to devise, mediate and sanction a school's collectively 'agreed' or public philosophy, (manifested through its 'policy'), is the academic staff and the governors. This again is not unproblematic, since to view the public philosophy of the school as the outcome of negotiation amongst individuals who each retain their personal notion of what schooling is all about, may imply a democratic sharing of power which in reality may well not exist. The policy of the school therefore might be viewed as a reflection of the manifest outcome of those with formal power to effectively formulate, proclaim and uphold a philosophy which is agreeable to dominant groups of power holders, whether their power be formal or otherwise, with the school's 'character' being mediated through that policy through negotiations amongst the principle subcultures associated with a school. Thus a school may be judged upon, for example, ability to maintain discipline, teaching of the three R's, the quality of teacher–pupil relationships and so on. Clearly, it is not only the formation and maintenance of school policy which shapes character and reputation but also the expectations of dominant groups in and out of school. Perhaps the *key* individual in shaping school policy is, traditionally at least, the headteacher, who normally possesses the power of veto and who normally is the mediator between staff and that other increasingly powerful group of policy shapers, the school governors.

Management and the supply teacher

It has been suggested (Musgrove 1972; Alexander 1984) that the power held
by headteachers is considerably more than administrative in nature and that
they in fact use their schools as vehicles for the maintenance of their personal
philosophy of schooling through the appointment of staff who, in their
opinion, will contribute to that philosophy. If this is so, then the arrival of a
supply teacher for a substantial amount of time and in whose appointment the
head had absolutely no part, must be the potential source of considerable
anxiety for that head. This was reflected by the comments of one particular
head who confessed that 'The supply teacher today is in a very fortunate
position; he has become a rare commodity. However, in the days when there
existed a choice between two or three reliefs, one normally phoned around
[fellow heads] a bit before choosing.' It was interesting, however, that
'telephoning around' amongst heads within the CEA was not entirely a thing
of the past. During interviews three heads openly admitted telephoning the
heads of schools where I had taught prior to my, usually substantial,
placement at their own school. Each head interviewed acknowledged the
presence of a powerful inter-headteacher grapevine which existed across the
whole city and confirmed that the opportunity still existed for the checking a
newcomer's credentials, and furthermore that many of them still regularly
employed this method of appraisal. When the CEA supply-teaching coordi-
nator was approached she maintained that although no formal method of
assessment existed, certain supply teachers did attract reputations, usually of
an 'unhelpful' nature, for although a headteacher might occasionally telephone in requesting a specific supply teacher again, more often than not the
call was concerned with negative, albeit unofficial, feedback. Thus the
general rule within the supply office was 'no news is good news'. In this way
the office constructed an impression of relative 'abilities' of teachers out on
the circuit, and very often they employed this picture as a guide to sending
particular supply teachers to particular schools. In this way a supply teacher
carries around a reputation within that authority, and failure at a school could
very possibly have detrimental consequences for teachers either in relation to
their supply-teaching career or should they decide to apply for permanent
posts within the LEA. Headteachers' concern over their lack of control over
the appointment of supply teachers in their schools was quite marked.
Sometimes this concern would manifest itself in the form of veiled warnings
such as, 'Would you believe that a supply teacher could destroy a class in just
two days? Well it has happened here', and the equally cautionary, 'Supply
teachers . . . are either very good or very bad in my experience. There are
supply teachers who I have had removed from my school, and there is no way
that I will have them on these premises again, and I certainly let the office
know that!'

Predictably perhaps, expectations of heads and other staff correlated
strongly with the envisaged length of placement. For instance, in a school

where I was due to remain for just two days the advice was to 'just enjoy them', whereas in a longer-term placement I was advised to 'establish good and firm relations as quickly as possible'. Expectations also depended upon the collectively 'agreed' (public) philosophy of the school. For instance, the 'demanding' head of Lakeside School regarded supply teachers as being 'something of an élite. They must be very strong, very capable and very adaptable. They must have the ability to work through the mesh of schemes and approaches of different schools. . . . The ability to assess a situation and work upon it directly and effectively is crucial.' Whereas at the more relaxed atmosphere of Moss Lane:

> The relief-teacher is running a holding operation. He should be keeping the class in order and doing basic teaching. If he can keep reasonable discipline and conduct a reasonable curriculum, then anything more than that is a bonus. Furthermore, a good relief teacher needs to be able to adjust to the disciplines of the particular school he's in.

Clearly, I was afforded more licence at the latter school, and indeed my stay there was markedly less stressful than was my time at Lakeside. The requirement common to both headteachers, however, was that of integration; that I should not rock the boat and that I should adapt to their particular ways of operating as quickly and as unobtrusively as possible.

Fitting in

From previous experiences of joining the staff of new schools it has always been the case that the new teacher is gradually eased in and initially granted a certain amount of licence in doing so. The new teacher undergoes a kind of informal probationary period. In my experience of supply teaching there was no such assistance, although the period of unofficial probation certainly *did* take place. That it was easier to integrate into some schools than others will hopefully become clear, but at schools where the collectively 'agreed' philosophy and pedagogy was at distinct odds with my personal philosophy and pedagogy, it became necessary to employ strategies of what Woods (1980) calls 'Impression management', whereby 'individuals try to manage the impressions others have of them'. The period of time required to adapt into any school therefore correlated strongly with the degree of cohesion between my personal pedagogy and the collective pedagogy of the particular school I was working in. In some instances adaptation required minimal adjustment, whereas in others the process was never properly completed and could result in a considerably stressful stay.

A key factor in assisting the teacher to cope and survive in any particular school structure is as will hopefully become clear, the structure itself. By integrating into the structure and becoming part of it, the teacher earns access to a variety of strategies which can only be safely implemented through membership of, or privy knowledge of, that particular institution. The peculiar case of the part-time supply teacher's potentially continual round of schools which are likely to widely differ in philosophy and practice, coupled with the exceptions of heads and staff should require little elucidation, and it is highly significant that the majority of supply teachers interviewed expressed a preference for working in one or perhaps a few schools which they had 'got to know' and, equally important, where the school had got to know them. Furthermore, those schools tended to be those which the supply teacher regarded as operating along pedagogic lines in sympathy with their own. Institutional location can be an invaluable asset to the teacher, for not until that teacher becomes identified with a particular school culture will they obtain licence to fully implement that school's range of support mechanisms. Given the importance of pedagogic empathy as an aid towards successful integration, it is not surprising that the majority of supply teachers preferred working at certain schools to others and that over a period of time they often found themselves working at just one or two schools at which they had become known by staff and pupils and which they knew operated along pedagogic lines they could easily relate to. As one supply teacher pointed out, 'When I first began supply teaching about five years ago . . . I worked at about eight different schools. You soon work out though which ones are easiest. [Q. Easiest?] Yes, the least stressful. I now work at three schools and have two sort of 'standbys' in case of emergencies.' Not surprisingly, perhaps, the heads themselves admitted that they too had preference for certain supply teachers and that they kept a list of those they could contact in times of need, despite this being contrary to official CEA policy. But in a period of burgeoning demand and mounting difficulties in obtaining supply cover, schools have increasingly found themselves denied any choice whatsoever.

Coping, conforming and competence

As mentioned above, the socialization period into a new school is normally a phased and aided process for the new teacher, but in my own experience of suppy teaching this proved to be the exception rather than the rule with the vast majority of introductions being at best cursory. This might be interpreted as a reflection of the trust and esteem accorded supply teachers by their full-time colleagues in recognition of their flexibility and resilience; however, there was strong evidence to suggest the contrary. It was the view of many of the full-time staff that if supply teaching was not being used as a vehicle to return to teaching (after, for instance, having produced and reared a family), then supply teachers were likely to be either failed teachers from other schools within the authority who were unable to gain a full-time post, or otherwise they were in it simply for 'pin-money' and therefore not serious about teaching as a career. Wary of such attitudes and the attendant appraisal by

other full-time staff, supply teachers often complained of feelings of isolation, and in response deliberately left minimal evidence of their stay by which
they might be judged as 'teacher' by, for example, doing all work upon
loose-leaf paper and taking it home with them. Furthermore, there existed a
feeling amongst many supply teachers, myself included, that to call upon
assistance from outside the classroom to deal with a difficult situation was
likely to be regarded as a reflection of a lack of control by other staff and may
serve to impugn their apparent competence. This resulted in pressure to
contain any incidents within their own classrooms which served to further
isolate them. However, as is highlighted below, this isolation can be used to
the distinct advantage of the supply teacher towards persuading others that,
whatever the reality of the situation, they are at least 'coping' within a school.

Despite the fact that switching from one school to another often
demanded quite dramatic shifts in age-range, routine, curriculum and pedagogy, the expectation of adaptation remained. It is not surprising then that
whereas some moves between schools required little in the way of personal
adaptation, others demanded recourse to fairly radical strategies in order to at
least give the impression that not only was I 'competent', but also that I was
actually conforming.

The ethos of 'privacy' which, Lortie (1975) argues, is jealously guarded
by experienced teachers and which leads to the isolation of teachers within the
traditionally closed classroom, can serve as a vital tool in implementing
personal pedagogic preferences in the comparative secrecy and safety of the
classroom. Fortunately, such privacy was a feature normally inherited from
the absent class teacher and I was not therefore required to engineer it myself;
I simply maintained or modified it. Thus in each classroom available, views
in for the casual passer-by would be screened off by varying degrees with
posters, children's work or some equivalent device. In one exceptional
circumstance a teacher in an adjacent room had taken it upon himself to paint
out with yellow paint the entire bottom four or so feet of an extensive set of
windows which overlooked a narrow expanse of playground bordered by a
ten-foot high wall. This, he informed me, was so that the children would not
be 'distracted from their lessons' by any playground activity, but interestingly it also served as the preferred route of the headteacher in his frequent
journeying between the junior and infant buildings. Deprived of a view into
the classroom, heads would often 'pop in' with various messages or 'just see
how things were going'. Other heads revealed that they also questioned the
children themselves about their new teacher or looked through their exercise
books in order to gauge the type and standard of work being undertaken. But
with the vast majority of outsiders deprived a view into the classroom, the
next most significant clue as to what might actually be occurring in a room at
any given time is noise. Denscombe (1980) has suggested that the amount of
noise emanating from a classroom may serve as an indicator to outsiders as to
the level of control that a teacher has over the pupils and may subsequently be
used to measure a teacher's competence. Perhaps it is no coincidence that

those teachers deemed to be 'good at discipline' often left their classroom doors ajar for no apparent reason other than to demonstrate their apparent mastery over the pupils. The importance attached to noise and its relation to control and competence was clearly demonstrated through a series of incidents at Moss Lane. The following occurred early on during my time there:

> During a PE lesson one afternoon the children became particularly noisy towards the climax of an intensely competitive team game. The cheering of teams and shouting of encouragement was rather loud but thankfully not terribly prolonged. We then returned to the classroom where the children got changed to go out to break. Back in the staffroom it transpired that one of the teachers had been showing her class a video in the library, which was adjacent to the hall where the PE lesson had been held and that she had had to suspend operations for a 'full thirty seconds' (presumably during the climax of the game) 'due to excessive noise'. This was not taken lightly by the rest of the staff and I was informed by the Deputy Head that I should try to keep them under tighter control, particularly during risky lessons such as PE. Upon protesting that at no time did I consider them to be beyond my control, the teacher in question announced, 'Well it didn't sound like it to me'.

I had acted in clear breach of established norms within that school and my discipline had been deemed as 'lacking'. What's more, there existed a clearly defined category of what were regarded as 'risky lessons' in terms of noise and control amongst the staff. One such activity was art, and for many of the teachers art lessons normally involved simple exercises in draughtmanship or the colouring in of outlines reproduced from children's drawing books. The following conversation took place in the staffroom one breaktime:

> Mr H.: We're actually doing some painting today [noises of exaggerated surprise from fellow staff]. Well, I do try to do it at least once a term so we'll get it over and done with today.
>
> Ms T.: Oh, I hate painting. I avoid doing it whenever I possibly can.

Another 'risky lesson' was PE:

> Ms B.: [upon receiving news of a visiting lecturer] Great, that means that we can't do PE tomorrow in the hall!
>
> Ms T.: Oh you lucky thing you.

However, failure to come up to scratch in terms of the internal, if informal, rules governing 'acceptable' and 'non-acceptable' curriculum and pedagogy was not the only method of incurring disapproval. For example, fuelled by the enthusiasm of Lakeside School the previous term, I began in earnest to replace the previous occupants' display work on the classroom wall with work done by the present class. In order to complete this as quickly as possible we began work on a variety of large and colourful friezes centred around different themes. When we eventually ran out of space we decided to renew the corridor display with one of our own. Whereas at Lakeside School this had proved an effective and acceptable activity, at Moss Lane I was eventually taken aside by the acting deputy head, who informed me that he considered that I'd done by far enough display work for now and that I'd 'better leave some for Mr Stewart to do when he returned'. Obviously I was beginning to set an unwelcome precedent, for traditionally work at 'our end of the corridor' (i.e. the upper juniors) did not involve an emphasis on display work and that was the way it must remain. Clearly, then, I was constantly under pressure to conform to a generally held notion of what teachers *should* be doing and the way in which they should be doing it, depending on which school I was working in. But how can this be to the advantage of the supply teacher?

The dual features of 'privacy' and 'control' have been highlighted by Denscombe (1982), who suggests that there operates within schools a 'hidden pedagogy' amongst teachers which centres on a shared belief that privacy and control are the basic prerequisites for successful teaching. This belief is passed down through generations of teachers, has developed from the day-to-day requirements and exigencies of teaching providing 'the grounds for estimating their [the teachers'] practical competence'. As has been pointed out, privacy was indeed a feature of primary classrooms and one which was maintained by teachers, and it is also clear that 'control' over one's charges is essential if one wishes to be considered 'competent'; however, there were further expectations, for example: 'Arrived to take a class whose room bordered on to the main assembly hall. The deputy head informed me that lower school assembly was taking place that morning and I therefore needed to keep them as quiet and as busy as possible.' Interesting here was the additional requirement that I should keep the class 'busy'. It was normally assumed that as long as the class was engaged in an acceptable activity and they appeared to be busy, then learning was taking place. Sharp and Green (1975) suggest that keeping them busy ('busyness') not only carries with it underlying connotations of a questionable method of social control, but also serves as an indispensable aid for the teacher towards competent management of the classroom. Certainly, as a supply teacher it proved a potent strategy towards the fulfilment of effective impression management, for as long as they appeared to be doing something properly (i.e. quietly and busily), then everyone, including the majority of children, was happy and I was 'in control'. I quickly developed a survival pack of crossword puzzles, games and other activities which pupils could engage in during those risky parts of a lesson when some of the children had finished all of their work and had nothing left to do. Also, I soon learned to give them 'work' to do from the blackboard during registration, an activity designed ostensibly to give them extra practice in essential numeracy skills, but equally to keep them occupied and quiet thus reducing the threat of noise and disorder and therefore maintaining the impression to outsiders that 'my class' were not only engaged in useful learning but also under firm control.

Initial interaction

A highly mobile part-time supply teacher will not have the benefits associated with institutional location. These are benefits which must be earned through a successful period of teaching in a variety of schools which might then request that the teacher return for future work there. Indeed, a measure of one's success at a particular school was whether or not at the end of the placement the headteacher asked for your telephone number. Thus an element of *real* choice begins to emerge dependent upon performance, but until that happens she must constantly undergo the process of establishing relations and 'proving' herself within schools if she is to achieve a lower degree of mobility within the LEA and enjoy some of the benefits associated with institutional location.

In order to achieve this as quickly and as smoothly as possible, the incoming teacher must attempt to establish as quickly as possible what life is *likely* to be like in that school. Under normal circumstances there exist a number of aids of varying reliability towards acquiring knowledge of a school, for instance telephoning prior to arrival, observing the nature of the catchment area and the outward appearance of the school and classroom. Occasionally, there was time enough to be given a tour of the school and an explanation of procedures, timetable and expectations of work and behaviour and so on. Such information, however, was not always helpful, as in the case of arriving to relieve a headteacher of a class one morning at extremely short notice:

> Arrived at the school at 9.30 am. The headteacher was taking the class (twenty-eight 9 and 10 year olds) for maths. He welcomed me enthusiastically and loudly informed me that they were 'generally a nice class'. He then proceeded to warn me of particular individuals to be 'on the look-out for' and pointed out the slow table who got 'easily bored'. He then left me with, 'Don't let them get away with anything Mr Lovett'.

However, it is not only the teacher who requires information about a new class but also *vice versa*. This period of initial encounter and the ensuing negotiation of some sort of consensus was a most crucial period of interaction between myself and any new class, for it was during these early stages that both myself and the pupils assessed one another and began to formulate a tentative definition of what life in that classroom was going to be like from that moment onwards. As Ball (1984) has pointed out, 'these . . . encounters are of crucial significance not only for understanding what comes later but in actually providing for what comes later'. This is the time that teacher and pupils to attempt to establish a working relationship based upon mutually acceptable terms; but upon what criteria do they base their negotiations and what decides the eventual outcome?

The common ground which both teachers and pupils share is a personal view of schooling that has evolved from their own experience of schools both inside and outside of institutions. All have been socialized in one way or another into perspectives upon schooling, and consequently all have an idea of what classroom life is *supposed* to be like at least. But no class can be realistically viewed as a unified group but rather, as Kleinig (1982) has pointed out, consists of 'thirty or more children with different backgrounds, temperaments, levels of achievement, interests and expectations, packed without reference to their own desires into not very comfortable classrooms'.

Teachers have the advantage, however, in that they are normally in the position of holding formal power, initially at least, and must to rely upon their own knowledge and experience of teaching to initiate a relationship which will be acceptable not only to themself but also the majority of pupils in that class. Under ordinary circumstances both teacher and pupils might be expected to have access to a variety of information which informs them in advance of what they may expect from one another, but with supply teachers there rarely exists any such point of reference. The onus is therefore upon individuals and groups within the classroom to elicit from the teacher significant behaviour which might indicate the likely nature of the impending relationship. There was sometimes, time allowing, a good deal of advice given beforehand, for instance a typical rundown on a class:

> I think you'll find them a nice class, but watch out for these two [pointing to a desk] and make sure that this one doesn't sit next to that one. This one'll try it on and I should take care over this one and that one. Any problems and send [X] to fetch me from my office. These on this table can be relied upon and [Y] is usually quite sensible.

Pupils, however, have no access to such information regarding their new teacher. They hold a view about what a teacher might be like, but one of the most salient features about teachers is that they all differ. They will therefore set out to discover the nature of this new teacher by attempting to elicit responses which they can then translate into a meaningful picture. Having begun to acquire such knowledge, they would then attempt to explore new possibilities of classroom life by attempting to establish new parameters and norms in conjunction with the new teacher's attempts to establish their own definition of the situation. Thus it became a process of negotiation between the teacher and dominant groups or individuals within the class, manifesting itself in a continual series of what might initially be considered trivial incidents. For example:

> Arrived in good time and was shown to my classroom [in an annexe overlooking a playground]. I was left alone and began looking at the timetable, registers and some exercise books left on the desk. As children began to arrive they started to congregate in groups outside the classroom windows, and were obviously aware that I was their new teacher for the week. Eventually, one of them came in and began fumbling in his desk. Asked if Mr [A.] normally allowed them inside

before the bell, he replied 'No sir'. I sent him out. This was witnessed by children in the playground who flocked around him upon his ejection from the classroom.

However trivial such an incident might appear, its significance should not be underestimated. However genuine his mission, it provided an early opportunity for him on behalf of his classmates to test my reaction to previously established norms. My immediate response was to refer to those norms in an attempt to assert that as far as I was concerned life was to carry on as normal. Thus negotiation always began with a series of minor incidents, as on another occasion in a later school:

> Children came quietly into registration and sat at their tables. One girl came in and immediately sat on top of her desk and wished me a cheerful 'good morning'. Asked whether or not she normally sat on top of her desk she replied, 'no sir' and sat down on her chair. This was watched by the whole class.

Again she had behaved in deliberate breach of previously established classroom norms and had done so in order to monitor my response not only for her own benefit but also for the rest of the class.

It was also interesting that renegotiation of previously established routines and norms was not only confined to teacher and pupils but also occurred amongst pupils who would often attempt renegotiation amongst themselves attempting to capitalize on my lack of knowledge of the situation. For example:

> While discussing the timetable with the class the question of PE arose. The master timetable contained three periods of PE during the week, but the teacher had only been giving them one. Some class members asked for the full three periods, others were more than content with the one. We eventually agreed upon two. This did not please everyone, but the majority found it acceptable.

The events surrounding the negotiations of classroom life as experienced during the initial periods of interaction have so far been discussed in the context of establishing some sort of working consensus acceptable to the majority. It would, however, be naïve to assume that all pupils are working towards consensus. There were always those whose action ran contrary to any notion of consensus and appeared to deliberately provoke confrontation with me as a new teacher. These intermittent skirmishes (Hargreaves 1975) may involve an intrinsic satisfaction to the perpetrator since the occasional sanctions imposed by the teacher are regarded as worthwhile, for the resulting prestige and attention rewarded as a result by the rest of the class. Riseborough certainly doesn't underestimate the importance of such actions and describes schools as 'teacher processing organizations' (1981) whose pupils through the continual process of what he terms 'the dialectic of teaching and learning' (1986), may attempt to make or break teachers according to their needs. The process of working out whether or not I possessed the necessary managerial skills to defend what I consider to be acceptable parameters of interaction was not only constant and stressful but also potentially dangerous. Furthermore, I learnt to my cost on more than one occasion that what began as sporadic incidents had a tendency to multiply in both frequency and intensity if taken too lightly, and might involve more and more children. This of course is not only experienced by supply teachers but also by full-time teachers, with potentially devastating consequences, for although the teacher initially holds more power than the pupils, that power is circumscribed, and:

> if it is used unfairly or unreasonably from the subjective perspective of the children, then they will change from their tactical compliance to more offensive strategies leading to a breakdown of the working consensus. They will defend themselves, often through forms of 'disorder', thus increasing the survival threat experienced by the teacher.

For example, at one school a very experienced teacher had arrived in September to take up a senior post and also act as class teacher to what were regarded as a 'difficult' class of upper juniors. After six weeks she was forced to leave the school. The pupils version of events was relayed to me by one of the girls:

> The trouble with her was that she never let us get away with nothing. She was always jumping down our throats. One thing she'd do was keep us all in at break for something that just one of us did, like Martin falling off his chair. It got so that we never had any breaks. But the more she kept us in the more we mucked about [laughing]. We really ganged up on her!

Here, the teacher had clearly over-reacted in the pupils' view and they met her over-reaction with over-reaction of their own.

The critical importance of initial interaction is clearly recognized by teacher cultures in all schools. Common snippets of advice included 'sit on them hard' and 'try to keep their heads down' are reminiscent of similar panaceas for successful teaching as offered during the probationary year (i.e. 'don't smile at them until Christmas') but do serve to reflect the universal concern of teachers that the establishment of control is vital if 'successful' teaching is to take place. Important, however, is the requirement that not only must an acceptable classroom relationship be set up between teacher and pupils as well as pupils and pupils, but this must also be acceptable to significant outsiders and be in sympathy with the general school ethos. It is this situation that the supply teacher has to contend with time and again in the course of her/his work.

Conclusion

Space does not allow for a lengthy exposition of later experiences, but the examples given will hopefully help serve to illustrate how in the course of my work as supply teacher it quickly became necessary to implement and maintain strategies in order to impress upon others that not only was I coping in any given class but also that I was conforming in terms of the collective pedagogy of the school. This is not in essence very different from what happens to any other teacher, but the supply teacher has little choice over destination, is expected to undergo this process continually and must adapt to a school or risk being labelled 'unsuitable', or worse still 'incompetent'. In addition to such pressures, supply teachers through the very nature of their work do not have automatic recourse to either institutional support nor anything more than the most basic support from teaching organizations. They are subject to methods of work which may be considered extraordinary in conventional teaching terms, yet receive minimal benefits and rewards. In short, the supply teacher is expected to operate fully as a full-time teacher on the one hand, but is rewarded as a casual worker by staff, schools and LEAs both through minimal possible wage levels, few rights as workers and very restricted opportunities for career advancement.

I have attempted to highlight features which I personally feel were important in my role as supply teacher. Clearly, then, it is a personal perspective but one which I feel able to claim as being shared by a proportion of fellow supply teachers with whom I came into contact both during the course of the research and in similar situations since. There is strong evidence of a commonality of experience amongst supply teachers with respect to their experiences of expectations and conditions of work. Furthermore, supply teachers recognize the extraordinary demands placed upon them and the potential consequences of 'failure', but as an unorganized, part-time work-force without specific location or full trade-union protection, they are powerless to alter their position.

The situation is slowly beginning to change, however, since LEAs are realizing the crucial importance of maintaining a well-motivated pool of willing supply cover both in response to recent teacher unrest and the teachers' consequent strict observance of contractual terms, as well as the growing emphasis upon in-service training essential to the successful implementation of initiatives, particularly in the secondary sector, such as CPVE, TVEI and GCSE. Evidence of this concern is becoming more abundant with LEAs beginning to advertise for contracted supply teachers with built-in career opportunities available.

The effects of such developments on the position of those who can only work on a part-time basis, however, remains to be seen. It may be that they will benefit from the increasing recognition and importance becoming attached to the roles of their full-time colleagues, or conversely it may simply serve to widen the gulf between them and consolidate their position as a distinct subcategory of the teaching workforce *of* whom an extraordinary amount is expected, but *for* whom very little is provided.

References

Alexander, R. (1984) *Primary Teaching*, London, Holt, Rinehart & Winston.
Apple M. (1983) 'Work, Class and Teaching', in Walker, S. and Barton, L. (eds) *Gender Class and Education*, Lewes, Falmer Press.
Ball, S. (1984) 'Initial Encounters in the Classroom and the Process of Establishment', in Hammersley, M. and Woods, P. (eds) *Life in School: The Sociology of Pupil Culture*, Milton Keynes, Open University Press.
Becker, H. and Geer, B. (1971) 'Latent Culture', in Cosin, B. Dale, R. Esland, G. and Swift, D. (eds) *School and Sociology: A Sociological Reader*, London and Milton Keynes, Open University Press/Routledge & Kegan Paul.
Denscombe, M. (1980) 'Keeping 'em Quiet: The Significance of Noise for the Practical Activity of Teaching', in Woods, P. (ed.) (1980) *Teacher Strategies*, Beckenham, Croom Helm.
Denscombe, M. (1982) 'The "Hidden Pedagogy" and its Implications for Teacher Training', *British Journal of the Sociology of Education* 3, No. 3.
Earley, P. (1986) *Questions of Supply: An Exploratory Study of External Cover Arrangements*, Slough, NFER.
Glaser, B. and Strauss, A. (1967) *The Discovery of Grounded Theory: Strategies for Qualitative Research*, Chicago, Aldine.
Hargreaves, D. (1975) *Deviance in Classrooms*, London, Routledge & Kegan Paul.
Kleinig, J. (1982) *Philosophical Issues in Education*, Beckenham, Croom Helm.
Lawn, M. and Barton, L. (1985) 'Making Sociologists Confess', *British Journal of the Sociology of Education* 6, 1.
Lortie, D. (1975) *Schoolteacher*, Chicago, University of Chicago Press.
Musgrove, P. (1972) *The Sociology of Education*, London, Methuen.
Nias, J. (1984) 'The Definition and Maintenance of Self in Primary Teaching', *British Journal of the Sociology of Education*, 5, 3.
Riseborough, G. (1981) 'Teacher Careers and Comprehensive Schooling', *Sociology* 15, 3.
Riseborough, G. (1986) 'Pupils, Teachers' Careers and Schooling: An Empirical Study', Ball, S. and Goodson, I. (eds) *Teacher's Lives and Careers*, Lewes, Falmer Press.
Sharp, R. and Green, A. (1975) *Education and Social Control*, London, Routledge & Kegan Paul.
Smith, L. (1978) 'An Evolving Logic of Participant Observation, Educational Ethnography, and Other Case Studies', in Schulman, L. (ed.) *Review of Research in Education* 6, A.E.R.A.
Woods, P. (ed.) (1980) *Pupil Strategies*, Beckenham, Croom Helm.

12

What it means to 'feel like a teacher': the subjective reality of primary school teaching

Jennifer Nias

The rather curious title of this paper arises from remarks made to me by primary teachers, of between two and nine years' experience, whom I interviewed between twelve and thirteen years ago. Subsequent analysis of the notes I made during those interviews suggested that a main determinant of teachers' behaviour in classroom and school is a desire to preserve their self-image (Nias 1984, 1985, 1987). Since many of them take up the work with a firm commitment to it, they tend not to incorporate 'teacher' into self-image even though they may do the job successfully and for many years. In other words, as several said, 'I teach but I do not feel like a teacher'.

Eventually, some of those who entered the profession take up alternative careers (notably parenthood), and others, finding they cannot leave teaching, become 'privatized workers'. However, a proportion, satisfied that they 'feel like teachers', incorporate an occupational identity into their self-image (Nias 1985). Unfortunately, I did not at the time ask them what they meant by that phrase. Like Woods (1981), Pollard (1985) and Sikes *et al.* (1985) I had evidence, in and out of the classroom, that teachers act so as to safeguard their sense of identity, but none of us could indicate how that identity was experienced by teachers themselves.

The decision to undertake in 1985 the second stage in a longitudinal study of these ninety-nine one-year trained graduate primary teachers offered an opportunity to fill this gap. I wrote to all of my interviewees, asking for their movements to date and whether they would be willing to talk to me again. I also wrote to fifteen people who had qualified in 1976 or 1977, too late for my original enquiry, but whom I knew still to be teaching. Fifty-one of the first group replied, all but two saying they would be ready to meet me. (These two were both men, still teaching in the same school or neighbourhood in which they had been ten years earlier). Thirteen of the second group replied affirmatively. I decided to interview only those who were still working in infant, junior or middle schools, though in the event I also talked to one special-school teacher (a woman), three secondary teachers (two men and one woman), two adult-education tutors (both women), five college lecturers (two men, three women) and three mothers who had recently given up teaching. Altogether, I conducted forty-eight interviews (two of them by telephone), during teacher action, in the spring term 1985. There were seventeen men, thirty-one women, five headteachers (four men), seven deputy heads (of whom five were women), eight women doing part-time or supply work. I left the choice of place to individuals; twenty-four chose their places of work, and I met the rest in pubs or their own homes. The venue did not appear to affect the freedom with which they spoke. Interviews were semi-structured, following a loosely framed set of questions, and took place at times convenient to individuals. The shortest was about fifty minutes, the longest about three hours. About two-thirds were tape-recorded, with the rest I took rapid notes and wrote up a summary as soon as possible thereafter. In both cases transcripts or summaries were sent to individuals for validation, with the suggestion (of which only three took advantage) that they delete anything they did not want me to use, and with assurances of confidentiality. The main focus of my questions were motivation; job satisfaction and dissatisfaction; professional, personal and career development; personal experience of and reflections upon teaching, the place of work in life and future career plans.

All those who replied to my original letter knew me well (I had been tutor to the PGCE course which most of them attended and several had kept in touch since then). All of the forty-eight had taught 4 to 13 year olds (the approximate age range for which they trained) at some point, and thirty-four (thirteen men, twenty-two women) were still doing so. Only three (two still teaching) spoke with distaste of the experience. Most were succeeding, in career terms, or were enthusiastically resuming a career after child-rearing. Thus the evidence on which I have drawn is heavily biased. With few exceptions it reflects the experience of successful and committed teachers who had been working for between nine and eighteen years (though in the case of married women returners, the years worked varied from five to twelve). Most were happy to identify as teachers and could describe the subjective reality of that experience. What this paper does not set out to do is to analyse the experience of the bored, frustrated, unhappy or uncommitted teacher, ready or anxious to change jobs or occupations but unable to do so. It attempts to describe what 'feeling like a teacher' means to those who espouse the identity of 'primary teacher', not of those who have rejected or never accepted it.

The evidence used comes from two sources. All interviewees were asked if they 'felt like' teachers, and an explanation for the question was given. If they said that they did, I then asked them to explain this reply. In addition, I have drawn upon other responses in which individuals were talking more generally about their experiences of teaching.

Eight of my forty-eight interviewees did not see themselves as teachers. One man and one woman had drifted into it and were trapped by financial pressures and lack of alternative employment. Three women (one a college lecturer) and one man enjoyed some aspects of teaching but rejected what they saw as the socially imposed role of the primary teacher. The two adult-education tutors felt in their new jobs, 'You can go in as yourself, not with that teacher-person to hide behind', or 'There is no switch of personality, I am the same person while teaching as I am outside'. Two men, though enthusiastic about teaching, felt all adults were teachers and preferred not to split their occupation from their other roles. I have included their responses in my analysis.

'Being yourself'

Most of the remaining forty believed that to adopt the identity of 'teacher' was simply to 'be yourself' in the classroom. They expressed this idea in three similar but slightly different ways. Some stressed a sense of fit between self and occupation (e.g. 'I feel as if I've found my niche'; 'However annoyed I may be at the end of a day in school . . . I still feel I'm in the right job for me'; 'There's nothing else that I'd rather be doing, nothing that would suit me better'). Others saw little distinction between their identities at work and outside it; as one said, 'What's happening to you as a person can't be separated from what's happening to you as a teacher'. Similar responses included: 'I've mellowed as a person so I've mellowed as a teacher'; 'What you are as a person goes into your job'; 'Most of the things I do [with the children] I love doing myself'; 'For me, being happy in teaching was a question of realizing what sort of person I was'; 'I don't think you're any good as a teacher if you're no good as a person'. Lastly, some felt, as one said, that they 'would have been the same person no matter what job I went into'. For example, they saw themselves as 'Christians', 'carers', 'organizers', 'workaholics'.

Two people stressed how important it is for teachers to have a strong sense of personal identity. One said, 'If teachers are going to be any good, they've got to have a really strong concept of what they are themselves. Fortunately, I have.' The other who had left primary teaching recalled:

> I just wanted to get out. I was asking too much of myself. I couldn't give what I hadn't got inside me to give and I felt that having gone from school straight into university and back into school again, I had not had the opportunity to explore life and certainly not to explore my own creativity. And there I was trying to get the children to be creative individuals and doing all the things I seemed never to have done at school . . . I wanted to sit down and make puppets and play with paint

and put my fingers in. I loved just playing with children . . . I felt I
needed to become whole and find out who I was and . . . become a
personality in my own right.

'Being whole'

Many teachers linked, as this one did, the notions of 'being yourself' and
'being whole'. Some achieved 'wholeness' by blurring the boundaries
between their personal and professional lives. A woman said:

I tend to bring a lot of my personal life into school with the children.
They know a lot about what I'm doing all the time, so in that way
teaching is never separate from my personal life. They know all about
my cat, everything that happened to me the previous evening, they
know that I sail, they know that I paint, they know what my house is
like, so they're not separate lives at all.

And a man recalled:

Before I was married what I did during the day followed through
automatically, into the pub. So if I went for a drink, all I talked about
was school. It was a town pub with a wide range of people, actors, bus
drivers, postmen, alcoholics. I fulfilled the role of the educationist . . .
and I'd go into school the following morning and I'd talk in assembly
about the guy I'd met in the pub last night who had real tales to tell.
There wasn't any conflict between my two lives.

Many more found a sense of unity in school, particularly with their
classes. Typically: 'I enjoy doing drama with them, especially if it's some sort
of work that means . . . the whole class working together so that we're all
swept along'; 'I like the class response when we feel as if we're a class and "our
Miss is doing this" or "with our Miss we did so and so"'; 'I always had a great
class relationship . . . [I worked] to create a kind of group identity and I was
part of that'; 'It's a feeling that at the end of the day, at the end of a year, at the
end of a project you . . . can look back and say, "Yes, we all, as a class, found
it satisfying"'. A secondary teacher was trying to create a remedial unit 'seen
as having a oneness it never had before'. A head confessed, 'I think I'm trying,
probably, unwisely, to build up the same sort of thing I had with a class. I'm
regarding them as my class of 220 and I'm hoping I can go at least part of the
way [towards] that sense of oneness'. Other heads, recognizing that they had
permanently lost this aspect of 'feeling like a teacher', nevertheless regretted it
and repeatedly referred back to it.

What these excerpts do not convey is the non-verbal signs which every
teacher used when he/she was talking about the 'wholeness' of class teaching.
Without exception when they tried to explain what it was to feel at one with a
group of children, they cupped their hands or made enfolding movements

with hands and arms. They spoke eagerly, enthusiastically, often leaning forwards, their faces animated. What they seemed to me, as a listener, to be describing was a deeply satisfying sense of belonging. Certainly, their response to my questions was an affective rather than a cognitive one, as is further shown by the difficulty they had in reflecting analytically upon the notion of 'wholeness'.

There were two teachers, however, who did manage to explain in some way why 'wholeness' was important to them. Both talked about it in terms of feelings. Commenting upon the introduction of specialist teaching into a pair of classes, a man said:

> I began to feel . . . there's something wrong here. I began to think about it. It seemed that we were open to the charge of splitting the curriculum in half and we know this is wrong, because we know there are links between things . . . I thought to myself, 'But we can do that, that can't be the problem. We can do that quite easily because, for example, in a topic on the body, writing [for Jane] can easily be linked to maths work on body measurements [for me]. There's something else that must be missing'. And [it seemed] that it was a sort of psychological perception that is missing. There is a mood the children have; individuals are different and we don't think about it very much because it's not one of those things that we actually plan and mark like a piece of work, but it's there, and the child's mood from one day to the next is different and it carries him through the day. . . . Normally . . . his mood comes from the previous piece of work and there's a psychological strand running through the day. By psychological I'm talking about his feelings. If we split the day in half, there is a rupture, it's as if he starts anew the next day – in fact of course there is a sort of link from one day to the next, so I can't even say it's like another day . . . but with us there is that split and the child has to start anew in the afternoon.

Interviewer: 'Are you saying that anyone can build links between subjects but it requires one teacher in one class to build a link between feelings. Is that right? Teacher: 'Yes, that's right. I've had misgivings all along about the way we have been doing it.' A woman suggested:

> having that ['we're a class' feeling] isn't to do with curriculum, or the integrated day or anything . . . it's about feeling you're together. . . . What goes on in a classroom is mostly about feelings, just as it is in life generally. Feelings are infinitely more important in guiding how people act than ideas are. You have to accept the importance of feelings, your own and theirs, or you will never be happy as a teacher.

The desire to create 'wholeness' also showed itself in attempts to soften the barriers of role, age and status and to prevent the erection of new ones (particularly those of curriculum or timetabling). Several teachers attacked what they described as 'fragmentation' or 'splitting' of their pupils' learning experiences. Many talked enthusiastically, and in the case of some heads, nostalgically, about their involvement with children in extracurricular activities, clubs, on field trips and school journeys, in residential study centres. At the time of the interviews most, because of their support for industrial action, had abandoned such activities and all had stopped eating lunch with pupils. Many regretted this curtailment of their roles and looked forward to a resumption of those activities which blurred the boundaries between the instructional and other aspects of their jobs. The urge to work in an environment characterized by unity, not division, extended to staff relationships as well. In Nias (forthcoming) I have shown how important it was to my interviewees to feel they were 'pulling together' as part of a staff team. In the words of a head, 'The school was a part of me, the staff were a part of me . . . I couldn't separate myself from them'. Similarly, several spoke warmly of schools in which they 'felt part of the community', 'were seen as part of a close-knit community', 'were very much part of a great, big unit, we are rooted in the history of the place, we've got parents who came to the same school'. Two had taken jobs in village schools, one because in such a school 'we're constantly working towards a oneness with the community', the other for 'the sense of community intimacy which attracted me to a small school'. Four had chosen to move to 4–11 schools because in them they could be with the same children for most of the latter's school career and, 'if you're lucky, they come back from the high school to see you sometimes so you see them as they get older, too'. Three of the five people who had moved to jobs in initial training made a point of telling me their main aim was to try and bring theory and practice together for students. Asked to describe things he enjoyed doing as a teacher, one person replied, 'I find that very difficult – it's the wholeness of the thing, I think, the total experience'.

'Being natural'

Feeling 'whole' was very close, for many teachers, to being 'natural'. Several saw school as being 'unnatural' and wanted to find ways of 'having a compromise between letting [pupils] be childish and childlike and saying "When you're here . . . this is how we do it"'. Two men rejected the designation 'teacher' because, as one said, 'In any relationship between an adult and a child, teaching is a natural role to play'. Nearly a third used the family as a metaphor or an analogy for their favourite schools. One described working with her welfare helper in a special school as 'we're almost a mummy and daddy, with a family'; another said he treated the children in his class as he did his own children, 'behaving like a dad to them'. In several other teachers' minds, small village schools offered a 'natural', 'family' form of education. Indeed, four confessed, as one said, to 'having a pipedream about ending up in a village school where I can make education into a natural thing and my part in it a natural one. . . . The more you can equate the classroom to a family, the more effective the education.'

Yet families were valued more because they were seen as having a shared sense of purpose than for their affective ties. Typically: 'I would like the staff to be far more open and honest about teaching, and while they are actually there in the job, to work as a team. We're just not benefiting from everybody's experience, they're too isolated, everybody is. Nobody's happy because there isn't unity, there isn't that kind of family feeling about the school', and, 'When you know a class and they know you there's a lot of shared humour, a lot of things you know together. You become a unit, everyone looking out for the other and helping them. It's like a family, I suppose. You establish a sense of unity and with it a sense of purpose.'

'Establishing relationships with children'

Embedded in the notions of belonging and of education as an extension of family life is a belief that to teach, one must 'establish a relationship with pupils'. Several people were explicit about this: 'I've met kids that I taught when I first went there who are now working . . . They don't just say, "Aren't you Mr Jones?", they say, "Alright Sir?" and that's the difference. It's not a question of education, it's a question of relationships'; 'Teaching is getting the children interested in you. And they will only be interested in you when they have seen you are interested in them'; 'One of the problems of being a part-timer is that you can't build up that relationship with them – they don't care what I think of them . . . a lot of them just don't care and in little ways they show not a lack of respect so much as a lack of consideration, and that makes it more difficult'; 'You never say to a child, "Carry my bags"; you offer to carry theirs . . . and you make sure the teachers never sit while the children are standing. But it works both ways, I used to get them together and say "We're going on holiday this week, I'm going on holiday as well, don't spoil it for me"'; 'What a teacher is to any individual child could be something totally different, it's a function of the two personalities involved'. Many described their work in terms such as 'getting cooperation from the children', 'it's a joint effort between you and them', 'doing something you and the children enjoy together', 'it all comes down to this relationship between you and the children'. One put it very strongly: 'If you actually reach the level where you see yourself as an hourly paid imparter of knowledge to whom relationships are unimportant, I think that is when you cease to be a professional'. Several others made similar references to 'passing on information, not teaching' or 'telling them things, rather than teaching'.

If my interviewees said that they liked their work, I asked them to imagine that I knew nothing about schools, and to name several things which they did that they enjoyed. Only two could do this; the rest described their satisfactions in terms of relationships with individuals or groups. By contrast, no one had difficulty in naming things that he/she did which he/she did not enjoy. I have explored their responses further in Nias (forthcoming). In this context I wish only to note the difficulty which committed teachers appear to have in conceptualizing the pleasures of the job in instrumental terms. In the same way, many find it hard to think in terms of external measures for their success or failure. One said, 'You can look at it in terms of results, but you can also look at it in terms of your gut reaction to the class as a whole and how they feel about you and you feel about them'. Another suggested, 'You build up a relationship with the children and then you feel as if you're actually achieving something'.

In general, my interviewees found it very hard to describe what they meant by their 'relationship' with children. Occasionally, it was seen as playing a parental role, sometimes as relating to peers (e.g. 'It can be as close as another friend'; 'Some of those children I'd really like to keep as friends'). Very frequently it contains a marked element of humour; many teachers appear to gauge the state of their relationship with a class by the extent to which 'we can all have a laugh together', 'I can be myself, laugh and joke', or 'we can share a joke and then get down to work again'. However, to many teachers the relationship is more than being either a parent or a friend. Several people described teaching as 'communication with another human being' or 'learning to communicate with other people'. A woman reflected, 'I've come to realize that if you really want to educate children you've got to share yourself with them, as a person. They've got to know about you, your interests, your life out of school, the sort of person you are. But most of all, it means being open to them as a person, and that makes you vulnerable. Yes, being a teacher is being ready to be vulnerable'. A man put it bluntly, even angrily: 'To talk of teaching as having a relationship with children isn't a cosy thing; it doesn't mean "having a nice time" with them. It means committing yourself as a person'.

Concern, responsibility and control

This commitment has three main characteristics: concern, responsibility and control. Several teachers emphasized the caring aspects of their role, using terms such as 'being prepared to put their interests first', 'doing your best for all the children in your class'. Five, four of them men, put it more strongly than this. One said, 'There are one or two children that I love very dearly. There have been one or two children in the past twelve years I have loved totally . . . only one or two. The difference that having my own son has made to my relationships at school has not been that strong. I still have one or two children I'm really fond of, not as pupils, but as people.' Another said, 'I really loved them until I had my own children. Once I started having my own children, my relationship changed with the classes I taught. But up to my little girl being born I used to love the children in my class, I used to get very close to them; at the end of the summer term I used to be sad at losing them and having to pass them on to someone else.' One woman felt, 'Love comes into it too, that's part of what you experience as a teacher', while another could not face these demands: 'It was giving, giving, giving all day long . . . it drove me round the bend.'

Related to but more detached than affection for children is a sense of responsibility for them. Some people see that, as teachers, they must 'accept the children's dependence on you', 'feel a great responsibility for every child in my care', 'play an active part in what we want our future adults to be', 'accept that you will influence them by what you are, whether you want to or not'. 'It means', claimed a man,

> that you have got to accept them for what they are, and if an 8 year old says, 'I love you, Mr Smith', she means it, and you can't play with that, you cannot dismiss it, you cannot turn round to her and say, 'I love you as well, Sarah', if you don't mean it. And I think that's what feeling like a teacher is: when you realize what an awesome responsibility you bear. . . . If teachers realized just what influence they have on children, I think then they'd realize what being a teacher was.

Another man said:

> I feel privileged, I suppose, to belong to the teaching profession which I really do believe is perhaps the most important profession for changing the future – the future is really in our hands, so to speak . . . I feel a great responsibility in being a teacher. I don't think about it every minute of the day, but when I do, I handle this relationship I'm being given with great care because it's a very precious profession, I'm not involved in making money for anybody, not involved in running a big organiz-ation, or the country, I'm involved in running an organization to nurture children, which must be the most important function in the world. So I accept the responsibility of being a teacher as important.

Strongly related to both caring and responsibility is control. Virtually every teacher responded to my request to explain what it was to 'feel like a teacher' by saying that it was to be in control (e.g. 'It's doing things you're in control of to a large extent'; 'It's being in control of what goes on in the classroom'; 'To start with, it's your will against theirs').

However, people had different reasons for making this response. Ten teachers (five men and five women) were explicit about their felt personal need to control their lives and environments. Two spoke of local political developments (e.g. amalgamations, curriculum initiatives) making them feel that 'instead of me having control over what I'm doing, the outside situation is taking over'. Others talked of the gratification of 'feeling that it's all mine, I'm queen in my own classroom' or 'There can't be many jobs where you are so closely linked with a number of people and it's all revolving round you, where you are controlling things'. Two talked with enthusiasm of teaching as 'you're the one who is making it happen at first hand', or 'it's you who's instigating things in the classroom'. Four (all men) were even more direct: 'I think the relationship's concerned with control. I'm very egocentric and I need to feel, as a person, that I have some control, and it's easy with children, because they're open and they respond'; 'I suppose when it comes to the bottom line what I really want is the ability to know I'm in control'; 'I think control is a personal thing for me. I don't like the idea of having a situation that I can't control. I think I could teach myself to tolerate it but I don't think it comes naturally, I don't like things to be out of hand, I think that's why I like teaching the 9 year olds because they are easier to control than the older children'; '[I wanted promotion] because I want control over what I am doing and what the kids are doing'.

It is of course impossible to tell from the available evidence whether these people were being more frank than the others or whether they had different personality needs. Certainly, I spoke to three people who still found the exercise of classroom control inconsistent with their self-image. One reflected: Feeling like a teacher can have a negative side to it – unless you're careful you can find yourself taking advantage of the situation, that you have tremendous power over children.

Another said:

> Sometimes I feel like Billy Liar or Peter Pan in that I have to pinch myself to think that I'm 36 and people call me 'Sir'; and Mr Brown, when I feel just like a big soft kid half the time. I remember kids calling me Mr Brown when I was doing my teaching practice and I felt such a charlatan . . . I couldn't understand why anyone should defer to me. It took a long time before I could accept it.

and the third felt 'With teaching you're sort of God, aren't you? I find that very hard.' Many more remarked that they hated 'being a policeman'; the times 'when you can't do any teaching because you spend all day just keeping them down'; or 'children who force you to act in ways you know have nothing to do with teaching'.

Yet even these people accepted, as one man said, that as a teacher, 'You have to exercise authority. Treating children like human beings and yet maintaining discipline is a constant challenge.' Indeed, being willing to exercise authority was widely seen as the one necessary condition for 'feeling like a teacher'. Two teachers suggested, 'A teacher's relationship with children is quite distinctive. However much you care and however much you share with them, you assume an air of authority. I didn't have any authority for a couple of years, partly because I didn't really have any conviction that I was doing anything right', and, 'There is no way round it. If you want to be a teacher you have to find some way of establishing your control because it's a sort of barrier you have to get through. If you want to do the job, you have to do that because it is part of being a teacher. You cannot do the rest of the job, which I wanted to do, without getting over that first barrier.'

The related idea that teachers have constantly to strive for a balance between authority and friendliness, recurs over and over again. For example: '[In my first school] you could have a joke with them, you could be friendly up to a point, as you wanted to be, but beyond that they would show you some respect. I found that quite different from where I am now'; 'Being new it was hard trying to be approachable and yet getting the children to realize that there had to be a certain amount of distance. That was awfully hard, but then I think towards the end I got it reasonably right. The children could always come and speak to me and they would never be turned away, and yet they knew I was the teacher and they were the pupils'; 'I think you have to force yourself to do things which you don't like to do – that makes me very unhappy and perhaps it brings on the lows. It's the times when you're with a class, with discipline, and they know how far they can go with you, and you have a laugh and joke and have fun with them, both in and out of the classroom – that works best of all'.

Some people, echoing Waller (1961) and Geer (1968), feel that teachers and learners can never be equal, that the act of teaching necessarily involves the exercise of power. This tacit assumption was voiced in both negative terms (e.g. 'That's why I should be paid the same as a police inspector – I do the same job') and positive ones (e.g. 'Feeling like a teacher is feeling as though you're in control, that you know what response is right for you to make . . . that you're building up a relationship with the children').

Closely related to feeling in control, is the sense of being well-organized and purposeful – 'having specific ends in view, not muddling through, knowing what you're about', 'knowing what you want from and for children', 'being organized, so that in any teaching situation you have a sense of direction'.

However a sense of feeling in control was expressed, the end result for most people was that they became in the words of one man, 'more intuitive, relaxed and spontaneous'. Interviewees repeatedly spoke of being more relaxed in the classroom and the staffroom, of feeling more able to be 'adaptive and flexible', of 'being less of a worrier', 'more laid back', and above all more self-confident. As one person crisply responded, 'Feeling confident in what you do, that's what it all hinges on'.

At this point the circular nature of my argument becomes apparent. What these teachers seemed to be saying was: to 'feel like a teacher' is to feel you can be yourself in the classroom; to be yourself is to feel whole, to act naturally; to act naturally is to enter into a relationship with children in which caring and the exercise of responsibility are made possible by the existence of control; to feel in control enables you to 'be yourself' in the classroom and therefore to 'feel like a teacher'.

Rewards

Now these interviews took place when industrial action in the teaching profession was well under way and my interviewees frequently and cogently expressed dissatisfaction with the status and conditions of teaching as a career. Yet levels of satisfaction with teaching as an occupation were extremely high. Most interviewees, when invited to name things they did not enjoy doing found it hard to go beyond mundane chores such as playground duty on a cold day or routine activities such as marking. Many spontaneously made comments such as, 'It must be rare in a job to look forward to Monday mornings, but I do', 'I love every moment of it', 'I can't think of anything about it that I don't like'; 'There can't be many people that get up and look forward to going to work each day, but most days I do. There's the sense of satisfaction you get, that I get from a lesson or a day or a week, or whatever it is'. Several women told me their non-teaching husbands envied them their job satisfaction; one recalled, 'My husband used to say it was a pity that I was the one who had to give up work and have the baby. He felt that I had more satisfaction from my work than he got out of his'. A woman explained, 'When I was in the classroom . . . that was the only time that I'd ever felt – you know when people talk about 'finding themselves' – I was myself in the classroom. I was doing something in my own right that I was good at and it was the only time I felt it, I never felt it at university'. Another woman, returning to part-time teaching, described how 'I thought, "I've been out of teaching nine years. How on earth is this going to go?" I walked into the classroom and within two minutes it was all back. I was really thrilled . . . I thought, "This is something I know how to do"'. A man told me, 'I feel at one with my career . . . education is something in which I'm interested, involved, active, from my own point of view successful . . . I don't feel as if I ought to be anything else'.

Many teachers also felt useful and needed. Some talked of 'knowing I was making a contribution to the school'; one recalled that her first successful experience of teaching was when in a particular school – 'I found I had something to give and I really enjoyed it.' Several referred to their jobs as being 'worthwhile' (though the only one who felt that her job was socially valued was a teacher of mentally handicapped children) or talked about a continuing commitment to schools and education. Both men and women also talked of 'knowing I'm loved' and of the satisfaction they took from the warmth and responsiveness of their pupils.

Two teachers summed it up: a man said, 'The main thing I get out of teaching is a recognition of me as someone valuable', and a woman, talking about what she liked doing in the classroom, suddenly stopped and exclaimed, 'It's all the feedback things, isn't it – all the things that make you feel good about yourself'.

Self-esteem tended to generate enthusiasm. 'Teaching', said one, 'ought to be something that's an inspiration to you' (it clearly was to him). Others equated 'being a teacher' with conveying interests and enthusiasms to children, taking up new activities or fields of interest in order to keep this freshness and zest, retaining a sense of wonder at the working of children's minds. Two men described teaching as 'exciting'. One likened it to walking a tightrope, the other said, 'I hope I'm always close to the edge. There's that little tingle if you're not quite sure it'll work out . . . I like an edge to what I'm doing.' Many people said they talked a great deal about school and pupils when they were away from them (particularly if they were married to other teachers). One man recalled how he had abandoned another profession to take up teaching largely because in his local pub he used regularly to meet several teachers who had amusing or interesting tales to tell: 'I used to think it must be marvellous to have a job you wanted to talk about in the evenings. I couldn't forget mine quick enough'.

Costs

Yet the greater the enthusiasm teachers showed, the greater their fatigue. Even the most committed teachers talked of being 'incredibly tired', 'utterly exhausted', 'going home shattered but knowing you'd got to prepare for tomorrow', knowing that 'I'm not as energetic as I was ten years ago but the work's no less, and I do get terribly tired', 'getting run down and ill but still having to go on'. A head described how his teaching wife fell asleep as soon as she got home each day; a woman recalled meeting someone at a party who, unaware of her occupation, had said, 'They're funny people, teachers. They're always tired'. A late entrant whose daughter had decided to teach reported having said to her, 'You've seen me at weekends. Do you really want to finish every week feeling like that?'

Teaching was also perceived as requiring a long working day, partly because, as one man said, 'If you're keen on the school you'll spend a lot of time there'. A teaching head claimed, 'My day at school is basically 7.30 am to 4.30 pm with an hour's stop and then I work at night at home – if we're busier I come in at 7.00 am'. Even those who spent less time than this at school argued, as one woman did, 'One is always the teacher, because it's always school which is the most important thing and looking at things for children. When we go out and see things, it's always "Could we have that in school?" I don't know if that's got anything to do with feeling like a teacher, but it's like that all the time'. Another woman put it this way:

> You don't actually go into teaching unless you're a caring person. And the thing about caring is that you care twenty-four hours a day, you don't just care from nine till half past three and so you take your worries, your thoughts with you, you take your enthusiasms home with you. I mean, when I leave here I'll go and walk around [the town] and I'll have half an eye open on what I might be doing on Monday.

For many people, to 'feel like a teacher' is to accept that work is, as one woman claimed, 'our life, not just a career'.

The corollary of this is often the curtailment of other interests and activities or a sense of tension between them. A man, his wife also a teacher, had this to say:

> We used both to be involved in community activities. That has stopped, we can't keep it up. Many, many things. You mentioned gardening, the garden's gone to pot. When we have spare time we leave the town. We get in the car and we drive somewhere. Every weekend, on a Saturday we go away and we drive anywhere and wander the streets and look at the shops and drink a cup of coffee and sometimes go to a film and come back. Sometimes there's work on Sunday to do, but that's our relaxation. Apart from that, there isn't really anything else. Certainly nothing from Monday to Friday. We enter the week on Monday morning and come out of the tunnel on Friday night and we hardly see each other in between.

This kind of total involvement in work was reported by several teachers, both men and women. Sometimes, especially when school also provided a vigorous and interesting social life and/or the work was deemed particularly fulfilling, it was seen as one of the pleasures of teaching. Several people married to teachers chose to tell me that 'work makes an extra bond between us'. A typical comment was, 'Jean and I have exactly the same job and the discussion of the job and the doing of the work is part of our relationship at home because it started that way – we worked together before we did anything else.'

More often, however, interviewees commented on the tension caused for them by the time, energy and attention required by their jobs. In extreme cases it led to an individual giving up teaching:

> I think too much is expected of teachers very often. I would come home every night shattered at four o'clock with two or three hours work to do, if I was going to do my job properly. Who else has to do that? Weekends – I'd spend Saturdays sometimes rummaging round for materials, sometimes taking the kids out. I didn't have a life to myself, I really didn't. It was work, work, work. I wasn't talking to any adults unless I made a big effort and I was usually too tired anyway. The long holidays just disintegrated into recovering from the terms . . . you were always thinking . . . and the dreams I had . . . it was constantly with me, I just couldn't get away from it, you can't just switch off at four o'clock, I couldn't. I think it's an awful job.

Those still in the profession were aware of the pressures it created for them. Sometimes they felt diminished as a person for example:

> I never do anything for me, to contribute to my own growth, not properly. This holidays, for example, I've done a lot of etching which I want to finish and it's been lovely just spending days doing it, and I've got a book on landscape painters – I want to read that properly but I

won't have time to do it and I know when I get back to work I'll be too involved in other things. I resent that – it makes me very unhappy and bad-tempered.

More often, they reported a conflict between work and family life. Two men spoke of 'a difference in commitment' after the birth of their first child. Three others told me about the continuing tension between their domestic and professional commitments (e.g. 'After [my son] was born, all I wanted to do at 3.45 pm was come home. The fact that most nights I didn't gave me a feeling of resentment':

> It's been an ongoing dilemma. When I do things in the evenings, which I do quite often, connected with the school – things like PTA meetings, open nights, occasional kids' ice-skating or whatever it might be – and tell [my wife] that I'm going to be home very late, she accepts it but she doesn't like it. She still can't understand, because I go home and talk about certain teachers who give the minimum and she has said in as many words 'Why can't you be like them?' . . . I do wonder, and I know she does, whether we would have had as many difficulties as we have had with our children, had I been there more of the time and had I devoted more of my energy to them, rather than school . . . it's been the cause of conflict several times.

Three married women with no children said (in the words of one), [My husband] has never complained . . . but sometimes I think if he didn't have the telly to keep him company . . . I feel the stress inside myself – you're pulling two ways'. Four women and one man reported that their enthusiasm for their jobs had contributed to the breakdown of their marriages (e.g. 'He said I was always talking about school'; 'I was working most evenings, or out at school – we saw less and less of each other') and four women said that they had regretfully decided to abandon their careers in favour of parenthood because, as one said, 'I asked other people, "How do you manage teaching and running a home?" and they all replied, "We don't"'. One man claimed, '[Not to have children] was a conscious decision because I've always thought it would be unfair on them to be their father, because I would never have given the sort of job dedication to children that they'd deserve'. To be sure, many married teachers of both sexes had found successful strategies for reconciling the demands of job and home life (Nias, forthcoming), but the tension was always there in the background, 'waiting', as one said, 'to catch you unawares when you least need it'.

Living with paradox

On the face of it many of my interviewees appeared to be giving inconsistent responses. They felt whole and in control, yet tired and under stress, they loved teaching but talked of giving it up. Finally, therefore, I want to address their apparent inconsistencies and to argue that the subjective reality of teaching is the experience of living with paradox.

The notion that dilemmas form an inescapable part of primary teachers' work was sensitively explored in Berlak and Berlak (1981). Trying simultaneously to accomplish irreconcilable ends undoubtedly places a great strain upon teachers and may have been underestimated as a source of stress for many of them. However, many of my interviewees seem to be suggesting that teaching itself is a contradictory activity and that, by implication, it needs to be understood in philosophical as well as sociological terms.

To the best of my knowledge, none of my interviewees has ever studied Froebel or Rousseau, or was aware that in their pursuit of the 'whole' and the 'natural' they were supported by two hundred years of educational thought. Yet to 'feel like a teacher' was, for most of them, to feel at one with themselves, both inside the classroom and away from it. Indeed, some could not distinguish between their occupational and other selves; for them work was as much part of being as were any of their other activities. To those who did make a distinction between their professional and other identities, teaching, at its best, offered opportunities for personal growth and fulfilment. Working as teachers they felt competent, extended, successful, valued (though seldom by parents or society at large), useful, occasionally loved, and, as a result, relaxed and self-confident. In their daily work and their careers, they actively pursued 'wholeness', deliberately blurring the boundaries between their personal and professional lives, trying to teach an undivided curriculum to many-faceted children, valuing unbroken development over the total span of a pupil's school life, seeking the integration of school and community, cultivating in their classes a sense of group identity and prizing highly their own place within these groups. Both as teachers and as staff members they preferred to 'pull together', their metaphors and their body language emphasized supporting, holding, enfolding, belonging. In describing their most powerful educational aims and experiences, they used words like 'organic' and 'oneness'.

This emphasis on wholeness led them to conceptualize teaching not as 'imparting knowledge' but as 'building relationships'. Though few, as far as I know, are familiar with existentialist thought and none had studied the educational writings of Martin Buber, they aspired to become an 'I' to the 'Thou' of every child, making themselves available as resources for and facilitators of the development of each unique personality. What is more, they recognized this as a demanding task, requiring the commitment of themselves as total individuals to all their pupils.

Even the agnostics and atheists appeared also to be influenced by the Christian tradition. They spoke of their pupils as human beings of equal worth to themselves, cared for and accepted moral responsibility for them. They therefore also accepted the need to control them.

Now each of these ways of thinking about teaching imposes both practical and philosophical strains on the teacher. In practical terms, the contemporary debate on the primary school curriculum (especially as it relates to specialist teaching and multi-culturalism), exigencies of cost and staffing, accountability pressures (particularly from those who take a narrow or instrumental view of the curriculum) make it increasingly difficult for teachers to work in environments which are not divided (in terms of time, curriculum and personnel) or constrained. The aftermath of industrial action and the debate about teachers' roles and responsibilities challenges those who see learning as extending outside the classroom and beyond the limits of the school day. As the Oracle Project has made abundantly clear, the managerial difficulties of relating to and answering the learning of each individual within a large class places impossible demands on the teacher. The impact (e.g. school closures, teacher redeployment) of falling roles and financial cuts reduce security and break up established relationships. Small wonder that teachers feel under stress if the conditions of their working lives prevent them from behaving in ways that they perceive as 'organic' or 'natural'. Nor is it surprising that they adopt 'coping strategies' (Hargreaves 1978; Pollard 1985) to alleviate the tension induced by this conflict.

More fundamentally, however, primary-school teachers in England – unlike their French counterparts (Osborn 1985) – appear to have a conception of teaching which imposes upon them the need continually to live and work with paradox. The very nature of teaching, as they seem to experience it, is contradictory. Teachers must nurture the whole while attending to the parts, liberate their pupils to grow in some directions by checking growth in others, foster and encourage progress by controlling it, show love and interest by curbing and chastising.

Indeed, there is some evidence that these teachers were themselves aware of the paradoxical nature of their task, particularly as it related to their definition of self. In particular, they saw themselves facing three quandaries.

First, they could not become the sort of teachers they wanted to be without first accepting the need also to behave in ways they found disagreeable. One talked of 'learning that you've got to establish yourself and your authority first – let them dislike you so they can like you later'. Another said, 'I have learnt that you must dominate the children in order to free them . . . I quite accept that now, it's just the pain of doing it'. A third, having described in detail his distaste for the custodial role he felt was forced upon him, explained, 'What I offer the children is the possibility of using the security of my control to try and develop themselves', while someone else argued, 'The only way to stop the teacher–pupil relationship being a negative one, based on power, is to make sure that it's you who has the power'.

Second, they could encounter children as individuals and care for them only if they were also aware of and valued themselves. One of them put it this way: 'I don't think anyone could teach young children unless they're both egocentric and selfless. You've got to be very sure of who you are yourself and yet quite prepared to forget who you are, not forget it, but put who you are second to who the kids are'.

Third, they could not be fulfilled by their work unless they allowed themselves to be depleted by its demands. I asked several people, 'Why do you let the school take so much of you?' The typical reply was, 'I enjoy giving it. . . .'

My claim is therefore that to adopt the identity of an English primary-school teacher is to accept the paradoxical nature of the task, as well as the difficulties inherent in carrying it out. It is also therefore inexorably to live with tension. Leaving practicalities aside, one is still left with the central contradictions of teaching as an activity. Those who claim that they can be themselves in and through their work – that is, they can 'feel like teachers' – are signalling that they have learnt to live with paradox. To define teachers' conditions of service, to increase funding, to improve the management of schools may all reduce the practical burden on teachers, but they do not alter the nature of the work itself. Nor, unless we change the philosophical bases of primary teaching – the apparent, though often unacknowledged influence of Pestalozzi, Forebel, Rousseau, Buber, Rogers and the Christian tradition – are we likely to do so. In any case, before we decide that such a change is desirable, we should, I suggest, listen to what committed teachers are themselves saying about their work.

References

Berlak, A. and Berlak, H. (1981) *The Dilemmas of Schooling*, London, Methuen.

Geer, B. (1968) 'Teaching', in N. Bennett and D. McNamara (eds) *Focus on Teaching*, London, Longmans.

Hargreaves, A. (1978) 'The significance of classroom strategies', in L. Barton and R. Meigham (eds) *Sociological Interpretation of Schooling and Classrooms*, Driffield, Nafferton.

Nias, J. (1984b) 'The definition and maintenance of self in primary teaching', *British Journal of Sociology of Education* 5, 3: 267–280.

Nias, J. (1985) 'A more distant drummer: teacher development as the development of self', in L. Barton and S. Walker (eds) *Education and Social Change*, Beckenham, Croom Helm.

Nias, J. (1987) 'Learning the job while playing a part: staff development in the early years of teaching', in G. Southworth (ed.) *Readings in Primary Management*, Lewes, Falmer Press.

Nias, J. (forthcoming) *Teachers and their work*, London, Methuen.

Osborne, M. (1985) 'Profiles of a typical French and English primary teacher', mimeo, Teacher's Conceptions of Their Professional Responsibility Project, University of Bristol.

Pollard, A. (1985) *The Social World of the Primary School*, Eastbourne, Holt Rinehart.

Sikes, P., Measor, L. and Woods, P. (1985) *Teacher Careers: Crisis and Continuities*, Lewes, Falmer Press.

Waller, W. (1961) (new edn), *Sociology of Teaching*, New York, Russell & Russell.

Woods, P. (1981) 'Strategy, commitment and identity: making and breaking the teacher role', in L. Barton and S. Walker (eds) *Schools, Teachers and Teaching*, Barcombe, Falmer Press.

Index

216   *Index*